C-1678   CAREER EXAMINATION SERIES

This is your
PASSBOOK for...

Staff Analyst Trainee

Test Preparation Study Guide
Questions & Answers

COPYRIGHT NOTICE

This book is SOLELY intended for, is sold ONLY to, and its use is RESTRICTED to individual, bona fide applicants or candidates who qualify by virtue of having seriously filed applications for appropriate license, certificate, professional and/or promotional advancement, higher school matriculation, scholarship, or other legitimate requirements of education and/or governmental authorities.

This book is NOT intended for use, class instruction, tutoring, training, duplication, copying, reprinting, excerption, or adaptation, etc., by:

1) Other publishers
2) Proprietors and/or Instructors of "Coaching" and/or Preparatory Courses
3) Personnel and/or Training Divisions of commercial, industrial, and governmental organizations
4) Schools, colleges, or universities and/or their departments and staffs, including teachers and other personnel
5) Testing Agencies or Bureaus
6) Study groups which seek by the purchase of a single volume to copy and/or duplicate and/or adapt this material for use by the group as a whole without having purchased individual volumes for each of the members of the group
7) Et al.

Such persons would be in violation of appropriate Federal and State statutes.

PROVISION OF LICENSING AGREEMENTS – Recognized educational, commercial, industrial, and governmental institutions and organizations, and others legitimately engaged in educational pursuits, including training, testing, and measurement activities, may address request for a licensing agreement to the copyright owners, who will determine whether, and under what conditions, including fees and charges, the materials in this book may be used them. In other words, a licensing facility exists for the legitimate use of the material in this book on other than an individual basis. However, it is asseverated and affirmed here that the material in this book CANNOT be used without the receipt of the express permission of such a licensing agreement from the Publishers. Inquiries re licensing should be addressed to the company, attention rights and permissions department.

All rights reserved, including the right of reproduction in whole or in part, in any form or by any means, electronic or mechanical, including photocopying, recording, or by any information storage and retrieval system, without permission in writing from the Publisher.

Copyright © 2024 by
National Learning Corporation

212 Michael Drive, Syosset, NY 11791
(516) 921-8888 • www.passbooks.com
E-mail: info@passbooks.com

PUBLISHED IN THE UNITED STATES OF AMERICA

PASSBOOK® SERIES

THE *PASSBOOK® SERIES* has been created to prepare applicants and candidates for the ultimate academic battlefield – the examination room.

At some time in our lives, each and every one of us may be required to take an examination – for validation, matriculation, admission, qualification, registration, certification, or licensure.

Based on the assumption that every applicant or candidate has met the basic formal educational standards, has taken the required number of courses, and read the necessary texts, the *PASSBOOK® SERIES* furnishes the one special preparation which may assure passing with confidence, instead of failing with insecurity. Examination questions – together with answers – are furnished as the basic vehicle for study so that the mysteries of the examination and its compounding difficulties may be eliminated or diminished by a sure method.

This book is meant to help you pass your examination provided that you qualify and are serious in your objective.

The entire field is reviewed through the huge store of content information which is succinctly presented through a provocative and challenging approach – the question-and-answer method.

A climate of success is established by furnishing the correct answers at the end of each test.

You soon learn to recognize types of questions, forms of questions, and patterns of questioning. You may even begin to anticipate expected outcomes.

You perceive that many questions are repeated or adapted so that you can gain acute insights, which may enable you to score many sure points.

You learn how to confront new questions, or types of questions, and to attack them confidently and work out the correct answers.

You note objectives and emphases, and recognize pitfalls and dangers, so that you may make positive educational adjustments.

Moreover, you are kept fully informed in relation to new concepts, methods, practices, and directions in the field.

You discover that you are actually taking the examination all the time: you are preparing for the examination by "taking" an examination, not by reading extraneous and/or supererogatory textbooks.

In short, this PASSBOOK®, used directedly, should be an important factor in helping you to pass your test.

STAFF ANALYST TRAINEE

DUTIES
Staff Analyst Trainees, under supervision, with some latitude for independent judgment, receive training in and assist in professional and technical work in the preparation and administration of departmental budgets; the preparation and conduct of administrative and procedural studies and analyses of the organization and operations of City agencies, and in personnel administration; perform related work.

SCOPE OF THE EXAMINATION
The multiple-choice test may include questions on descriptive statistics; arithmetic reasoning; ability to collect and analyze data; ability to interpret written materials; written communication, including ability to review and edit correspondence, reports and other written documents; and other related areas. Such questions will be concerned with budgeting, procedural, organizational and operational studies and personnel administration.

HOW TO TAKE A TEST

I. YOU MUST PASS AN EXAMINATION

A. WHAT EVERY CANDIDATE SHOULD KNOW

Examination applicants often ask us for help in preparing for the written test. What can I study in advance? What kinds of questions will be asked? How will the test be given? How will the papers be graded?

As an applicant for a civil service examination, you may be wondering about some of these things. Our purpose here is to suggest effective methods of advance study and to describe civil service examinations.

Your chances for success on this examination can be increased if you know how to prepare. Those "pre-examination jitters" can be reduced if you know what to expect. You can even experience an adventure in good citizenship if you know why civil service exams are given.

B. WHY ARE CIVIL SERVICE EXAMINATIONS GIVEN?

Civil service examinations are important to you in two ways. As a citizen, you want public jobs filled by employees who know how to do their work. As a job seeker, you want a fair chance to compete for that job on an equal footing with other candidates. The best-known means of accomplishing this two-fold goal is the competitive examination.

Exams are widely publicized throughout the nation. They may be administered for jobs in federal, state, city, municipal, town or village governments or agencies.

Any citizen may apply, with some limitations, such as the age or residence of applicants. Your experience and education may be reviewed to see whether you meet the requirements for the particular examination. When these requirements exist, they are reasonable and applied consistently to all applicants. Thus, a competitive examination may cause you some uneasiness now, but it is your privilege and safeguard.

C. HOW ARE CIVIL SERVICE EXAMS DEVELOPED?

Examinations are carefully written by trained technicians who are specialists in the field known as "psychological measurement," in consultation with recognized authorities in the field of work that the test will cover. These experts recommend the subject matter areas or skills to be tested; only those knowledges or skills important to your success on the job are included. The most reliable books and source materials available are used as references. Together, the experts and technicians judge the difficulty level of the questions.

Test technicians know how to phrase questions so that the problem is clearly stated. Their ethics do not permit "trick" or "catch" questions. Questions may have been tried out on sample groups, or subjected to statistical analysis, to determine their usefulness.

Written tests are often used in combination with performance tests, ratings of training and experience, and oral interviews. All of these measures combine to form the best-known means of finding the right person for the right job.

II. HOW TO PASS THE WRITTEN TEST

A. NATURE OF THE EXAMINATION

To prepare intelligently for civil service examinations, you should know how they differ from school examinations you have taken. In school you were assigned certain definite pages to read or subjects to cover. The examination questions were quite detailed and usually emphasized memory. Civil service exams, on the other hand, try to discover your present ability to perform the duties of a position, plus your potentiality to learn these duties. In other words, a civil service exam attempts to predict how successful you will be. Questions cover such a broad area that they cannot be as minute and detailed as school exam questions.

In the public service similar kinds of work, or positions, are grouped together in one "class." This process is known as *position-classification*. All the positions in a class are paid according to the salary range for that class. One class title covers all of these positions, and they are all tested by the same examination.

B. FOUR BASIC STEPS

1) Study the announcement

How, then, can you know what subjects to study? Our best answer is: "Learn as much as possible about the class of positions for which you've applied." The exam will test the knowledge, skills and abilities needed to do the work.

Your most valuable source of information about the position you want is the official exam announcement. This announcement lists the training and experience qualifications. Check these standards and apply only if you come reasonably close to meeting them.

The brief description of the position in the examination announcement offers some clues to the subjects which will be tested. Think about the job itself. Review the duties in your mind. Can you perform them, or are there some in which you are rusty? Fill in the blank spots in your preparation.

Many jurisdictions preview the written test in the exam announcement by including a section called "Knowledge and Abilities Required," "Scope of the Examination," or some similar heading. Here you will find out specifically what fields will be tested.

2) Review your own background

Once you learn in general what the position is all about, and what you need to know to do the work, ask yourself which subjects you already know fairly well and which need improvement. You may wonder whether to concentrate on improving your strong areas or on building some background in your fields of weakness. When the announcement has specified "some knowledge" or "considerable knowledge," or has used adjectives like "beginning principles of…" or "advanced … methods," you can get a clue as to the number and difficulty of questions to be asked in any given field. More questions, and hence broader coverage, would be included for those subjects which are more important in the work. Now weigh your strengths and weaknesses against the job requirements and prepare accordingly.

3) Determine the level of the position

Another way to tell how intensively you should prepare is to understand the level of the job for which you are applying. Is it the entering level? In other words, is this the position in which beginners in a field of work are hired? Or is it an intermediate or advanced level? Sometimes this is indicated by such words as "Junior" or "Senior" in the class title. Other jurisdictions use Roman numerals to designate the level – Clerk I, Clerk II, for example. The word "Supervisor" sometimes appears in the title. If the level is not indicated by the title, check the description of duties. Will you be working under very close supervision, or will you have responsibility for independent decisions in this work?

4) Choose appropriate study materials

Now that you know the subjects to be examined and the relative amount of each subject to be covered, you can choose suitable study materials. For beginning level jobs, or even advanced ones, if you have a pronounced weakness in some aspect of your training, read a modern, standard textbook in that field. Be sure it is up to date and has general coverage. Such books are normally available at your library, and the librarian will be glad to help you locate one. For entry-level positions, questions of appropriate difficulty are chosen – neither highly advanced questions, nor those too simple. Such questions require careful thought but not advanced training.

If the position for which you are applying is technical or advanced, you will read more advanced, specialized material. If you are already familiar with the basic principles of your field, elementary textbooks would waste your time. Concentrate on advanced textbooks and technical periodicals. Think through the concepts and review difficult problems in your field.

These are all general sources. You can get more ideas on your own initiative, following these leads. For example, training manuals and publications of the government agency which employs workers in your field can be useful, particularly for technical and professional positions. A letter or visit to the government department involved may result in more specific study suggestions, and certainly will provide you with a more definite idea of the exact nature of the position you are seeking.

III. KINDS OF TESTS

Tests are used for purposes other than measuring knowledge and ability to perform specified duties. For some positions, it is equally important to test ability to make adjustments to new situations or to profit from training. In others, basic mental abilities not dependent on information are essential. Questions which test these things may not appear as pertinent to the duties of the position as those which test for knowledge and information. Yet they are often highly important parts of a fair examination. For very general questions, it is almost impossible to help you direct your study efforts. What we can do is to point out some of the more common of these general abilities needed in public service positions and describe some typical questions.

1) General information

Broad, general information has been found useful for predicting job success in some kinds of work. This is tested in a variety of ways, from vocabulary lists to questions about current events. Basic background in some field of work, such as sociology or economics, may be sampled in a group of questions. Often these are principles which have become familiar to most persons through exposure rather than through formal training. It is difficult to advise you how to study for these questions; being alert to the world around you is our best suggestion.

2) Verbal ability

An example of an ability needed in many positions is verbal or language ability. Verbal ability is, in brief, the ability to use and understand words. Vocabulary and grammar tests are typical measures of this ability. Reading comprehension or paragraph interpretation questions are common in many kinds of civil service tests. You are given a paragraph of written material and asked to find its central meaning.

3) Numerical ability

Number skills can be tested by the familiar arithmetic problem, by checking paired lists of numbers to see which are alike and which are different, or by interpreting charts and graphs. In the latter test, a graph may be printed in the test booklet which you are asked to use as the basis for answering questions.

4) Observation

A popular test for law-enforcement positions is the observation test. A picture is shown to you for several minutes, then taken away. Questions about the picture test your ability to observe both details and larger elements.

5) Following directions

In many positions in the public service, the employee must be able to carry out written instructions dependably and accurately. You may be given a chart with several columns, each column listing a variety of information. The questions require you to carry out directions involving the information given in the chart.

6) Skills and aptitudes

Performance tests effectively measure some manual skills and aptitudes. When the skill is one in which you are trained, such as typing or shorthand, you can practice. These tests are often very much like those given in business school or high school courses. For many of the other skills and aptitudes, however, no short-time preparation can be made. Skills and abilities natural to you or that you have developed throughout your lifetime are being tested.

Many of the general questions just described provide all the data needed to answer the questions and ask you to use your reasoning ability to find the answers. Your best preparation for these tests, as well as for tests of facts and ideas, is to be at your physical and mental best. You, no doubt, have your own methods of getting into an exam-taking mood and keeping "in shape." The next section lists some ideas on this subject.

IV. KINDS OF QUESTIONS

Only rarely is the "essay" question, which you answer in narrative form, used in civil service tests. Civil service tests are usually of the short-answer type. Full instructions for answering these questions will be given to you at the examination. But in case this is your first experience with short-answer questions and separate answer sheets, here is what you need to know:

1) Multiple-choice Questions

Most popular of the short-answer questions is the "multiple choice" or "best answer" question. It can be used, for example, to test for factual knowledge, ability to solve problems or judgment in meeting situations found at work.

A multiple-choice question is normally one of three types—
- It can begin with an incomplete statement followed by several possible endings. You are to find the one ending which *best* completes the statement, although some of the others may not be entirely wrong.
- It can also be a complete statement in the form of a question which is answered by choosing one of the statements listed.

- It can be in the form of a problem – again you select the best answer.

Here is an example of a multiple-choice question with a discussion which should give you some clues as to the method for choosing the right answer:

When an employee has a complaint about his assignment, the action which will *best* help him overcome his difficulty is to
   A. discuss his difficulty with his coworkers
   B. take the problem to the head of the organization
   C. take the problem to the person who gave him the assignment
   D. say nothing to anyone about his complaint

In answering this question, you should study each of the choices to find which is best. Consider choice "A" – Certainly an employee may discuss his complaint with fellow employees, but no change or improvement can result, and the complaint remains unresolved. Choice "B" is a poor choice since the head of the organization probably does not know what assignment you have been given, and taking your problem to him is known as "going over the head" of the supervisor. The supervisor, or person who made the assignment, is the person who can clarify it or correct any injustice. Choice "C" is, therefore, correct. To say nothing, as in choice "D," is unwise. Supervisors have and interest in knowing the problems employees are facing, and the employee is seeking a solution to his problem.

2) True/False Questions

The "true/false" or "right/wrong" form of question is sometimes used. Here a complete statement is given. Your job is to decide whether the statement is right or wrong.

SAMPLE: A roaming cell-phone call to a nearby city costs less than a non-roaming call to a distant city.

This statement is wrong, or false, since roaming calls are more expensive.

This is not a complete list of all possible question forms, although most of the others are variations of these common types. You will always get complete directions for answering questions. Be sure you understand *how* to mark your answers – ask questions until you do.

V. RECORDING YOUR ANSWERS

Computer terminals are used more and more today for many different kinds of exams.

For an examination with very few applicants, you may be told to record your answers in the test booklet itself. Separate answer sheets are much more common. If this separate answer sheet is to be scored by machine – and this is often the case – it is highly important that you mark your answers correctly in order to get credit.

An electronic scoring machine is often used in civil service offices because of the speed with which papers can be scored. Machine-scored answer sheets must be marked with a pencil, which will be given to you. This pencil has a high graphite content which responds to the electronic scoring machine. As a matter of fact, stray dots may register as answers, so do not let your pencil rest on the answer sheet while you are pondering the correct answer. Also, if your pencil lead breaks or is otherwise defective, ask for another.

Since the answer sheet will be dropped in a slot in the scoring machine, be careful not to bend the corners or get the paper crumpled.

The answer sheet normally has five vertical columns of numbers, with 30 numbers to a column. These numbers correspond to the question numbers in your test booklet. After each number, going across the page are four or five pairs of dotted lines. These short dotted lines have small letters or numbers above them. The first two pairs may also have a "T" or "F" above the letters. This indicates that the first two pairs only are to be used if the questions are of the true-false type. If the questions are multiple choice, disregard the "T" and "F" and pay attention only to the small letters or numbers.

Answer your questions in the manner of the sample that follows:

32. The largest city in the United States is
    A. Washington, D.C.
    B. New York City
    C. Chicago
    D. Detroit
    E. San Francisco

1) Choose the answer you think is best. (New York City is the largest, so "B" is correct.)
2) Find the row of dotted lines numbered the same as the question you are answering. (Find row number 32)
3) Find the pair of dotted lines corresponding to the answer. (Find the pair of lines under the mark "B.")
4) Make a solid black mark between the dotted lines.

VI. BEFORE THE TEST

Common sense will help you find procedures to follow to get ready for an examination. Too many of us, however, overlook these sensible measures. Indeed, nervousness and fatigue have been found to be the most serious reasons why applicants fail to do their best on civil service tests. Here is a list of reminders:

- Begin your preparation early – Don't wait until the last minute to go scurrying around for books and materials or to find out what the position is all about.
- Prepare continuously – An hour a night for a week is better than an all-night cram session. This has been definitely established. What is more, a night a week for a month will return better dividends than crowding your study into a shorter period of time.
- Locate the place of the exam – You have been sent a notice telling you when and where to report for the examination. If the location is in a different town or otherwise unfamiliar to you, it would be well to inquire the best route and learn something about the building.
- Relax the night before the test – Allow your mind to rest. Do not study at all that night. Plan some mild recreation or diversion; then go to bed early and get a good night's sleep.
- Get up early enough to make a leisurely trip to the place for the test – This way unforeseen events, traffic snarls, unfamiliar buildings, etc. will not upset you.
- Dress comfortably – A written test is not a fashion show. You will be known by number and not by name, so wear something comfortable.

- Leave excess paraphernalia at home – Shopping bags and odd bundles will get in your way. You need bring only the items mentioned in the official notice you received; usually everything you need is provided. Do not bring reference books to the exam. They will only confuse those last minutes and be taken away from you when in the test room.
- Arrive somewhat ahead of time – If because of transportation schedules you must get there very early, bring a newspaper or magazine to take your mind off yourself while waiting.
- Locate the examination room – When you have found the proper room, you will be directed to the seat or part of the room where you will sit. Sometimes you are given a sheet of instructions to read while you are waiting. Do not fill out any forms until you are told to do so; just read them and be prepared.
- Relax and prepare to listen to the instructions
- If you have any physical problem that may keep you from doing your best, be sure to tell the test administrator. If you are sick or in poor health, you really cannot do your best on the exam. You can come back and take the test some other time.

VII. AT THE TEST

The day of the test is here and you have the test booklet in your hand. The temptation to get going is very strong. Caution! There is more to success than knowing the right answers. You must know how to identify your papers and understand variations in the type of short-answer question used in this particular examination. Follow these suggestions for maximum results from your efforts:

1) Cooperate with the monitor

The test administrator has a duty to create a situation in which you can be as much at ease as possible. He will give instructions, tell you when to begin, check to see that you are marking your answer sheet correctly, and so on. He is not there to guard you, although he will see that your competitors do not take unfair advantage. He wants to help you do your best.

2) Listen to all instructions

Don't jump the gun! Wait until you understand all directions. In most civil service tests you get more time than you need to answer the questions. So don't be in a hurry. Read each word of instructions until you clearly understand the meaning. Study the examples, listen to all announcements and follow directions. Ask questions if you do not understand what to do.

3) Identify your papers

Civil service exams are usually identified by number only. You will be assigned a number; you must not put your name on your test papers. Be sure to copy your number correctly. Since more than one exam may be given, copy your exact examination title.

4) Plan your time

Unless you are told that a test is a "speed" or "rate of work" test, speed itself is usually not important. Time enough to answer all the questions will be provided, but this does not mean that you have all day. An overall time limit has been set. Divide the total time (in minutes) by the number of questions to determine the approximate time you have for each question.

5) Do not linger over difficult questions

If you come across a difficult question, mark it with a paper clip (useful to have along) and come back to it when you have been through the booklet. One caution if you do this – be sure to skip a number on your answer sheet as well. Check often to be sure that you have not lost your place and that you are marking in the row numbered the same as the question you are answering.

6) Read the questions

Be sure you know what the question asks! Many capable people are unsuccessful because they failed to *read* the questions correctly.

7) Answer all questions

Unless you have been instructed that a penalty will be deducted for incorrect answers, it is better to guess than to omit a question.

8) Speed tests

It is often better NOT to guess on speed tests. It has been found that on timed tests people are tempted to spend the last few seconds before time is called in marking answers at random – without even reading them – in the hope of picking up a few extra points. To discourage this practice, the instructions may warn you that your score will be "corrected" for guessing. That is, a penalty will be applied. The incorrect answers will be deducted from the correct ones, or some other penalty formula will be used.

9) Review your answers

If you finish before time is called, go back to the questions you guessed or omitted to give them further thought. Review other answers if you have time.

10) Return your test materials

If you are ready to leave before others have finished or time is called, take ALL your materials to the monitor and leave quietly. Never take any test material with you. The monitor can discover whose papers are not complete, and taking a test booklet may be grounds for disqualification.

VIII. EXAMINATION TECHNIQUES

1) Read the general instructions carefully. These are usually printed on the first page of the exam booklet. As a rule, these instructions refer to the timing of the examination; the fact that you should not start work until the signal and must stop work at a signal, etc. If there are any *special* instructions, such as a choice of questions to be answered, make sure that you note this instruction carefully.

2) When you are ready to start work on the examination, that is as soon as the signal has been given, read the instructions to each question booklet, underline any key words or phrases, such as *least, best, outline, describe* and the like. In this way you will tend to answer as requested rather than discover on reviewing your paper that you *listed without describing*, that you selected the *worst* choice rather than the *best* choice, etc.

3) If the examination is of the objective or multiple-choice type – that is, each question will also give a series of possible answers: A, B, C or D, and you are called upon to select the best answer and write the letter next to that answer on your answer paper – it is advisable to start answering each question in turn. There may be anywhere from 50 to 100 such questions in the three or four hours allotted and you can see how much time would be taken if you read through all the questions before beginning to answer any. Furthermore, if you come across a question or group of questions which you know would be difficult to answer, it would undoubtedly affect your handling of all the other questions.

4) If the examination is of the essay type and contains but a few questions, it is a moot point as to whether you should read all the questions before starting to answer any one. Of course, if you are given a choice – say five out of seven and the like – then it is essential to read all the questions so you can eliminate the two that are most difficult. If, however, you are asked to answer all the questions, there may be danger in trying to answer the easiest one first because you may find that you will spend too much time on it. The best technique is to answer the first question, then proceed to the second, etc.

5) Time your answers. Before the exam begins, write down the time it started, then add the time allowed for the examination and write down the time it must be completed, then divide the time available somewhat as follows:
   - If 3-1/2 hours are allowed, that would be 210 minutes. If you have 80 objective-type questions, that would be an average of 2-1/2 minutes per question. Allow yourself no more than 2 minutes per question, or a total of 160 minutes, which will permit about 50 minutes to review.
   - If for the time allotment of 210 minutes there are 7 essay questions to answer, that would average about 30 minutes a question. Give yourself only 25 minutes per question so that you have about 35 minutes to review.

6) The most important instruction is to *read each question* and make sure you know what is wanted. The second most important instruction is to *time yourself properly* so that you answer every question. The third most important instruction is to *answer every question*. Guess if you have to but include something for each question. Remember that you will receive no credit for a blank and will probably receive some credit if you write something in answer to an essay question. If you guess a letter – say "B" for a multiple-choice question – you may have guessed right. If you leave a blank as an answer to a multiple-choice question, the examiners may respect your feelings but it will not add a point to your score. Some exams may penalize you for wrong answers, so in such cases *only*, you may not want to guess unless you have some basis for your answer.

7) Suggestions
   a. Objective-type questions
      1. Examine the question booklet for proper sequence of pages and questions
      2. Read all instructions carefully
      3. Skip any question which seems too difficult; return to it after all other questions have been answered
      4. Apportion your time properly; do not spend too much time on any single question or group of questions

5. Note and underline key words – *all, most, fewest, least, best, worst, same, opposite,* etc.
6. Pay particular attention to negatives
7. Note unusual option, e.g., unduly long, short, complex, different or similar in content to the body of the question
8. Observe the use of "hedging" words – *probably, may, most likely,* etc.
9. Make sure that your answer is put next to the same number as the question
10. Do not second-guess unless you have good reason to believe the second answer is definitely more correct
11. Cross out original answer if you decide another answer is more accurate; do not erase until you are ready to hand your paper in
12. Answer all questions; guess unless instructed otherwise
13. Leave time for review

b. Essay questions
 1. Read each question carefully
 2. Determine exactly what is wanted. Underline key words or phrases.
 3. Decide on outline or paragraph answer
 4. Include many different points and elements unless asked to develop any one or two points or elements
 5. Show impartiality by giving pros and cons unless directed to select one side only
 6. Make and write down any assumptions you find necessary to answer the questions
 7. Watch your English, grammar, punctuation and choice of words
 8. Time your answers; don't crowd material

8) Answering the essay question

Most essay questions can be answered by framing the specific response around several key words or ideas. Here are a few such key words or ideas:

M's: manpower, materials, methods, money, management
P's: purpose, program, policy, plan, procedure, practice, problems, pitfalls, personnel, public relations

a. Six basic steps in handling problems:
 1. Preliminary plan and background development
 2. Collect information, data and facts
 3. Analyze and interpret information, data and facts
 4. Analyze and develop solutions as well as make recommendations
 5. Prepare report and sell recommendations
 6. Install recommendations and follow up effectiveness

b. Pitfalls to avoid
 1. *Taking things for granted* – A statement of the situation does not necessarily imply that each of the elements is necessarily true; for example, a complaint may be invalid and biased so that all that can be taken for granted is that a complaint has been registered

2. *Considering only one side of a situation* – Wherever possible, indicate several alternatives and then point out the reasons you selected the best one
3. *Failing to indicate follow up* – Whenever your answer indicates action on your part, make certain that you will take proper follow-up action to see how successful your recommendations, procedures or actions turn out to be
4. *Taking too long in answering any single question* – Remember to time your answers properly

IX. AFTER THE TEST

Scoring procedures differ in detail among civil service jurisdictions although the general principles are the same. Whether the papers are hand-scored or graded by machine we have described, they are nearly always graded by number. That is, the person who marks the paper knows only the number – never the name – of the applicant. Not until all the papers have been graded will they be matched with names. If other tests, such as training and experience or oral interview ratings have been given, scores will be combined. Different parts of the examination usually have different weights. For example, the written test might count 60 percent of the final grade, and a rating of training and experience 40 percent. In many jurisdictions, veterans will have a certain number of points added to their grades.

After the final grade has been determined, the names are placed in grade order and an eligible list is established. There are various methods for resolving ties between those who get the same final grade – probably the most common is to place first the name of the person whose application was received first. Job offers are made from the eligible list in the order the names appear on it. You will be notified of your grade and your rank as soon as all these computations have been made. This will be done as rapidly as possible.

People who are found to meet the requirements in the announcement are called "eligibles." Their names are put on a list of eligible candidates. An eligible's chances of getting a job depend on how high he stands on this list and how fast agencies are filling jobs from the list.

When a job is to be filled from a list of eligibles, the agency asks for the names of people on the list of eligibles for that job. When the civil service commission receives this request, it sends to the agency the names of the three people highest on this list. Or, if the job to be filled has specialized requirements, the office sends the agency the names of the top three persons who meet these requirements from the general list.

The appointing officer makes a choice from among the three people whose names were sent to him. If the selected person accepts the appointment, the names of the others are put back on the list to be considered for future openings.

That is the rule in hiring from all kinds of eligible lists, whether they are for typist, carpenter, chemist, or something else. For every vacancy, the appointing officer has his choice of any one of the top three eligibles on the list. This explains why the person whose name is on top of the list sometimes does not get an appointment when some of the persons lower on the list do. If the appointing officer chooses the second or third eligible, the No. 1 eligible does not get a job at once, but stays on the list until he is appointed or the list is terminated.

X. HOW TO PASS THE INTERVIEW TEST

The examination for which you applied requires an oral interview test. You have already taken the written test and you are now being called for the interview test – the final part of the formal examination.

You may think that it is not possible to prepare for an interview test and that there are no procedures to follow during an interview. Our purpose is to point out some things you can do in advance that will help you and some good rules to follow and pitfalls to avoid while you are being interviewed.

What is an interview supposed to test?

The written examination is designed to test the technical knowledge and competence of the candidate; the oral is designed to evaluate intangible qualities, not readily measured otherwise, and to establish a list showing the relative fitness of each candidate – as measured against his competitors – for the position sought. Scoring is not on the basis of "right" and "wrong," but on a sliding scale of values ranging from "not passable" to "outstanding." As a matter of fact, it is possible to achieve a relatively low score without a single "incorrect" answer because of evident weakness in the qualities being measured.

Occasionally, an examination may consist entirely of an oral test – either an individual or a group oral. In such cases, information is sought concerning the technical knowledges and abilities of the candidate, since there has been no written examination for this purpose. More commonly, however, an oral test is used to supplement a written examination.

Who conducts interviews?

The composition of oral boards varies among different jurisdictions. In nearly all, a representative of the personnel department serves as chairman. One of the members of the board may be a representative of the department in which the candidate would work. In some cases, "outside experts" are used, and, frequently, a businessman or some other representative of the general public is asked to serve. Labor and management or other special groups may be represented. The aim is to secure the services of experts in the appropriate field.

However the board is composed, it is a good idea (and not at all improper or unethical) to ascertain in advance of the interview who the members are and what groups they represent. When you are introduced to them, you will have some idea of their backgrounds and interests, and at least you will not stutter and stammer over their names.

What should be done before the interview?

While knowledge about the board members is useful and takes some of the surprise element out of the interview, there is other preparation which is more substantive. It *is* possible to prepare for an oral interview – in several ways:

1) Keep a copy of your application and review it carefully before the interview

This may be the only document before the oral board, and the starting point of the interview. Know what education and experience you have listed there, and the sequence and dates of all of it. Sometimes the board will ask you to review the highlights of your experience for them; you should not have to hem and haw doing it.

2) Study the class specification and the examination announcement

Usually, the oral board has one or both of these to guide them. The qualities, characteristics or knowledges required by the position sought are stated in these documents. They offer valuable clues as to the nature of the oral interview. For example, if the job involves supervisory responsibilities, the announcement will usually indicate that knowledge of modern supervisory methods and the qualifications of the candidate as a supervisor will be tested. If so, you can expect such questions, frequently in the form of a hypothetical situation which you are expected to solve. NEVER go into an oral without knowledge of the duties and responsibilities of the job you seek.

3) Think through each qualification required

Try to visualize the kind of questions you would ask if you were a board member. How well could you answer them? Try especially to appraise your own knowledge and background in each area, *measured against the job sought*, and identify any areas in which you are weak. Be critical and realistic – do not flatter yourself.

4) Do some general reading in areas in which you feel you may be weak

For example, if the job involves supervision and your past experience has NOT, some general reading in supervisory methods and practices, particularly in the field of human relations, might be useful. Do NOT study agency procedures or detailed manuals. The oral board will be testing your understanding and capacity, not your memory.

5) Get a good night's sleep and watch your general health and mental attitude

You will want a clear head at the interview. Take care of a cold or any other minor ailment, and of course, no hangovers.

What should be done on the day of the interview?

Now comes the day of the interview itself. Give yourself plenty of time to get there. Plan to arrive somewhat ahead of the scheduled time, particularly if your appointment is in the fore part of the day. If a previous candidate fails to appear, the board might be ready for you a bit early. By early afternoon an oral board is almost invariably behind schedule if there are many candidates, and you may have to wait. Take along a book or magazine to read, or your application to review, but leave any extraneous material in the waiting room when you go in for your interview. In any event, relax and compose yourself.

The matter of dress is important. The board is forming impressions about you – from your experience, your manners, your attitude, and your appearance. Give your personal appearance careful attention. Dress your best, but not your flashiest. Choose conservative, appropriate clothing, and be sure it is immaculate. This is a business interview, and your appearance should indicate that you regard it as such. Besides, being well groomed and properly dressed will help boost your confidence.

Sooner or later, someone will call your name and escort you into the interview room. *This is it.* From here on you are on your own. It is too late for any more preparation. But remember, you asked for this opportunity to prove your fitness, and you are here because your request was granted.

What happens when you go in?

The usual sequence of events will be as follows: The clerk (who is often the board stenographer) will introduce you to the chairman of the oral board, who will introduce you to the other members of the board. Acknowledge the introductions before you sit down. Do not be surprised if you find a microphone facing you or a stenotypist sitting by. Oral interviews are usually recorded in the event of an appeal or other review.

Usually the chairman of the board will open the interview by reviewing the highlights of your education and work experience from your application – primarily for the benefit of the other members of the board, as well as to get the material into the record. Do not interrupt or comment unless there is an error or significant misinterpretation; if that is the case, do not hesitate. But do not quibble about insignificant matters. Also, he will usually ask you some question about your education, experience or your present job – partly to get you to start talking and to establish the interviewing "rapport." He may start the actual questioning, or turn it over to one of the other members. Frequently, each member undertakes the questioning on a particular area, one in which he is perhaps most competent, so you can expect each member to participate in the examination. Because time is limited, you may also expect some rather abrupt switches in the direction the questioning takes, so do not be upset by it. Normally, a board member will not pursue a single line of questioning unless he discovers a particular strength or weakness.

After each member has participated, the chairman will usually ask whether any member has any further questions, then will ask you if you have anything you wish to add. Unless you are expecting this question, it may floor you. Worse, it may start you off on an extended, extemporaneous speech. The board is not usually seeking more information. The question is principally to offer you a last opportunity to present further qualifications or to indicate that you have nothing to add. So, if you feel that a significant qualification or characteristic has been overlooked, it is proper to point it out in a sentence or so. Do not compliment the board on the thoroughness of their examination – they have been sketchy, and you know it. If you wish, merely say, "No thank you, I have nothing further to add." This is a point where you can "talk yourself out" of a good impression or fail to present an important bit of information. Remember, *you close the interview yourself.*

The chairman will then say, "That is all, Mr. _____, thank you." Do not be startled; the interview is over, and quicker than you think. Thank him, gather your belongings and take your leave. Save your sigh of relief for the other side of the door.

How to put your best foot forward

Throughout this entire process, you may feel that the board individually and collectively is trying to pierce your defenses, seek out your hidden weaknesses and embarrass and confuse you. Actually, this is not true. They are obliged to make an appraisal of your qualifications for the job you are seeking, and they want to see you in your best light. Remember, they must interview all candidates and a non-cooperative candidate may become a failure in spite of their best efforts to bring out his qualifications. Here are 15 suggestions that will help you:

1) Be natural – Keep your attitude confident, not cocky

If you are not confident that you can do the job, do not expect the board to be. Do not apologize for your weaknesses, try to bring out your strong points. The board is interested in a positive, not negative, presentation. Cockiness will antagonize any board member and make him wonder if you are covering up a weakness by a false show of strength.

2) Get comfortable, but don't lounge or sprawl

Sit erectly but not stiffly. A careless posture may lead the board to conclude that you are careless in other things, or at least that you are not impressed by the importance of the occasion. Either conclusion is natural, even if incorrect. Do not fuss with your clothing, a pencil or an ashtray. Your hands may occasionally be useful to emphasize a point; do not let them become a point of distraction.

3) Do not wisecrack or make small talk

This is a serious situation, and your attitude should show that you consider it as such. Further, the time of the board is limited – they do not want to waste it, and neither should you.

4) Do not exaggerate your experience or abilities

In the first place, from information in the application or other interviews and sources, the board may know more about you than you think. Secondly, you probably will not get away with it. An experienced board is rather adept at spotting such a situation, so do not take the chance.

5) If you know a board member, do not make a point of it, yet do not hide it

Certainly you are not fooling him, and probably not the other members of the board. Do not try to take advantage of your acquaintanceship – it will probably do you little good.

6) Do not dominate the interview

Let the board do that. They will give you the clues – do not assume that you have to do all the talking. Realize that the board has a number of questions to ask you, and do not try to take up all the interview time by showing off your extensive knowledge of the answer to the first one.

7) Be attentive

You only have 20 minutes or so, and you should keep your attention at its sharpest throughout. When a member is addressing a problem or question to you, give him your undivided attention. Address your reply principally to him, but do not exclude the other board members.

8) Do not interrupt

A board member may be stating a problem for you to analyze. He will ask you a question when the time comes. Let him state the problem, and wait for the question.

9) Make sure you understand the question

Do not try to answer until you are sure what the question is. If it is not clear, restate it in your own words or ask the board member to clarify it for you. However, do not haggle about minor elements.

10) Reply promptly but not hastily

A common entry on oral board rating sheets is "candidate responded readily," or "candidate hesitated in replies." Respond as promptly and quickly as you can, but do not jump to a hasty, ill-considered answer.

11) Do not be peremptory in your answers

A brief answer is proper – but do not fire your answer back. That is a losing game from your point of view. The board member can probably ask questions much faster than you can answer them.

12) Do not try to create the answer you think the board member wants

He is interested in what kind of mind you have and how it works – not in playing games. Furthermore, he can usually spot this practice and will actually grade you down on it.

13) Do not switch sides in your reply merely to agree with a board member

Frequently, a member will take a contrary position merely to draw you out and to see if you are willing and able to defend your point of view. Do not start a debate, yet do not surrender a good position. If a position is worth taking, it is worth defending.

14) Do not be afraid to admit an error in judgment if you are shown to be wrong

The board knows that you are forced to reply without any opportunity for careful consideration. Your answer may be demonstrably wrong. If so, admit it and get on with the interview.

15) Do not dwell at length on your present job

The opening question may relate to your present assignment. Answer the question but do not go into an extended discussion. You are being examined for a *new* job, not your present one. As a matter of fact, try to phrase ALL your answers in terms of the job for which you are being examined.

Basis of Rating

Probably you will forget most of these "do's" and "don'ts" when you walk into the oral interview room. Even remembering them all will not ensure you a passing grade. Perhaps you did not have the qualifications in the first place. But remembering them will help you to put your best foot forward, without treading on the toes of the board members.

Rumor and popular opinion to the contrary notwithstanding, an oral board wants you to make the best appearance possible. They know you are under pressure – but they also want to see how you respond to it as a guide to what your reaction would be under the pressures of the job you seek. They will be influenced by the degree of poise you display, the personal traits you show and the manner in which you respond.

ABOUT THIS BOOK

This book contains tests divided into Examination Sections. Go through each test, answering every question in the margin. We have also attached a sample answer sheet at the back of the book that can be removed and used. At the end of each test look at the answer key and check your answers. On the ones you got wrong, look at the right answer choice and learn. Do not fill in the answers first. Do not memorize the questions and answers, but understand the answer and principles involved. On your test, the questions will likely be different from the samples. Questions are changed and new ones added. If you understand these past questions you should have success with any changes that arise. Tests may consist of several types of questions. We have additional books on each subject should more study be advisable or necessary for you. Finally, the more you study, the better prepared you will be. This book is intended to be the last thing you study before you walk into the examination room. Prior study of relevant texts is also recommended. NLC publishes some of these in our Fundamental Series. Knowledge and good sense are important factors in passing your exam. Good luck also helps. So now study this Passbook, absorb the material contained within and take that knowledge into the examination. Then do your best to pass that exam.

EXAMINATION SECTION

EXAMINATION SECTION
TEST 1

DIRECTIONS: Each question or incomplete statement is followed by several suggested answers or completions. Select the one that BEST answers the question or completes the statement. *PRINT THE LETTER OF THE CORRECT ANSWER IN THE SPACE AT THE RIGHT.*

Questions 1-5.

DIRECTIONS: Each of Questions 1 through 5 consists of a passage which contains one word that is incorrectly used because it is not in keeping with the meaning that the quotation is evidently intended to convey. Determine which word is incorrectly used. Select from the choices lettered A, B, C, and D the word which, when substituted for the incorrectly used word, would BEST to convey the meaning of the quotation.

1. Whatever the method, the necessity to keep up with the dynamics of an organization is the point on which many classification plans go awry. The budgetary approach to "positions," for example, often leads to using for recruitment and pay purposes a position authorized many years earlier for quite a different purpose than currently contemplated—making perhaps the title, the class, and the qualifications required inappropriate to the current need. This happens because executives overlook the stability that takes place in job duties and fail to reread an initial description of the job before saying, as they scan a list of titles, "We should fill this position right away." Once a classification plan is adopted, it is pointless to do anything less than provide for continuous, painstaking maintenance on a current basis, else once different positions that have actually become similar to each other remain in different classes, and some former cognates that have become quite different continue in the same class. Such a program often seems expensive. But to stint too much on this out-of-pocket cost may create still higher hidden costs growing out of lowered morale, poor production, delayed operating programs, excessive pay for simple work, and low pay for responsible work (resulting in poorly qualified executives and professional men)—all normal concomitants of inadequate, hasty, or out-of-date classification.   1.____

    A. evolution   B. personnel   C. disapproved   D. forward

2. At first sight, it may seem that there is little or no difference between the usable-ness of a manual and the degree of its use. But there is a difference. A manual may have all the qualities which make up the usable manual and still not be used. Take this instance as an example: Suppose you have a satisfactory manual but issue instructions from day to day through the avenue of bulletins, memorandums, and other informational releases. Which will the employee use, the manual or the bulletin which passes over his desk? He will,   2.____

of course, use the latter, for some obsolete material will not be contained in this manual. Here we have a theoretically usable manual which is unused because of the other avenues by which procedural information may be issued.
   A. countermand   B. discard   C. intentional   D. worthwhile

3. By reconcentrating control over its operations in a central headquarters, a firm is able to extend the influence of automation to many, if not all, of its functions—from inventory and payroll to production, sales, and personnel. In so doing, businesses freeze all the elements of the corporate function in their relationship to one another and to the overall objectives of the firm. From this total systems concept, companies learn that computers can accomplish much more than clerical and accounting jobs. Their capabilities can be tapped to perform the traditional applications (payroll processing, inventory control, accounts payable, and accounts receivable) as well as newer applications such as spotting deviations from planned programs (exception reporting), adjusting planning schedules, forecasting business trends, simulating market conditions, and solving production problems. Since the officer manage is a manager of information and each of these applications revolve around the processing of data, he must take an active role in studying and improving the system under his care.
   A. maintaining   B. inclusion   C. limited   D. visualize

3._____

4. In addition to the formal and acceptance theories of the source of authority, although perhaps more closely related to the latter, is the belief that authority is generated by personal qualifies of technical competence. Under this heading is the individual who has made, in effect, subordinates of others through sheer force of personality, and the engineer or economist who exerts influence by furnishing answers or sound advice. These may have no actual organizational authority, yet their advice may be so eagerly sought and so unerringly followed that it appears to carry the weight of an order. But, above all, one cannot discount the importance of formal authority with its institutional foundations. Buttressed by the qualities of leadership implicit in the acceptance theory, formal authority is basic to the managerial job. Once abrogated, it may be delegated or withheld, used or misused, and be effective in capable hands or be ineffective in inept hands.
   A. selected   B. delegation   C. limited   D. possessed

4._____

5. Since managerial operations in organization, staffing, directing, and controlling are designed to support the accomplishment of enterprise objectives, planning logically precedes the execution of all other managerial functions. Although all the functions intermesh in practice, planning is unique in that it establishes the objectives necessary for all group effort. Besides, plans must be made to accomplish these objectives before the manager knows what kind of organization relationships and personal qualifications are needed, along which course subordinates are to be directed, and what kind of control is to be applied. And, of course, each of the other managerial functions must be planned if they are to be effective.

5._____

Planning and control are inseparable—the Siamese twins of management. Unplanned action cannot be controlled, for control involves keeping activities on course by correcting deviations from plans. Any attempt to control without plans would be meaningless, since there are no way anyone can tell whether he is going where he wants to go—the task of control—unless first he knows where he wants to go—the task of planning. Plans thus preclude the standards of control.
    A. coordinating   B. individual   C. furnish   D. follow

Questions 6-7.

DIRECTIONS: Questions 6 and 7 are to be answered SOLELY on the basis of information given in the following paragraph.

In-basket tests are often used to assess managerial potential. The exercise consists of a set of papers that would be likely to be found in the in-basket of an administrator or manager at any given time, and requires the individuals participating in the examination to indicate how they would dispose of each item found in the in-basket. In order to handle the in-basket effectively, they must successfully manage their time, refer and assign some work to subordinates, juggle potentially conflicting appointments and meetings, and arrange for follow-up of problems generated by the items in the in-basket. In other words, the in-basket test is attempting to evaluate the participants' abilities to organize their work, set priorities, delegate control, and make decisions.

6. According to the above paragraph, to succeed in an in-basket test, an administrator must
   A. be able to read very quickly
   B. have a great deal of technical knowledge
   C. know when to delegate work
   D. arrange a lot of appointments and meetings

7. According to the above paragraph, all of the following abilities are indications of managerial potential EXCEPT the ability to
   A. organize and control   B. manage time
   C. write effective reports   D. make appropriate decisions

Questions 8-9.

DIRECTIONS: Questions 8 and 9 are to be answered SOLELY on the basis of information given in the following paragraph.

One of the biggest mistakes of government executives with substantial supervisory responsibility is failing to make careful appraisals of performance during employee probationary periods. Many a later headache could have been avoided by prompt and full appraisal during the early months of an employee's assignment. There is not much more to say about this except to emphasize the common prevalence of this oversight, and to underscore that for its consequences, which are many and sad, the offending managers have no one to blame but themselves.

8. According to the above paragraph, probationary periods are
   A. a mistake, and should not be used by supervisors with large responsibilities
   B. not used properly by government executives
   C. used only for those with supervisory responsibility
   D. the consequences of management mistakes

8._____

9. The one of the following conclusions that can MOST appropriately be drawn from the above paragraph is that
   A. management's failure to appraise employees during their probationary period is a common occurrence
   B. there is not much to say about probationary periods, because they are unimportant
   C. managers should blame employees for failing to use their probationary periods properly
   D. probationary periods are a headache to most managers

9._____

Questions 10-12.

DIRECTIONS: Questions 11 and 12 are to be answered SOLELY on the basis of the information given in the following paragraph.

The common sense character of the merit system seems so natural to most Americans that many people wonder why it should ever have been inoperative. After all, the American economic system, the most phenomenal the world has ever known, is also founded on a rugged selective process which emphasizes the personal qualities of capacity, industriousness, and productivity. The criteria may not have always been appropriate and competition has not always been fair, but competition there was, and the responsibilities and the rewards—with exceptions, of course—have gone to those who could measure up in terms of intelligence, knowledge, or perseverance. This has been true not only in the economic area, in the money-making process, but also in achievement in the professions and other walks of life.

10. According to the above paragraph, economic awards in the United States have
    A. always been based on appropriate, fair criteria
    B. only recently been based on a competitive system
    C. not gone to people who compete too ruggedly
    D. usually gone to those people with intelligence, knowledge, and perseverance

10._____

11. According to the above paragraph, a merit system is
    A. an unfair criterion on which to base rewards
    B. unnatural to anyone who is not American
    C. based only on common sense
    D. based on the same principles as the American economic system

11._____

12. According to the above paragraph, it is MOST accurate to say that 12.____
    A. the United States has always had a civil service merit system
    B. civil service employees are very rugged
    C. the American economic system has always been based on a merit objective
    D. competition is unique to the American way of life

Questions 13-15.

DIRECTIONS: The management study of employee absence due to sickness is an effective tool in planning. Questions 13 through 15 are to be answered SOLELY on the data given below.

Number of Days Absent Per Worker (Sickness)	1	2	3	4	5	6	7	8 or Over
Number of Workers	76	23	6	3	1	0	1	0
Total Number of Workers	400							
Period Covered	January 1 – December 31							

13. The total number of man-days lost due to illness was 13.____
    A. 110   B. 137   C. 144   D. 164

14. What percent of the workers had 4 or more days absence due to sickness? 14.____
    A. .25%   B. 2.5%   C. 1.25%   D. 12.5%

15. Of the 400 workers studied, the number who lost no days due to sickness was 15.____
    A. 190   B. 236   C. 290   D. 346

Questions 16-18.

DIRECTIONS: In the graph below, the lines labeled "A" and "B" represent the cumulative progress in the work of two file clerks, each of whom was given 500 consecutively numbered applications to file in the proper cabinets over a five-day work week. Questions 16 through 18 are to be answered SOLELY upon the data provided in the graph.

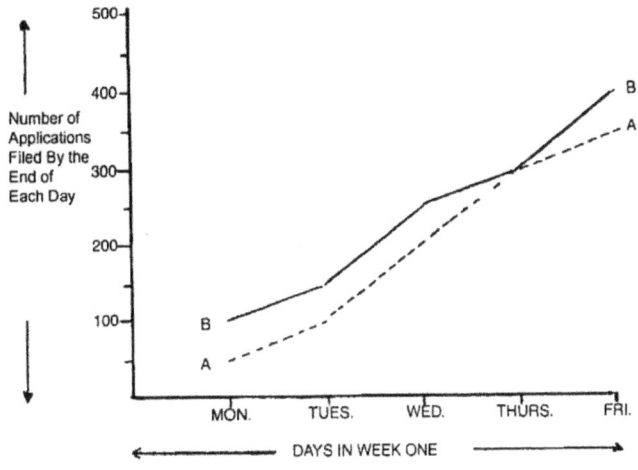

16. The day during which the LARGEST number of applications was filed by both clerks was
    A. Monday   B. Tuesday   C. Wednesday   D. Friday

17. At the end of the second day, the percentage of applications STILL to be filed was
    A. 25%   B. 50%   C. 66%   D. 75%

18. Assuming that the production pattern is the same the following week as the week shown in the chart, the day on which the file clerks will FINISH this assignment will be
    A. Monday   B. Tuesday   C. Wednesday   D. Friday

Questions 19-21.

DIRECTIONS: The following chart shows the differences between the rates of production of employees in Department D in 2009 and 2019. Questions 19 through 21 are to be answered SOLELY on the basis of the information given in the chart.

Number of Employees Producing Work-Units Within Range in 2009	Number of Work-Units Produced	Number of Employees Producing Work-Units Within Range in 2019
7	500 – 1000	4
14	1001 – 1500	11
26	1501 – 2000	28
22	2001 – 2500	36
17	2501 – 3000	39
10	3001 – 3500	23
4	3501 - 4000	9

19. Assuming that within each range of work-units produced the average production was at the mid-point at that range (e.g., category 500 – 1000 = 750), then the AVERAGE number of work-units produced per employee in 2009 fell into the range
    A. 1001 – 1500   B. 1501 – 2000   C. 2001 – 2500   D. 2501 – 3000

20. The ratio of the number of employees producing more than 2000 work-units in 2009 to the number of employees producing more than 2000 work-units in 2019 is MOST NEARLY
    A. 1:2   B. 2:3   C. 3:4   D. 4:5

21. In Department D, which of the following were GREATER in 2019 than in 2009?
    I. Total number of employees
    II. Total number of work-units produced
    III. Number of employees producing 2000 or fewer work-units
    The CORRECT answer is
    A. I, II, III   B. I, II   C. I, III   D. II, III

22. Unit S's production fluctuated substantially from one year to another. In 2018, Unit S's production was 100% greater than in 2017. In 2019, production decreased by 25% from 2018. In 2020, Unit S's production was 10% greater than in 2019.
On the basis of this information, it is CORRECT to conclude that Unit S's production in 2020 exceeded Unit S's production in 2017 by
    A. 65%   B. 85%   C. 95%   D. 135%

22.____

23. Agency "X" is moving into a new building. It has 1500 employees presently on its staff and does not contemplate much variance from this level. The new building contains 100 available offices, each with a maximum capacity of 30 employees. It has been decided that only 2/3 of the maximum capacity of each office will be utilized.
The TOTAL number of offices that will be occupied by Agency "X" is
    A. 30   B. 66   C. 75   D. 90

23.____

24. One typist completes a form letter every 5 minutes and another typist completes one every 6 minutes.
If the two typists start together, they will again start typing new letters simultaneously _____ minutes later and will have completed _____ letters by that time.
    A. 11; 30   B. 12; 24   C. 24; 12   D. 30; 11

24.____

25. During one week, a machine operator produces 10 fewer pages per hour of work than he usually does.
If it ordinarily takes him six hours to produce a 300-page report, it will take him _____ hours longer to produce that same 300-page report during the week when he produces more slowly.
    A. 1½   B. 1²/₃   C. 2   D. 2¾

25.____

KEY (CORRECT ANSWERS)

		Incorrect Words
1.	A	stability
2.	D	obsolete
3.	D	freeze
4.	D	abrogated
5.	C	preclude

6.	C	16.	C
7.	C	17.	D
8.	B	18.	B
9.	A	19.	C
10.	D	20.	A

11.	D	21.	B
12	C	22.	A
13.	D	23.	C
14.	C	24.	D
15.	C	25.	A

EXAMINATION SECTION
TEST 1

DIRECTIONS: Each question or incomplete statement is followed by several suggested answers or completions. Select the one that BEST answers the question or completes the statement. *PRINT THE LETTER OF THE CORRECT ANSWER IN THE SPACE AT THE RIGHT.*

1. The one of the following which has had GREATEST effect upon size of the budget of large cities in the last twenty years is
   A. change in the organization of the city resulting from new charters
   B. increase in services rendered by the city
   C. development of independent authorities
   D. increase in the city's ability to borrow money
   E. increase in the size of the city

1._____

2. The one of the following services for which cities receive the LEAST amount of direct financial assistance from state governments is
   A. education   B. welfare   C. housing
   D. roads   E. museums

2._____

3. Major problems which face most large cities, including New York, arise from the vertical sandwiching of governments in a single area and from the many independent governments that crowd the boundaries of the central city.
   Of the following methods of solving these problems, the one which has been MOST successful in the past has been to
   A. decentralize the administration of the central city
   B. create various supra-municipal authorities which tend to integrate the activities of the metropolitan area
   C. bring the metropolitan population under a single local government
   D. set up intermunicipal coordinating agencies to solve area administrative and economic problems
   E. allow each government element in the metropolitan area to work out its own solution

3._____

4. By means of the *debt limit*, the states regulate many facets of the debt of the cities.
   The one of the following factors which is NOT regulated in this manner is the
   A. purpose for which the debt is incurred
   B. amount of debt which may be incurred
   C. terms of the notes or bonds issued by the city
   D. forms of debts which may be incurred
   E. source from which the money may be borrowed

4._____

5. The one of the following which is a characteristic of NEITHER the state nor the federal governments, but which is a characteristic of the government of cities is that the latter
   A. is not sovereign but an agent
   B. does not have the power to raise taxes
   C. cannot enter into contracts
   D. may not make treaties with foreign countries
   E. may not coin money

5.____

Questions 6-8.

DIRECTIONS: Questions 6 through 8 are to be answered on the basis of the following paragraph.

The regressive uses of discipline is ubiquitous. Administrative architects who seek the optimum balance between structure and morale must accordingly look toward the identification and isolation of disciplinary elements. The whole range of disciplinary sanctions, from the reprimand to the dismissal presents opportunities for reciprocity and accommodation of institutional interests. When rightly seized upon, these opportunities may provide the moment and the means for fruitful exercise of leadership and collaboration.

6. The one of the following ways of reworking the ideas presented in this paragraph in order to be BEST suited for presentation in an in-service training course in supervision is:
   A. When one of your men does something wrong, talk it over with him. Tell him what he should have done. This is a chance for you to show the man that you are on his side and that you would welcome him on your side.
   B. It is not necessary to reprimand or to dismiss an employee because he needs disciplining. The alert foreman will lead and collaborate with his subordinates making discipline unnecessary.
   C. A good way to lead the men you supervise is to take those opportunities which present themselves to use the whole range of disciplinary sanctions from reprimand to dismissal as a means for enforcing collaboration.
   D. Chances to punish a man in your squad should be welcomed as opportunities to show that you are a "*good guy*" who does not bear a grudge.
   E. Before you talk to a man or have him report to the office for something he has done wrong, attempt to lead him and get him to work with you. Tell him that his actions were wrong, that you expect him not to repeat the same wrong act, and that you will take a firmer stand if the act is repeated.

6.____

7. Of the following, the PRINCIPAL point made in the paragraph is that
   A. discipline is frequently used improperly
   B. it is possible to isolate the factors entering into a disciplinary situation
   C. identification of the disciplinary elements is desirable

7.____

D. disciplinary situations may be used to the advantage of the organization
E. obtaining the best relationship between organizational form and spirit, depend upon the ability to label disciplinary elements

8. The MOST novel idea presented in the paragraph is that 8.____
   A. discipline is rarely necessary
   B. discipline may be a joint action of man and supervisor
   C. there are disciplinary elements which may be identified
   D. a range of disciplinary sanctions exist
   E. it is desirable to seek for balance between structure and morale

9. When, in the process of developing a classification plan, it has been decided that certain positions all have distinguishing characteristics sufficiently similar to justify treating them alike in the process of selecting appointees and establishing pay rates or scales, then the kind of employment represented by such positions will be called a "class." 9.____
   According to this paragraph, a group of positions is called a class if they
   A. have distinguishing characteristics
   B. represent a kind of employment
   C. can be treated in the same manner for some functions
   D. all have the same pay rates
   E. are treated in the same manner in the development of a classification plan

Questions 10-12.

DIRECTIONS: Questions 10 through 12 are to be answered on the basis of the following paragraph.

The fundamental characteristic of the type of remote control which management needs to bridge the gap between itself and actual operations is the more effective use of records and reports—more specifically, the gathering and interpretation of the facts contained in records and reports. Facts, for management purposes, are those data (narrative and quantitative) which express in simple terms the current standing of the agency's program, work and resources in relation to the plans and policies formulated by management. They are those facts or measures (1) which permit management to compare current status with past performance and with its forecasts for the immediate future, and (2) which provide management with a reliable basis for long-range forecasting.

10. According to the above statement, a characteristic of a type of management control 10.____
    A. is the kind of facts contained in records and reports
    B. is narrative and quantitative data
    C. is its remoteness from actual operations
    D. is the use of records
    E. which expresses in simple terms the current standing of the agency's program, provides management with a reliable basis for long-range forecasting

11. For management purposes, facts are, according to the paragraph, 11.____
    A. forecasts which can be compared to current status
    B. data which can be used for certain control purposes
    C. a fundamental characteristic of a type of remote control
    D. the data contained in records and reports
    E. data (narrative and quantitative) which describe the plans and policies formulated by management

12. An inference which can be drawn from this statement is that 12.____
    A. management which has a reliable basis for long-range forecasting has at its disposal a type of remote control which is needed to bridge the gap between itself and actual operations
    B. data which do not express in simple terms the current standing of the agency's program, work and resources in relationship to the plans and policies formulated by management, may still be facts for management purposes
    C. data which express relationships among the agency's program, work, and resources are management facts
    D. the gap between management and actual operations can only be bridged by characteristics which are fundamentally a type of remote control
    E. management compares current status with past performance in order to obtain a reliable basis for long-range forecasting

Questions 13-14.

DIRECTIONS: Questions 13 and 14 are to be answered on the basis of the following paragraph.

People must be selected to do the tasks involved and must be placed on a payroll in jobs fairly priced. Each of these people must be assigned those tasks which he can perform best: the work of each must be appraised, and good and poor work singled out appropriately. Skill in performing assigned tasks must be developed, and the total work situation must be conducive to sustained high performance. Finally, employees must be separated from the work force either voluntarily or involuntarily because of inefficient or unsatisfactory performance or because of curtailment of organizational activities.

13. A personnel function which is NOT included in the above description is 13.____
    A. classification   B. training   C. placement
    D. severance   E. service rating

14. The underlying implied purpose of the policy enunciated in the above paragraph is 14.____
    A. to plan for the curtailment of the organizational program when it becomes necessary
    B. to single out appropriate skill in performing assigned tasks
    C. to develop and maintain a high level of performance by employees

D. that training employees in relation to the total work situation is essential if good and poor work are to be singled out
E. that equal money for equal work results in a total work situation which insures proper appraisal

15. Changes in program must be quickly and effectively translated into organizational adjustments if the administrative machinery is to be fully adapted to current operating needs. Continuous administrative planning is indispensable to the successful and expeditious accomplishment of such organization changes.
According to this statement,
   A. the absence of continuous administrative planning must result in out-moded administrative machinery
   B. continuous administrative planning is necessary for changes in program
   C. if changes in program are quickly and effectively translated into organizational adjustments, the administrative machinery is fully adapted to current operating needs
   D. continuous administrative planning results in successful and expeditious accomplishment of organization changes
   E. if administrative machinery is not fully adapted to current operating needs, then continuous administrative planning is absent

15.____

16. The first-line supervisor executes policy as elsewhere formulated. He does not make policy. He is the element of the administrative structure closest to the employee group.
From this point of view, it follows that a MAJOR function of the first-line supervisor is to
   A. suggest desirable changes in procedure to top management
   B. prepare time schedules showing when his unit will complete a piece of work so that it will dovetail with the requirements of other units
   C. humanize policy so as to respect employee needs and interests
   D. report danger points to top management in order to forestall possible bottlenecks
   E. discipline employees who continuously break departmental rules

16.____

17. During a supervisory staff meeting, the department head said to the first-line supervisors, "*The most important job you have is to get across to the employees in your units the desirability of achieving our department's aims and the importance of the jobs they are performing toward reaching our goals.*"
In general, adoption of this point of view would tend to result in an organization
   A. in which supervisors would be faced by many disciplinary problems caused by employee reaction to the program
   B. in which less supervision is required of the work of the average employee
   C. having more clearly defined avenues of communication
   D. lacking definition; supervisors would tend to forget their primary mission of getting the assigned work completed as efficiently as possible
   E. in which most employees would be capable of taking over a supervisory position when necessary

17.____

18. A supervisor, in assigning a man to a job, generally followed the policy of fitting the man to the job.
    This procedure is
    A. *undesirable*; the job should be fitted to the man
    B. *desirable*; primary emphasis should be on the work to be accomplished
    C. *undesirable*; the policy does not consider human values
    D. *desirable*; setting up a definite policy and following it permits careful analysis
    E. *undesirable*; it is not always possible to fit the available man to the job

19. Assume that one of the units under your jurisdiction has 40 typists. Their skill range from 15 to 80 words a minute.
    The MOST feasible of the following methods to increase the typing output of this unit is to
    A. study the various typing jobs to determine the skill requirements for each type of work and assign to each typist tasks commensurate with her skill
    B. assign the slow typists to clerical work and hire new typists
    C. assign such tasks as typing straight copy to the slower typists
    D. reduce the skill requirements necessary to produce a satisfactory quantity of work
    E. simplify procedures and keep records, memoranda, and letters short and concise

20. In a division of a department, private secretaries were assigned to members of the technical staff since each required a secretary who was familiar with his particular field and who could handle various routine matters without referring to anyone. Other members of the staff depended for their dictation and typing work upon a small pool consisting of two stenographers and two typists. Because of turnover and the difficulty of recruiting new stenographers and typists, the pool had to be discontinued.
    Of the following, the MOST satisfactory way to provide stenographic and typing service for the division is to
    A. organize the private secretaries into a decentralized pool under the direction of a supervisor to whom nontechnical staff members would send requests for stenographic and typing assistance
    B. organize the private secretaries into a central pool under the direction of a supervisor to whom all staff members would send requests for stenographic and typing assistance
    C. train clerks as typists and typists as stenographers
    D. relieve stenographers and typists of jobs that can be done by messengers or clerks
    E. conserve time by using such devices as indicating minor corrections on a final draft in such a way that they can be erased and by using duplicating machines to eliminate typing many copies

21. Even under perfect organizational conditions, the relationships between the line units and the units charged with budget planning and personnel management may be precarious at times.
    The one of the following which is a MAJOR reason for this is that
    A. service units assist the head of the agency in formulating and executing policies
    B. line units frequently find lines of communication to the agency head blocked by service units
    C. there is a natural antagonism between planners and doers
    D. service units tend to become line in attitude and emphasis, and to conflict with operating units
    E. service units tend to function apart from the operating units

22. The one of the following which is the CHIEF reason for training supervisors is that
    A. untrained supervisors find it difficult to train their subordinates
    B. most persons do not start as supervisors and consequently are in need of supervisory training
    C. training permits a higher degree of decentralization of the decision-making process
    D. training permits a higher degree of centralization of the decision-making process
    E. coordinated actions on the part of many persons pre-supposes familiarity with the procedures to be employed

23. The problem of determining the type of organization which should exist is inextricably interwoven with the problem of recruitment.
    In general, this statement is
    A. *correct*; since organizations are man-made, they can be changed
    B. *incorrect*; the organizational form which is most desirable is independent of the persons involved
    C. *correct*; the problem of organization cannot be considered apart from employee qualifications
    D. *incorrect*; organizational problems can be separated into many parts and recruitment is important in only few of these
    E. *correct*; a good recruitment program will reduce the problems of organization

24. The conference as an administrative tool is MOST valuable for solving problems which
    A. are simple and within a familiar frame of reference
    B. are of long standing
    C. are novel and complex
    D. are not solvable
    E. require immediate solution

25. Of the following, a recognized procedure for avoiding conflicts in the delegation of authority is to 25.____
    A. delegate authority so as to preserve control by top management
    B. provide for a workable span of control
    C. preview all assignments periodically
    D. assign all related work to the same control
    E. use the linear method of assignment

KEY (CORRECT ANSWERS)

1.	B		11.	B
2.	E		12.	A
3.	C		13.	A
4.	E		14.	C
5.	A		15.	A
6.	A		16.	C
7.	D		17.	B
8.	B		18.	B
9.	C		19.	A
10.	D		20.	A

21. D
22. C
23. C
24. C
25. D

TEST 2

DIRECTIONS: Each question or incomplete statement is followed by several suggested answers or completions. Select the one that BEST answers the question or completes the statement. *PRINT THE LETTER OF THE CORRECT ANSWER IN THE SPACE AT THE RIGHT.*

1. A danger which exists in any organization as complex as that required for administration of a large city is that each department comes to believe that it exists for its own sake.
   The one of the following which has been attempted in some organizations as a cure for this condition is to
   A. build up the departmental esprit de corps
   B. expand the functions and jurisdictions of the various departments so that better integration is possible
   C. develop a body of specialists in the various subject matter fields which cut across departmental lines
   D. delegate authority to the lowest possible echelon
   E. systematically transfer administrative personnel from one department to another

1.____

2. At best, the organization chart is ordinarily and necessarily an idealized picture of the intent of top management, a reflection of hopes and aims rather than a photograph of the operating facts within an organization.
   The one of the following which is the BASIC reason for this is that the organization chart
   A. does not show the flow of work within the organization
   B. speaks in terms of positions rather than of live employees
   C. frequently contains unresolved internal ambiguities
   D. is a record of past organization or of proposed future organization and never a photograph of the living organization
   E. does not label the jurisdiction assigned to each component unit

2.____

3. The drag of inadequacy is always downward. The need in administration is always for the reverse; for a department head to project his thinking to the city level, for the unit chief to try to see the problems of the department.
   The inability of a city administration to recruit administrators who can satisfy this need usually results in departments characterized by
   A. disorganization   B. poor supervision
   C. circumscribed viewpoints D. poor public relations
   E. a lack of programs

3.____

4. When, as a result of a shift in public sentiment, the elective officers of a city are changed, is it desirable for career administrators to shift ground without performing any illegal or dishonest act in order to conform to the policies of the new elective officers?
   A. *No*; the opinions and beliefs of the career officials are the result of long experience in administration and are more reliable than those of politicians.

4.____

B. *Yes*; only in this way can citizens, political officials, and career administrators alike have confidence in the performance of their respective functions.
C. *No*; a top career official who is so spineless as to change his views or procedures as a result of public opinion is of little value to the public service.
D. *Yes*; legal or illegal, it is necessary that a city employee carry out the orders of his superior officers
E. *No*; shifting ground with every change in administration will preclude the use of a constant overall policy.

5. Participation in developing plans which will affect levels in the organization in addition to his own, will contribute to an individual's understanding of the entire system. When possible, this should be encouraged.
This policy is, in general,
    A. *desirable*; the maintenance of any organization depends upon individual understanding
    B. *undesirable*; employees should participate only in those activities which affect their own level, otherwise conflicts in authority may arise
    C. *desirable*; an employee's will to contribute to the maintenance of an organization depends to a great extent on the level which he occupies
    D. *undesirable*; employees can be trained more efficiently and economically in an organized training program than by participating in plan development
    E. *desirable*; it will enable the employee to make intelligent suggestions for adjustment of the plan in the future

5.____

6. Constant study should be made of the information contained in reports to isolate those elements of experience which are static, those which are variable and repetitive, and those which are variable and due to chance.
Knowledge of those elements of experience in his organization which are static or constant will enable the operating official to
    A. fix responsibility for their supervision at a lower level
    B. revise the procedure in order to make the elements variable
    C. arrange for follow-up and periodic adjustment
    D. bring related data together
    E. provide a frame of reference within which detailed standards for measure-meant can be installed

6.____

7. A chief staff officer, serving as one of the immediate advisors to the department head, has demonstrated a special capacity for achieving internal agreements and for sound judgment. As a result he has been used more and more as a source of counsel and assistance by the department head. Other staff officers and line officials as well have discovered that it is wise for them to check with this colleague in advance on all problematical matters handed up to the department head.
Developments such as this are
    A. *undesirable*; they disrupt the normal lines for flow of work in an organization

7.____

B. *desirable*; they allow an organization to make the most of its strength wherever such strength resides
C. *undesirable*; they tend to undermine the authority of the department head and put it in the hands of a staff officer who does not have the responsibility
D. *desirable*; they tend to resolve internal ambiguities in organization
E. *undesirable*; they make for bad morale by causing *cut throat* competition

8. A common difference among executives is that some are not content unless they are out in front of everything that concerns their organization, while others prefer to run things by pulling strings, by putting others out in front and by stepping into the breach only when necessary.
   Generally speaking, an advantage this latter method of operation has over the former is that it
   A. results in a higher level of morale over a sustained period of time
   B. gets results by exhortation and direct stimulus
   C. makes it necessary to calculate integrated moves
   D. makes the personality of the executive felt further down the line
   E. results in the executive getting the reputation for being a good fellow

9. Administrators frequently have to get facts by interviewing people. Although the interview is a legitimate fact-gathering technique, it has definite limitations which should not be overlooked.
   The one of the following which is an important limitation is that
   A. people who are interviewed frequently answer questions with guesses rather than admit their ignorance
   B. it is a poor way to discover the general attitude and thinking of supervisors interviewed
   C. people sometimes hesitate to give information during an interview which they will submit in written form
   D. it is a poor way to discover how well employees understand departmental policies
   E. the material obtained from the interview can usually be obtained at lower cost from existing records

10. It is desirable and advantageous to leave a maximum measure of planning responsibility to operating agencies or units, rather than to remove the responsibility to a central planning staff agency.
    Adoption of the former policy (decentralized planning) would lead to
    A. *less effective* planning; operating personnel do not have the time to make long-term plans
    B. *more effective* planning; operating units are usually better equipped technically than any staff agency and consequently are in a better position to set up valid plans
    C. *less effective* planning; a central planning agency has a more objective point of view than any operating agency can achieve
    D. *more effective* planning; plans are conceived in terms of the existing situation and their execution is carried out with the will to succeed

E. *less effective* planning; there is little or no opportunity to check deviation from plans in the proposed set-up

Questions 11-15.

DIRECTIONS: The following sections appeared in a report on the work production of two bureaus of a department. Questions 10 through 12 are to be answered on the basis of the following information. Throughout the report, assume that each month has 4 weeks.

Each of the two bureaus maintains a chronological file. In Bureau A, every 9 months on the average, this material fills a standard legal size file cabinet sufficient for 12,000 work units. In Bureau B, the same type of cabinet is filled in 18 months. Each bureau maintains three complete years of information plus a current file. When the current file cabinet is filled, the cabinet containing the oldest material is emptied, the contents disposed of and the cabinet used for current material. The similarity of these operations makes it possible to consolidate these files with little effort.

Study of the practice of using typists as filing clerks for periods when there is no typing work showed (1) Bureau A has for the past 6 months completed a total of 1,500 filing work units a week using on the average 200 man-hours of trained file clerk time and 20 man-hours of typist time, (2) Bureau B has in the same period completed a total of 2,000 filing work units a week using on the average 125 man-hours of trained file clerk time and 60 hours of typist time. This includes all work in chronological files. Assuming that all clerks work at the same speed and that all typists work at the same speed, this indicates that work other than filing should be found for typists or that they should be given some training in the filing procedures used. It should be noted that Bureau A has not been producing the 1,600 units of technical (not filing) work per 30 day period required by Schedule K, but is at present 200 units behind. The Bureau should be allowed 3 working days to get on schedule.

11. What percentage (approximate) of the total number of filing work units completed in both units consists of the work involved in the maintenance of the chronological files?
    A. 5%   B. 10%   C. 15%   D. 20%   E. 25%

    11.____

12. If the two chronological files are consolidated, the number of months which should be allowed for filling a cabinet is
    A. 2   B. 4   C. 6   D. 8   E. 14

    12.____

13. The MAXIMUM number of file cabinets which can be released for other uses as a result of the consolidation recommended is
    A. 0
    B. 1
    C. 2
    D. 3
    E. not determinable on the basis of the data given

    13.____

14. If all the filing work for both units is consolidated without any diminution in the amount to be done and all filing work is done by trained file clerks, the number of clerks required (35-hour work week) is

    A. 4   B. 5   C. 6   D. 7   E. 8

14.____

15. In order to comply with the recommendation with respect to Schedule K, the present work production of Bureau A must be increased by
    A. 50%
    B. 100%
    C. 150%
    D. 200%
    E. an amount which is not determinable on the basis of the data given

15.____

16. A certain training program during World War II resulted in training of thousands of supervisors in industry. The methods of this program were later successfully applied in various governmental agencies. The program was based upon the assumption that there is an irreducible minimum of three supervisory skills. The one of these skills among the following is
    A. to know how to perform the job at hand well
    B. to be able to deal personally with workers, especially face-to-face
    C. to be able to imbue workers with the will to perform the job well
    D. to know the kind of work that is done by one's unit and the policies and procedures of one's agency
    E. the "know-how" of administrative and supervisory processes

16.____

17. A comment made by an employee about a training course was, *We never have any idea how we are getting along in that course."*
The fundamental error in training methods to which this criticism points is
    A. insufficient student participation
    B. failure to develop a feeling of need or active want for the material being presented
    C. the training sessions may be too long
    D. no attempt may have been made to connect the new material with what was already known
    E. no goals have been set for the students

17.____

18. Assume that you are attending a departmental conference on efficiency ratings at which it is proposed that a man-to-man rating scale be introduced.
You should point out that, of the following, the CHIEF weakness of the man-to-man rating scale is that
    A. it involves abstract numbers rather than concrete employee characteristics
    B. judges are unable to select their own standards for comparison
    C. the standard for comparison shifts from man to man for each person rated
    D. not every person rated is given the opportunity to serve as a standard for comparison
    E. standards for comparison will vary from judge to judge

18.____

6 (#2)

19. Assume that you are conferring with a supervisor who has assigned to his subordinates efficiency ratings which you believe to be generally too low. The supervisor argues that his ratings are generally low because his subordinates are generally inferior.
Of the following, the evidence MOST relevant to the point at issue can be secured by comparing efficiency ratings assigned by this supervisor
   A. with ratings assigned by other supervisors in the same agency
   B. this year with ratings assigned by him in previous years
   C. to men recently transferred to his unit with ratings previously earned by these men
   D. with the general city average of ratings assigned by all supervisors to all employees
   E. with the relative order of merit of his employees as determined independently by promotion test marks

19.____

20. The one of the following which is NOT among the most common of the compensable factors used in wage evaluation studies is
   A. initiative and ingenuity required
   B. physical demand
   C. responsibility for the safety of others
   D. working conditions
   E. presence of avoidable hazards

20.____

21. If independent functions are separated, there is an immediate gain in conserving special skills. If we are to make optimum use of the abilities of our employees, these skills must be conserved.
Assuming the correctness of this statement, it follows that
   A. if we are not making optimum use of employee abilities, independent functions have not been separated
   B. we are making optimum use of employee abilities if we conserve special skills
   C. we are making optimum use of employee abilities if independent functions have been separated
   D. we are not making optimum use of employee abilities if we do not conserve special skills
   E. if special skills are being conserved, independent functions need not be separated

21.____

22. A reorganization of the bureau to provide for a stenographic pool instead of individual unit stenographer will result in more stenographic help being available too each unit when it is required, and consequently will result in greater productivity for each unit. An analysis of the space requirements shows that setting up a stenographic pool will require a minimum of 400 square feet of good space. In order to obtain this space, it will be necessary to reduce the space available for technical personnel, resulting in lesser productivity for each unit.
On the basis of the above discussion, it can be stated that in order to obtain greater productivity for each unit,

22.____

A. a stenographic pool should be set up
B. further analysis of the space requirement should be made
C. it is not certain as to whether or not a stenographic pool should be set up
D. the space available for each technician should be increased in order to compensate for the absence of a stenographic pool
E. a stenographic pool should not be set up

23. The adoption of a single consolidated form will mean that most of the form will not be used in any one operation. This would create waste and confusion. This conclusion is based upon the unstated hypothesis that
    A. if waste and confusion are to be avoided, a single consolidated form should be used
    B. if a single consolidated form is constructed, most of it can be used in each operation
    C. if waste and confusion are to be avoided, most of the form employed should be used
    D. most of a single consolidated form is not used
    E. a single consolidated form should not be used

23.____

24. Assume that you are studying the results of mechanizing several hand operations.
    The type of data which would be MOST useful in proving that an increase in mechanization is followed by a lower cost of operation is data which show that in
    A. some cases a lower cost of operation was not preceded by an increase in mechanization
    B. no case was a higher cost of operation preceded by a decrease in mechanization
    C. some cases a lower cost of operation was preceded by a decrease in mechanization
    D no case was a higher cost of operation preceded by an increase in mechanization
    E. some cases an increase in mechanization was followed by a decrease in cost of operation

24.____

25. The type of data which would be MOST useful in determining if an increase in the length of rest periods is followed by an increased rate of production is data which would indicate that _____ in the length of the rest period.

    A. *decrease* in the total production never follows an increase in
    B. *increase* in the total production never follows an increase
    C. *increase* in the rate of production never follows a decrease
    D. *decrease* in the total production may follow a decrease
    E. *increase* in the total production sometimes follows an increase

25.____

KEY (CORRECT ANSWERS)

1.	E	11.	C
2.	B	12.	C
3.	C	13.	B
4.	B	14.	D
5.	E	15.	E
6.	A	16.	B
7.	B	17.	E
8.	A	18.	E
9.	A	19.	C
10.	D	20.	E

21.	D
22.	C
23.	C
24.	D
25.	A

TEST 3

DIRECTIONS: Each question or incomplete statement is followed by several suggested answers or completions. Select the one that BEST answers the question or completes the statement. *PRINT THE LETTER OF THE CORRECT ANSWER IN THE SPACE AT THE RIGHT.*

1. You have been asked to answer a request from a citizen of the city. After giving the request careful consideration, you find that it cannot be granted. In answering the letter, you should begin by
    A. saying that the request cannot be granted
    B. discussing in detail the consideration you have to the request
    C. quoting the laws relating to the request
    D. explaining in detail why the request cannot be granted
    E. indicating an alternative method of achieving the end desired

    1.____

2. Reports submitted to the department head should be complete to the last detail. A far as possible, summaries should be avoided.
    This statement is, in general,
    A. *correct*; only on the basis of complete information can a proper decision be reached
    B. *incorrect*; if all reports submitted were of this character, a department head would never complete his work
    C. *correct*; the decision as to what is important and what is not can only be made by the person who is responsible for the action
    D. *incorrect*; preliminary reports, obviously, cannot be complete to the last detail
    E. *correct*; summaries tend to conceal the actual state of affairs and to encourage generalizations which would not be made if the details were known; consequently, they should be avoided if possible

    2.____

3. The supervisor of a large bureau, who was required in the course of business to answer a large number of letters from the public, completely formalized his responses, that is, the form and vocabulary of every letter he prepared were the same as far as possible.
    This method of solving the problem of how to handle correspondence is, in general
    A. *good*; it reduces the time and thought necessary for a response
    B. *bad*; the time required to develop a satisfactory standard form and vocabulary is usually not available in an active organization
    C. *good*; the use of standard forms causes similar requests to be answered in a similar way
    D. *bad*; the use of standard forms and vocabulary to the extent indicated results in letters in *officialese* hindering unambiguous explanation and clear understanding
    E. *good*; if this method were applied to an entire department, the answering of letters could be left to clerks and the administrators would be free for more constructive work

    3.____

25

4. Of the following systems of designating the pages in a looseleaf manual subject to constant revision and addition, the MOST practicable one is to use _____ for main divisions and _____ for subdivisions.
   A. decimals; integers
   B. integers; letters
   C. integers; decimals
   D. letters; integers
   E. integers; integers

4.____

5. A subordinate submits a proposed draft of a form which is being revised to facilitate filling in the form on a typewriter. The draft shows that the captions for each space will be printed below the space to be filled in.
   This proposal is
   A. *undesirable*; it decreases visibility
   B. *desirable*; it makes the form easy to understand
   C. *undesirable*; it makes the form more difficult to understand
   D. *desirable*; it increases visibility
   E. *undesirable*; it is less compact than other layouts

5.____

6. The one of the following which is NOT an essential element of an integrated reporting system for work-measurement is a
   A. uniform record form for accumulating data and instructions for its maintenance
   B. procedure for routing reports upward through the organization and routing summaries downward
   C. standard report form for summarizing basic records and instructions for its preparation
   D. method for summarizing, analyzing and presenting data from several reports
   E. looseleaf revisable manual which contains all procedural materials that are reasonably permanent and have a substantial reference value

6.____

7. Forms control only accomplishes the elimination, consolidation, and simplification of forms. It contributes little to the elimination, consolidation, and simplification of procedures.
   This statement is
   A. *correct*; the form is static while the procedure is dynamic; consequently, control of one does not necessarily result in control of the other
   B. *incorrect*; forms frequently dictate the way work is laid out; consequently, control of one frequently results in control of the other
   C. *correct*; the procedure is primary and the form secondary; consequently, control of procedure will also control form
   D. *incorrect*; the form and procedure are identical from the viewpoint of work control; consequently, control of one means control of the other
   E. *correct*; the assurance that forms are produced and distributed economically has little relationship to the consolidation and simplification of procedures

7.____

8. Governmental agencies frequently attempt to avoid special interest group pressures by referring them to the predetermined legislative policy, or to the necessity for rules and regulations applying generally to all groups and situations.
   Of the following, the MOST important weakness of this formally correct position is that
   A. it is not tenable in the face of determined opposition
   B. it tends to legalize and formalize the informal relationships between citizen groups and the government
   C. the achievement of an agency's aims is in large measure dependent upon its ability to secure the cooperation and support of special interest groups
   D. independent groups which participate in the formulation of policy in their sphere of interest tend to criticize openly and to press for changes in the direction of their policy
   E. agencies following this policy find it difficult to decentralize their public relation activities as subdivisions can only refer to the agency's overall policy

8.____

9. One of the primary purposes of the performance budget is to improve the ability to examine budgetary requirement by groups who have not been engaged in the construction of the budget.
   This is accomplished by
   A. making line by line appropriations
   B. making lump sum appropriations by department
   C. enumerating authorization for all expenditures
   D. standardizing the language used and the kinds of authorizations permitted
   E. permitting examination on the level of accomplishment

9.____

10. When engaged in budget construction or budget analysis, there is no point in trying to determine the total or average benefits to be obtained from total expenditures for a particular commodity or function.
    The validity of this argument is USUALLY based upon the
    A. viewpoint that it is not possible to construct a functional budget
    B. theory (or phenomenon) of diminishing utility
    C. hypothesis that as governmental budgets provide in theory for minimum requirements, there is no need to determine total benefits
    D. assumption that such determinations are not possible
    E. false hypothesis that a comparison between expected and achieved results does not aid in budget construction

10.____

Questions 11-12.

DIRECTIONS: Questions 11 and 12 are to be answered on the basis of the following paragraph.

Production planning is mainly a process of synthesis. As a basis for the positive act of bringing complex production elements properly together, however, analysis is necessary, especially if improvement is to be made in an existing organization. The necessary analysis requires customary means of orientation and preliminary fact gathering with emphasis, however, on the recognition of administrative goals and of the relationship among work steps.

11. The entire process described is PRIMARILY one of 11.____
    A. taking apart, examining, and recombining
    B. deciding what changes are necessary, making the changes and checking on their value
    C. fact finding so as to provide the necessary orientation
    D. discovering just where the emphasis in production should be placed and then modifying the existing procedure so that it is placed properly
    E. recognizing administrative goals and the relationship among work steps

12. In production planning according to the above paragraph, analysis is used PRIMARILY as 12.____
    A. a means of making important changes in an organization
    B. the customary means of orientation and preliminary fact finding
    C. a development of the relationship among work steps
    D. a means for holding the entire process intact by providing a logical basis
    E. a method to obtain the facts upon which a theory can be built

Questions 13-15.

DIRECTIONS: Questions 13 through 15 are to be answered on the basis of the following paragraph.

Public administration is policy-making. But it is not autonomous, exclusive or isolated policy-making. It is policy-making on a field where mighty forces contend, forces engendered in and by society. It is policy-making subject to still other and various policy makers. Public administration is one of a number of basic political processes by which these people achieves and controls government.

13. From the point of view expressed in the above paragraph, public administration is 13.____
    A. becoming a technical field with completely objective processes
    B. the primary force in modern society
    C. a technical field which should be divorced from the actual decision-making function
    D. basically anti-democratic
    E. intimately related to politics

14. According to the above paragraph, public administration is NOT entirely 14.____
    A. a force generated in and by society
    B. subject at times to controlling influences
    C. a social process
    D. policy-making relating to administrative practices
    E. related to policy-making at lower levels

15. The above paragraph asserts that public administration
    A. develops the basic and controlling policies
    B. is the result of policies made by many different forces
    C. should attempt to break through its isolated policy-making and engage on a broader field
    D. is a means of directing government
    E. is subject to the political processes by which acts are controlled

Questions 16-18.

DIRECTIONS: Questions 16 through 18 are to be answered on the basis of the following chart.

In order to understand completely the source of an employee's insecurity on his job, it is necessary to understand how he came to be, who he is and what kind of person he is away from his job. This would necessitate an understanding of those personal assets and liabilities which the employee brings to the job situation. These arise from his individual characteristics and his past experiences and established patterns of interpersonal relations. This whole area is of tremendous scope, encompassing everything included within the study of psychiatry and interpersonal relations. Therefore, it has been impracticable to consider it in detail. Attention has been focused on the relatively circumscribed area of the actual occupational situation. The factors considered those which the employee brings to the job situation and which arise from his individual characteristics and his past experience and established patterns of interpersonal relations are: intellectual-level or capacity, specific aptitudes, education, work experience, health, social and economic background, patterns of interpersonal relations and resultant personality characteristics.

16. According to the above paragraph, the one of the following fields of study which would be of LEAST importance in the study of the problem is the
    A. relationships existing among employees
    B. causes of employee insecurity in the job situation
    C. conflict, if it exists, between intellectual level and work experience
    D. distribution of intellectual achievement
    E. relationship between employee characteristics and the established pattern of interpersonal relations in the work situation

17. According to the above paragraph, in order to make a thoroughgoing and comprehensive study of the sources of employee insecurity, the field of study should include
    A. only such circumscribed areas as are involved in extra-occupational situations
    B. a study of the dominant mores of the period
    C. all branches of the science of psychology
    D. a determination of the characteristics, such as intellectual capacity, which an employee should bring to the job situation
    E. employee personality characteristics arising from previous relationships with other people

18. It is implied by this paragraph that it would be of GREATEST advantage to bring 18.____
to this problem a comprehensive knowledge of
    A. all established patterns of interpersonal relations
    B. the milieu in which the employee group is located
    C. what assets and liabilities are presented in the job situation
    D. methods of focusing attention on relatively circumscribed regions
    E. the sources of an employee's insecurity on his job

Questions 19-20.

DIRECTIONS: Questions 19 and 20 are to be answered on the basis of the following paragraph.

If, during a study, some hundreds of values of a variable (such as annual number of latenesses for each employee in a department) have been noted merely in the arbitrary order in which they happen to occur, the mind cannot properly grasp the significance of the record, the observations must be ranked or classified in some way before the characteristics of the series can be comprehended, and those comparisons, on which arguments as to causation depend, can be made with other series. A dichotomous classification is too crude; if the values are merely classified according to whether they exceed or fall short of some fixed value, a large part of the information given by the original record is lost. Numerical measurements lend themselves with peculiar readiness to a manifold classification.

19. According to the above paragraph, if the values of a variable which are gathered 19.____
during a study are classified in a few subdivisions, the MOST likely result will be
    A. an inability to grasp the signification of the record
    B. an inability to relate the series with other series
    C. a loss of much of the information in the original data
    D. a loss of the readiness with which numerical measurements lend themselves to a manifold classification
    E. that the order in which they happen to occur will be arbitrary

20. The above paragraph advocates, with respect to numerical data, the use of 20.____
    A. arbitrary order   B. comparisons with other series
    C. a two-value classification D. a many value classification
    E. all values of a variable

Questions 21-25.

DIRECTIONS: Questions 21 through 25 are to be answered on the basis of the following chart.

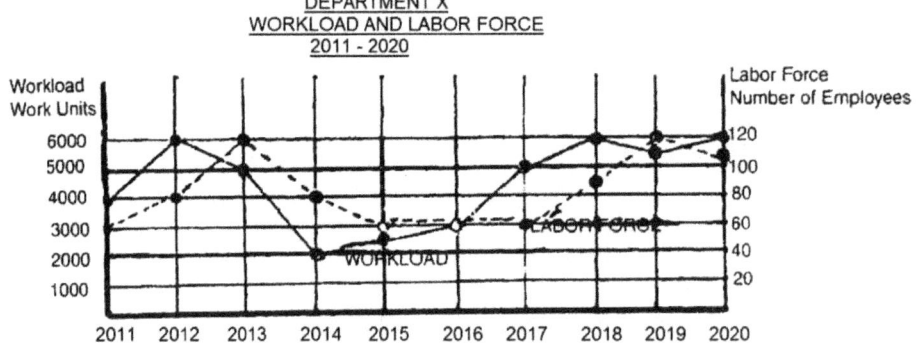

7 (#3)

21. The one of the following years for which average employee production was LOWEST was 21._____
    A. 2012   B. 2014   C. 2016   D. 2018   E. 2020

22. The average annual employee production for the ten-year period was, in terms of work units, MOST NEARLY 22._____
    A. 30   B. 50   C. 70   D. 80   E. 90

23. On the basis of the chart, it can be deduced that personnel needs for the coming year are budgeted on the basis of 23._____
    A. workload for the current year
    B. expected workload for the coming year
    C. no set plan
    D. average workload over the five years immediately preceding the period
    E. expected workload for the five coming years

24. The chart indicates that the operation is carefully programmed and that the labor force has been used properly. 24._____
    This opinion is
    A. *supported* by the chart; the organization has been able to meet emergency situations requiring much additional work without commensurate increase in staff
    B. *not supported* by the chart; the irregular workload shows a complete absence of planning
    C. *supported* by the chart; the similar shapes of the workload and labor force curves show that these important factors are closely related
    D. *not supported* by the chart; poor planning with respect to labor requirements is obvious from the chart
    E. *supported* by the chart; the average number of units of work performed in any 5-year period during the 10 years shows sufficient regularity to indicate a definite trend

25. The chart indicates that the department may be organized in such a way as to require a permanent minimum staff which is too large for the type of operation indicated. 25._____
    This opinion is
    A. *supported* by the chart; there is indication that the operation calls for an irreducible minimum number of employees and application of the most favorable work production records shows this to be too high for normal operation
    B. *not supported* by the chart; the absence of any sort of regularity makes it impossible to express any opinion with any degree of certainty
    C. *supported* by the chart; the expected close relationship between workload and labor force is displaced somewhat, a phenomenon which usually occurs as a result of a fixed minimum requirement
    D. *not supported* by the chart; the violent movement of the labor force curve makes it evident that no minimum requirements are in effect

E. *supported* by the chart; calculation shows that the average number of employees was 84 with an average variation of 17.8, thus indicating that the minimum number of 60 persons was too high for efficient operation

---

KEY (CORRECT ANSWERS)

1.	A		11.	A
2.	B		12.	E
3.	D		13.	E
4.	C		14.	D
5.	A		15.	D
6.	E		16.	D
7.	B		17.	E
8.	C		18.	B
9.	E		19.	C
10.	B		20.	D

21. B
22. B
23. A
24. D
25. A

EXAMINATION SECTION

TEST 1

DIRECTIONS: Each question or incomplete statement is followed by several suggested answers or completions. Select the one that BEST answers the question or completes the statement. *PRINT THE LETTER OF THE CORRECT ANSWER IN THE SPACE AT THE RIGHT.*

1. The new head of a central filing unit, after studying a procedure in use, decided that it was unsatisfactory. He thereupon drew up an entirely new procedure which made no use of and ignored the existing procedure.
   This plan of action is, in general,
   A. *satisfactory*; a new broom sweeps clean
   B. *unsatisfactory*; any plan should use available resources to the utmost before resorting to new creation
   C. *satisfactory*; in general, use of part of an old procedure and part of a new procedure results sin an unworkable patchwork arrangement
   D. *unsatisfactory*; before deciding that the existing procedure was unusable, he should have requested that an independent, unbiased agency study the problem
   E. *satisfactory*; it is usually less time consuming to construct a new plan than to remedy an old one

    1.____

2. Assume that you have broken a complex job into simpler and smaller components.
   After you have assigned a component to each employee, should you proceed to teach each employee a number of alternative methods for doing his job?
   A. *yes*; the more methods for performing a job an employee knows, the more chance there is that he will choose the one best suited to his abilities
   B. *No*; experienced employees should be permitted to decide how to perform the jobs assigned to them
   C. *Yes*; if several different methods are available, a desirable flexibility of operation results
   D. *No*; a single method for each job should be decided upon and taught
   E. *Yes*; the employees will have greater interest in their jobs

    2.____

3. Assume that you are the head of a major staff unit and that a line unit has requested from your unit a special report to be completed in one day. After reviewing the request, you decide that much tie would be saved if two items which you know are superfluous are omitted from the report. You discuss the matter with the head of the other unit and he still insists that the two items are essential for his purposes.
   The one of the following actions which you should take at this stage is to
   A. plan to complete the report, including the two items, as expeditiously as possible
   B. write a memorandum to the department head giving both opinions fairly and asking for a decision

    3.____

C. plan to complete the report without the two items, as expeditiously as possible
D. devise a plan for preparing the report without the two items which will permit you to add them later if they prove necessary although some time may be lost
E. again review the report with the line unit showing them why the two items are unnecessary

4. The one of the following functions of a supervisor which can be MOST successfully delegated is
   A. responsibility for accomplishing the unit's mission
   B. handling discipline
   C. checking completed work
   D. reporting to the bureau chief
   E. placing subordinates in the proper job

5. It is a standard operating procedure in an office which receives several thousand forms each week to have the file on clerk accumulate a week's receipts before filing them. The forms will not be examined for a period of one month after receipt.
   In comparison with daily filing, this procedure is, in general,
   A. *less satisfactory*; it keeps the files unnecessarily incomplete
   B. *more satisfactory*; it tends to reduce filing time
   C. *less satisfactory*; all information should be placed in a safe storage place as soon as possible
   D. *more satisfactory*; it tends to eliminate the prefiling period
   E. *less satisfactory*; it tends to build up an unnecessary period

6. Some organizations attempt to keep a constant backlog of work.
   This procedure is usually
   A. *undesirable*; reports are not ready when they are needed
   B. *desirable*; it tends to insure continuity of work flow
   C. *undesirable*; production records are too difficult to keep
   D. *desirable*; it tends to keep the employees under constant pressure
   E. *undesirable*; it tends to keep the employees under constant pressure

7. The first few times a procedure is carried through, a close check should be kept of all work times.
   The PRIMARY reason for this is to
   A. be able to present a clear picture of the situation
   B. determine if the employees understand the procedure
   C. evaluate the efficiency which may have been presented by the new procedure
   D. determine the efficiency of the employees
   E. permit revision of schedules

3 (#1)

8. The one of the following pieces of information which is of LEAST importance in setting up the schedule for a given job is the time
   A. which is required to perform each component of the job
   B. when the source material will be available
   C. the job will take under adverse conditions
   D. by which the job must be completed
   E. employees will be available

9. Every employee should have a thorough knowledge of the organization of which he is a part.
   Of the following, the BEST justification for the above opinion is that
   A. the feeling of being a member of a team develops a responsible attitude toward one's everyday duties
   B. in an emergency, an employee may be called upon to perform duties other than his own
   C. the intricate details of an organization as complicated as a city department cannot easily be reduced to an organization chart
   D. an understanding of the different specialized units in an organization is often necessary to achieve the organization's given objective
   E. many city jobs are technical; thus, each employee should be trained to have more than a single narrow skill

10. The one of the following which is NOT a good rule in administering discipline is for you as a supervisor to
    A. reprimand the employee in private even though the fault was committed before others
    B. allow the employee a chance to reply to your criticism if he wishes
    C. be as specific as possible in criticizing the employee for his faults
    D. be sure you have all the facts before you reprimand an employee for an error he has committed
    E. allow an extended period to elapse after an error has been committed before reprimanding an employee

11. After you have submitted your annual evaluations of the work of your subordinates, one of them whose work has not been satisfactory complains to you that your evaluation was unjustified.
    For you to avoid discussing the evaluation but to point out two or three specific instances where the employee's work was below standard is
    A. *desirable*; an employee should be told what aspects of his work are unsatisfactory
    B. *undesirable*; once the evaluation has been submitted, there is no point in reconsidering it
    C. *desirable*; once the evaluation has been submitted, there is no point in reconsidering it but a discussion of the employee's weaknesses may help
    D. *undesirable*; it would have been better to explain how you arrived at your evaluation
    E. *desirable*; entering into a general argument is bad for the discipline of an organization

12. The chief of a central files bureau which has 50 employees customarily spends 12.____
a considerable portion of his time in spot-checking the files, reviewing material
being transferred from active to inactive files and similar activities.
From the viewpoint of the department top management, the MOST pertinent
evaluation which can be made on the basis of this information is that the
    A. supervisor is conscientious and hardworking
    B. bureau may need additional staff
    C. supervisor has not made a sufficient delegation of authority and
       responsibility
    D. bureau needs an in-service training course as the work of its employees
       requires an abnormal amount of review
    E filing system employed may be inadequate

13. Assume that you are in charge of a unit with 40 employees. The department 13.____
head requests immediate preparation of a special and rather complicated
report which will take about a day to complete if everyone in your unit works on
it.
After breaking the job into simple components and assigning each component
to an employee, should more than one person be instructed on the procedure
to be followed on each component?
    A. *No*; the procedure would be a waste of time in this instance
    B. *Yes*; it is always desirable to have a replacement available in the event of
       illness or any other emergency
    C. *No*; in general, as long as an employee's job performance is satisfactory,
       there is no need to train an alternate
    D. *Yes*; the presence of more than one person in a unit who can perform a
       given task tends to prevent the formation of a bottleneck
    E. *No*; there is, in general, no need to train more than one employee in the
       performance of a special job

14. A new employee who has shown that she is capable of performing superior work 14.____
during the first month of her employment falls far below this standard after the
first month.
For the supervisor to wait until the end of the probationary period and then
recommend that she be discharged if her work is still unsatisfactory is
    A. *undesirable*; she should have been discharged when her work became
       unsatisfactory
    B. *desirable*; there is no place in the civil service for unsatisfactory
       employees
    C. *undesirable*; he should immediately attempt to determine the cause of the
       poor performance
    D. *desirable*; the employee is entitled to an opportunity to prove herself
    E. *undesirable*; the employee is obviously capable of performing good work
       and simply requires some guidance from the supervisor

15. In order to make sure that work is completed on time, the unit supervisor should   15.____
    A. use the linear method of delegating responsibility
    B. pitch in and do as much of the work himself as he can
    C. schedule the work and keep himself informed of its progress
    D. not assign more than one person to any one task
    E. know the capabilities of his subordinates

16. One of the more effective ways to obtain optimum performance from employees   16.____
    is to keep them off balance by not letting them feel secure in the job; to permit
    an employee to feel secure is to invite him to settle into a comfortable rut.
    The point of view expressed in this statement is
    A. *correct*; studies have shown that the degree of effort put forth on a job
       generally varies directly with the degree of job insecurity
    B. *incorrect*; studies have shown that a relatively high degree of security is
       conducive to best job performance
    C. *correct*; while studies have shown that there is little relationship between
       security and job performance, what tendencies are present to support the
       point of view expressed
    D. *incorrect*; studies have shown that there is little relationship between
       security and job performance and what tendencies are present are
       opposed to the point of view expressed
    E. *correct*; while no specific studies have been made in this field, analogous
       studies made in similar fields show that permitting a feeling of security to
       develop results in decreased job performance

Questions 17-19.

DIRECTIONS: Questions 17 through 19 are to be answered on the basis of the following
            paragraph.

The supervisor of a large clerical and statistical division has assigned to one of the units
under his supervision the preparation of a special statistical report required by the department
head. The unit accepted the assignment without comment but soon ran into considerable
difficulty because no one in his unit had had any statistical training.

17. If a result of this lack of training is that the report is not completed on time,   17.____
    although everyone has done all that could be expected, the responsibility for
    the failure rests with
    A. the department head   B. the supervisor
    C. the unit head   D. the employees in the unit
    E. no one

18. This incident indicates that the supervisory staff has insufficient knowledge of   18.____
    employee
    A. capabilities
    B. reaction to increased demands
    C. on-the-job training needs
    D. work habits
    E. ability to perform ordinary assignments

19. After working on the report for two days, the unit head notifies the supervisor that he will not be able to get the report out in the required time. He states that his staff will be completely trained in another day or two and that after preparing the report will be a simple matter. At this stage, the supervisor decides to have the statistical unit prepare the report.
This action on the part of the supervisor is
   A. *undesirable*; the unit head should be given an incentive to continue with his training program which may produce good results
   B. *desirable*; it is the most effective way in which the supervisor can show his displeasure with the unit head's failure
   C. *undesirable*; it may adversely affect the morale of the unit
   D. *desirable*; it will generally result in a better report completed in a shorter time
   E. *undesirable*; the time spent training the unit will be completely wasted

20. A supervisor criticizes a subordinate's work by telling him that he is disappointed with it. The supervisor states that the work is completely unsatisfactory, shows where it is bad, and says that improvement is expected.
This approach is usually
   A. *good*; the employee knows just where he stands
   B. *poor*; some favorable comment should be made at the same time if possible
   C. *good*; it is good policy to keep this type of interview as short as possible
   D. *poor*; the employee should be asked to explain why his work is poor
   E. *good*; the supervisor did not criticize the subordinate in front of other employees

Questions 21-25.

DIRECTIONS: Column I below lists five kinds of statistical data which are to be transformed into a chart or a graph for incorporation into the department annual report. Column II lists nine different kinds of graphs or charts. For each type of information listed in Column I, select the chart or graph from Column II by means of which it should be demonstrated.

COLUMN I   COLUMN II

21. The relationship between employees' occupational classification and their salaries, for all employees by occupational classification, showing minimum, maximum, and average salary in each group.

22. A comparison of the number of employees in the department, the departmental budget the number of employees in the operating divisions and the operating division budget for each year over a ten-year period.

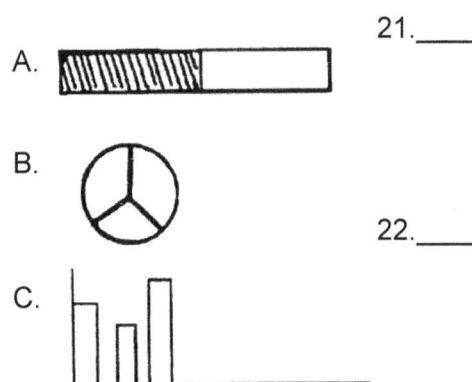

COLUMN I	COLUMN II
23. The amount of money spent for each of the department's 10 most important functions during the past year.	D.  23.____
24. The percentage of the department's budget spent for each of the department's activities for each year over a ten-year period.	E.  24.____
25. The number of each kind of employee employed in the department over a period of twenty years and the total number of employees in the department for each of these periods.	F. 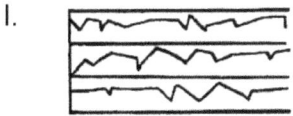 25.____
	G.
	H.
	I.

KEY (CORRECT ANSWERS)

1.	B	11.	D
2.	D	12.	C
3.	A	13.	A
4.	C	14.	C
5.	B	15.	C
6.	B	16.	B
7.	E	17.	B
8.	C	18.	A
9.	A	19.	D
10.	E	20.	B

21. F
22. D
23. C
24. H
25. G

TEST 2

DIRECTIONS: Each question or incomplete statement is followed by several suggested answers or completions. Select the one that BEST answers the question or completes the statement. *PRINT THE LETTER OF THE CORRECT ANSWER IN THE SPACE AT THE RIGHT.*

1. The report of the head of Unit Y to his bureau chief on the performance of a new clerical employee indicates that the performance is not up to the expected standard. After reading the report, the bureau chief transferred the employee to Unit X.
   This action on the part of the bureau chief was
   A. in line with good personal practice; an employee who does poorly in one place may do better in another
   B. premature; an attempt to discover the cause of the poor performance should be made first
   C. desirable; personnel reports become meaningless unless acted upon at once
   D. undesirable; unsatisfactory employees should be dismissed and not transferred from unit to unit
   E. in the best interest of the organization; whenever a supervisor cannot get along with a subordinate for whatever reason, it is desirable to transfer the subordinate

   1.____

2. Suppose that you have been consulted by a department head who wishes to initiate an in-service training course in his department. The department head suggests that, as a first step, a training course be initiated for supervisors in the department.
   This suggestion is BEST characterized as
   A. *undesirable*; the supervisors are generally the persons least in need of work incentives
   B. *desirable*; it is generally cheaper and more effective to train a few supervisors than a large number of employees
   C. *undesirable*; supervisors may be held up to ridicule if they are isolated for training
   D. *desirable*; trained supervisors are needed to train employees
   E. *undesirable*; employees should be trained before supervisors

   2.____

3. Any person thoroughly familiar with the specific steps in a particular class of work is well qualified to serve as a training course instructor in that work.
   This statement is erroneous CHIEFLY because
   A. it is practically impossible for any instructor to be acquainted with all the specific steps sin a particular class of work
   B. what is true of one class of work is not necessarily true of other types of work
   C. a qualified instructor cannot be expected to have detailed information about many specific fields

   3.____

D. the steps in any type of work are usually interrelated and not independent or unique
E. the quantity of information possessed by an instructor does not bear a direct relationship to the quality of instruction

4. Of the following, the MOST significant argument against making it compulsory for civil service employees to attend a training course is that
   A. unwilling trainees will be penalized in any event by non-promotion
   B. most training requires additional time and expense on the part of the trainee
   C. training is highly desirable but not absolutely essential for adequate job performance
   D. incompetent work is generally reflected in poor service ratings
   E. trainees must be receptive if training is to be successful

4.____

5. There are four basic systems of job evaluation which have been extensively used by government and industry.
   The one of the following which is NOT one of these is the _____ system.
   A. Benchmark   B. Factor Comparison
   C. Point   D. Job Classification
   E. Ranking

5.____

6. Of the following, the CHIEF advantage derived by filling all vacancies in an organization by promotion from below rather than from outside the organization is that such a procedure
   A. fills existing vacancies from the widest possible recruitment base
   B. stimulates individual employees to improve their work habits
   C. avoids personality difficulties likely to arise when an employee is assigned to supervise former colleagues
   D. indirectly coordinates the work of different units by interchange of personnel
   E. encourages reorientation and review of administrative procedures

6.____

7. Of the following, the CHIEF justification for a periodic classification audit is that
   A. salaries should be readjusted at frequent intervals
   B. some degree of personnel turnover should always be expected
   C. a career service requires regular promotion opportunities
   D. employees require frequent stimulation and encouragement
   E. positions frequently change over a period of time

7.____

8. A classification analyst sorts jobs horizontally and vertically.
   Of the following, the LEAST important job factor to be considered with respect to vertical placement is
   A. independence of action and decision
   B. consequence of errors
   C. kind and character of work performed
   D. degree of supervision received
   E. determination of policy

8.____

9. Assume that you have been assigned to prepare a plan for conducting a large scale job classification survey.
   Of the following, the BEST suggestion for reducing the number of appeals from the final allocations likely to be received after the classification study has been completed is to
   A. have supervisors check statements of employees on classification questionnaires
   B. allocate present positions to proposed classes according to jurisdictional assignments
   C. adjust salary to present level of work performed by employees
   D. allow employee participation throughout the classification process
   E. postpone controversial problems until simpler problems have been solved and a general blueprint laid down

10. A comment made by an employee about a training course was, *Oh, I suppose it's important for the job but it's a waste of time for me just to sit in that course and yawn while the instructor rambles on."*
    The fundamental error in training methodology to which this criticism points is failure to provide
    A. goals for the students
    B. for individual differences
    C. connecting links between new and old material
    D. for student participation
    E. motivation for the subject matter of the course

11. You are preparing a long report addressed to your superior on a study which you have conducted for him.
    The one of the following sections which should come FIRST in the report is a
    A. description of the working procedure utilized in the study
    B. description of the situation which exists
    C. summary of the conclusions of the survey
    D. discussion of possible objections to the report and their refutation
    E. description of the method of installing the recommendations

12. While setting up a reporting system to help the department planning section, an administrator proposed the policy that no overlap or duplication be permitted even if it meant that some minor areas were left uncovered.
    This policy is
    A. *undesirable*; overlap is frequently necessary
    B. *desirable*; the presence of overlap and duplication indicates defective planning
    C. *undesirable*; setting up general policy in advance of the specific reporting system may lead to inflexibility
    D. *desirable*; it is not necessary to get complete coverage in order to be able to plan operations
    E. *undesirable*; duplication is preferable to leaving any area uncovered

Questions 13-15.

DIRECTIONS: Questions 13 through 15 are to be answered on the basis of the following paragraph.

Prior to revising its child care program, a department feels that it is necessary to get some information from the mothers served by the existing program in order to determine where changes are required. A questionnaire is to be constructed to obtain this information.

13. Of the following points which can be taken into consideration in the construction of the questionnaire, the one which is of LEAST importance is
    A. that the data are to be put into punch cards
    B. the aspects of the program which seem to be in need of change
    C. the type of person who will fill out the questionnaire
    D. testing the questionnaire for ambiguity in advance of general distribution
    E. setting up a control group so that answers received can be compared to a standard

14. To discuss this questionnaire with all mothers who have been asked to answer it, before they actually fill it out, is
    A. *desirable*; the mothers may be able to offer valuable suggestions for changes in the form of the questionnaire
    B. *undesirable*; it is of some value but consumes too much valuable time
    C. *desirable*; cooperation and uniform interpretation will tend to be achieved
    D. *undesirable*; it may cause the answers to be biased
    E. *desirable*; the group will tend to support the program

15. Of the following items included in the questionnaire, the one which will be of LEAST assistance for comparing attitudes toward the program among different kinds of persons is
    A. name
    B. address
    C. age
    D. place of birth
    E. education

16. You have been asked, to prepare for public distribution, a statement dealing with a controversial matter.
    Of the following approaches, the one which would usually be MOST effective is to present your department's point of view
    A. as tersely as possible with no reference to any other matters
    B. developed from ideas and facts well known to most readers
    C. and show all the statistical data and techniques which were used in arriving at it
    D. in such a way that the controversial parts are omitted
    E. substantiated by supporting quotations from persons in the specialized field even if they are not well known

5 (#2)

17. During a conference of administrative staff personnel, the department head discussing the letter prepared for his signature stated, *"Use no more words than are necessary to express your meaning."*
Following this rule in letter writing is, in general,
    A. *desirable*; considerable time will be saved in the preparation of correspondence
    B. *undesirable*; it is frequently necessary to elaborate on an explanation in order to make certain that the reader will understand
    C. *desirable*; terse statements give government letters a business-like air which impresses readers favorably
    D. *undesirable*; terse statements are generally cold and formal and produce an unfavorable reaction in the reader
    E. *desirable*; the use of more words than are necessary is likely to obscure the meaning and tire the reader

17.____

18. While you are designing the layout for a departmental procedure manual, it is suggested that you carefully arrange your reading material so that there will be a minimum amount of blank space on the page.
Of the following judgments of this suggestion, the one which is the MOST valid basis for action is that it is
    A. *bad*; readability and ease of reference will be decreased
    B. *good*; the cost of production can be decreased considerably without any great disadvantage
    C. *of little or no importance*; more or less blank space on the page will not affect the value of the manual
    D. *good*; it will make for a smaller, easier to handle book
    E. *bad*; replacement of outdated pages is made more difficult by having more material on a page

18.____

19. After the planning of an employee's procedure manual had been completed, the suggestion was made that the manual should be prepared and arranged so that changes could be made readily.
Of the following decisions with respect to this suggestion, the one which is MOST desirable from the viewpoint of good administration is that the suggestions should
    A. not be considered as it is generally impossible to prepare a satisfactory manual which will take everything into consideration
    B. be followed only if it does not conflict with the planned layout
    C. be used even if it is somewhat more costly than the planned layout
    D. be noted and acted upon at the next revision of the manual
    E. not be considered as this type of manual is more difficult to maintain properly

19.____

20. Assume that you are in charge of preparing a procedure manual of about 100 pages for a large clerical unit. After you have decided to use a looseleaf format, one of your subordinates proposes that only one side of the page be printed.

20.____

This proposal is
- A. *good*; replacement of obsolete pages is made easier
- B. *poor*; cost is increased
- C. *good*; provision is automatically made for employee's notes
- D. *poor*; it will increase the size of the manual, making it more difficult to use
- E *good*; indexing will be made easier

21. It may be assumed that if all departments had qualified personnel officers, not all departments would be lacking adequate training programs. However, the most cursory examination of the situation will show that some departments do not have adequate training programs. Thus, we must conclude that some of them lack qualified personnel officers.
    The argument presented in the report is
    - A. *correct*; the conclusion follows logically from the assumption and the facts
    - B. *not correct*; what can be concluded is that no department has a qualified personnel officer
    - C. *not correct*; no conclusion with respect to the presence of personnel officers in departments can be drawn from the information
    - D. *not correct*; what can be concluded is that the absence of an adequate training program in a department implies the absence of a personnel officer
    - E. *correct*; but the conclusion is false as the hypothesis is not true

21.____

22. In a study of the relationship between a fixed discipline policy and the incidence of lateness, it would be MOST informative to have data proving the statement:
    - A. In those organizations in which there are no fixed discipline policy, the incidence of lateness is variable.
    - B. The incidence of lateness has not decreased in those organizations where fixed discipline policies have been abandoned.
    - C. The incidence of lateness and the discipline policy vary from organization to organization.
    - D. Discipline policies sometimes ignore the problem of lateness.
    - E. In organizations with a fixed discipline policy, the incidence of lateness is variable.

22.____

23. The data prove that an increase in the number of clerks performing filing work results in an increased cost per item filed.
    On the basis of these data, we can be certain that
    - A. if filing costs per item filed increase, it is caused by an increase in the number of clerks filing
    - B. if filing costs per item filed decrease, the number of clerks filing cannot be increasing
    - C. if the number of clerks filing is changed, the unit cost per filing will change
    - D. if the number of clerks filing is not increased, the cost per unit filed will not increase
    - E. if the number of clerks filing is decreased, the cost per item filed will decrease

23.____

24. Each unit either has sufficient space assigned to it or it has not. No unit which has insufficient space assigned to it has neglected to ask for additional space. From these data, we can state
    A. units with sufficient space have not asked for additional space
    B. only units which have sufficient space have not asked for additional space
    C. nothing about the relationship between the need for additional space and requests made for additional space
    D. all units which have requested additional space have insufficient space
    E. no units which have requested additional space have sufficient space

25. One argument which is presented against a strict career system in the civil service is as follows:
    The employees who are recruited today for low-level jobs become the administrators of tomorrow. At the present time the employees we are attracting for the low-level jobs are untrained and poorly educated. Thus, it follows that the administrators of tomorrow will be untrained and poorly educated.
    The one of the following which is a CORRECT criticism of the reasoning is that
    A. the argument is logically correct but the conclusion is false as the hypothesis that we are attracting untrained and poorly educated people for our low-level job is false
    B. the conclusion does not follow logically from hypotheses
    C. the argument is logically correct, but the conclusion is false because it is a false hypothesis that tomorrow's administrators will come from employees who hold low-level jobs
    D. the argument is logically correct and the conclusion is correct
    E. while the argument is logically correct and the hypotheses are not demonstrably false, the argument ignores the realities of the case that those who are untrained today may be trained tomorrow

KEY (CORRECT ANSWERS)

1.	B	11.	C
2.	D	12.	E
3.	E	13.	E
4.	E	14.	C
5.	A	15.	A
6.	B	16.	B
7.	E	17.	E
8.	C	18.	A
9.	D	19.	C
10.	D	20.	A

21. C
22. B
23. B
24. B
25. B

TEST 3

DIRECTIONS: Each question or incomplete statement is followed by several suggested answers or completions. Select the one that BEST answers the question or completes the statement. *PRINT THE LETTER OF THE CORRECT ANSWER IN THE SPACE AT THE RIGHT.*

1. Surveying modern administration, it becomes clear that there is GREATEST need at present for administrators with 1.____
    A. a good knowledge of personnel administration
    B. the ability to write good reports
    C. a working knowledge of modern methods analysis
    D. a broad rather than specialized viewpoint
    E. the ability to analyze complicated fiscal programs

2. The one of the following which is a fundamental obstacle to effective planning in MOST governmental agencies is 2.____
    A. inadequate staff or resources
    B. the absence of the properly centralized administration
    C. the absence of clearly defined objective and constituent programs
    D. the neglect of analysis of ways and means
    E. the absence of functional boundaries for units and individuals

3. A department consists of several independent bureaus, each responsible to the commissioner for its own planning, operation, and reporting, a central personnel unit and the commissioner's office consisting of a secretary and several clerks to handle public relations. 3.____
The one of the following *undesirable* characteristics which is MOST likely to arise in this organization is
    A. absence of planning
    B. weak and ineffectual leadership
    C. failure to have employees properly trained
    D. a lack of an easily understandable goal
    E. duplication of work

4. The one of the following practices which is MOST likely to lead to confusion, recrimination and jurisdictional conflict among the bureaus of a department is the failure to 4.____
    A. make clear and unambiguous assignments
    B. systematically subdivide the work
    C. explain general policy to those responsible for its achievement
    D. allocate equitably available resources
    E. set up uniform operating procedures for all units

5. The one of the following which is MOST likely to occur in an over-specialized administrative set-up is 5.____
    A. inability to recruit proper personnel to fill over-specialized positions
    B. improper supervision
    C. failure of employees to realize the broad implications of their work

D. lack of proper decentralization of authority, as emphasis on specialization goes hand-in-hand with over-centralization
E. inability to solve technical problems which are not entirely in one specialty

6. Of the following, the LEAST valid reason for a department head continuing to require that a weekly report be forwarded to him, is that the report forms a basis for
   A. measuring performance
   B. making decisions
   C. revising policy
   D. the execution of the mission of the unit which receives it
   E. the operation of the unit which is required to prepare it

6.____

7. Administrators must learn not to farm out essential functions to unintegrated agencies, but to organize all responsibilities in unified but decentralized hierarchies.
A problem which an administrator may be expected to face if he has not learned this is that
   A. the organization fails to develop administrators capable of independent action
   B. issues will not be posed at the level where decisions should be made
   C. relationships with the public will not be satisfactory
   D. it will be difficult to achieve administrative control or get agreement on departmental action
   E. individual agencies will be unable to complete the work scheduled

7.____

8. The central staff planning unit within any organization includes in its functions helping to plan policy at one extreme and planning detailed execution at the other extreme.
With respect to the actual execution, the planning activity should
   A. have no concern with it
   B. simply forward and explain new plans
   C. have only the responsibility of explaining in the form of plans the objectives of top management
   D. keep track of how the plans are working out but make no attempt to supervise their execution
   E. supervise the execution of new plans

8.____

9. The head of a department assigned final responsibility for the training function to the personnel office.
This assignment was
   A. *undesirable*; this type of centralization prevents a staff organization from carrying out staff functions
   B. *desirable*; experience has shown that centralization of this type results in more efficient and economic operation
   C. *undesirable*; the personnel office usually does not have the technical "know how" to carry this responsibility
   D. *desirable*; if training is left to the line officials, it never is accomplished
   E. *undesirable*; this responsibility must rest with the supervisor

9.____

3 (#3)

10. A department head insisted that operating officials participate in the development of new procedures along with the planning section.
Participation of this type is, on the whole,
    A. *desirable*; operating realities are more likely to be considered
    B. *undesirable*; the inclusion of conflicting views before the plan is drawn may result in no plan
    C. *desirable*; plans will be more flexible and objectives more clearly defined
    D. *undesirable*; the operating officials should decide to what extent they wish to participate with no pressure from the top
    E. *desirable*; to back down on a procedure once it has been decided upon is a sign of weakness

10.____

11. Much of the current criticism of the administration of large organizations is basically a criticism of our failure to place the same emphasis on accountability that we do on authority and responsibility.
The one of the following acts which is MOST likely to insure accountability for the discharge of responsibilities inherent in the delegation of authority is the
    A. establishment of appropriate reports and controls
    B. organization of a methods analysis section
    C. delegation of authority so made as to support functional or homogeneous activities
    D. delegation of authority so made as to preserve unity of command
    E. decentralization of responsibility and authority

11.____

12. This statement has been made:
A man who is a top-notch executive in one organization would make a top-notch executive in any other organization, even if the organizations are as diverse as a sales agency and a research foundation.
This statement is, in general,
    A. *correct*; the characteristics required for a good executive are invariant with respect to organization
    B. *incorrect*; there is no way of predicting how a good executive in one organization would be in any other
    C. *correct*; while the characteristics required for a good executive vary from organization to organization, the common core requirements are great enough to insure similar performance
    D. *incorrect*; although some prediction can be made, different types of organizations require different types of executives
    E. *correct*; success as an executive does not depend upon "characteristics" but on the man; if he is able to direct and execute in one organization he will be able to do so in any other

12.____

13. Reported information is not needed at levels higher than those at which decisions are made on the basis of the information reported.
This statement is, in general,
    A. *correct*; if no action is to be taken on the basis of the information, the information is unnecessary
    B. *incorrect*; all information is of importance in arriving at a sound decision

13.____

C. *correct*; levels below the one at which the decision is made have need of the information
D. *incorrect*; levels below the one at which the decision is made do not have need of the information
E. *correct*; decisions should be made on the basis of information reported

14. Of the following, the characteristic of an organization which BEST shows that the organizational hierarchy is effective is that
    A. the department head commands the respect of the employees
    B. the organization is sufficiently flexible to assume functions in fields not related to his major field of endeavor
    C. responsibility has been appropriately delegated throughout the organization
    D. the department continues to function effectively even though there is continual turnover in the higher supervisory ranks
    E. no employee in the organization is subject to orders from more than one source

15. It is only because the primary purpose of traditional discipline has been to preserve the structure of command that a need has arisen for ameliorative safeguards such as a formal statement of "cause," right of hearing, and right of appeal.
    The BEST current practice with respect to discipline is that
    A. few ameliorative safeguards of the kind enumerated are desirable as their presence hurts the public service
    B. discipline is a means of controlling deviations from established authority
    C. the safeguards enumerated are not sufficient for the protection of the employee
    D. discipline should be based upon education, persuasion, and consultation
    E. unquestioned obedience to each order should not be expected but that a supervisor should be prepared at all times to demonstrate the reasonableness of his requests

16. Of the following types of work, the one for which a manual process is MOST usually to be preferred over a mechanized process is one in which the transactions are very
    A. numerous   B. similar   C. dissimilar
    D. predictable   E. unpredictable

17. Work flow charts are used in an organization PRIMARILY because they
    A. indicate present and future objectives clearly
    B. are frequently used records
    C. clearly indicate when each operation will be performed
    D. summarize the work procedures of the organization
    E. tend to clarify thinking by presenting certain facts clearly

5 (#3)

18. With respect to a report prepared by an IBM installation, the one of the following changes which is LEAST likely to cause a change in the procedure for preparing the report is a change in the
    A. volume of work
    B. source documents
    C. final report
    D. employees assigned
    E. time allowed for the preparation of the report

19. The one of the following which is NOT necessarily a characteristic of a good buying procedure is that it
    A. provides for proper analysis of purchases made
    B. is simple
    C. makes provision for substitutions where possible and necessary
    D. makes sealed bids mandatory
    E. recruits many bidders

20. Data relating to the operation of any unit should be accumulated and periodically summarized and analyzed PRIMARILY in order to
    A. point out the most efficient and least efficient workers
    B. determine the relative value of each procedure
    C. locate the elements of an operation which are unusually efficient or inefficient
    D. evaluate the importance of maintaining operating records and quotas
    E. compare the work performed by comparable units

21. Of the following, the MAJOR function of an administrative planning and research staff units is to
    A. investigate trouble points in the organization
    B. reorganize inefficient units
    C. assist the executive to plan future operations
    D. conduct continuous investigations and planning
    E. write the necessary operation and procedure manuals

22. The one of the following which does NOT require definition when setting up a work measurement system is the
    A. level of work accomplishment at which to measure
    B. work unit in which to measure
    C. time unit by which to measure
    D. acceptable quota for each activity
    E. reporting system to be used

23. During a discussion of the time unit that would be appropriate to measure employee-time in a work measurement program in a public agency, the man-day was suggested.
    This unit is
    A. *satisfactory*; record keeping will be kept to a minimum
    B. *unsatisfactory*; it will be difficult to verify the unit against official time records

C. *satisfactory*; it will be easy to verify the unit against official time records
D. *unsatisfactory*; its use will unnecessarily complicate record keeping
E. *satisfactory*; it permits more meaningful comparisons to be made between equal periods of time

24. As part of a space layout survey, an administrator instructed his subordinates to study the flow of work and sequence of operating procedures.
His MAJOR purposes in doing this was to determine
    A. the physical distribution and movement of personnel, material, and equipment
    B. the amount of space which is available and the amount of space which will be required
    C. the order in which the component steps in the different procedures are performed
    D. what future requirements will be, based on observable present trend
    E. how the distribution of personnel to various organization units is related to their space requirements

25. Before discussing a proposed office layout, the administrative officer stated, *"We intend to have a minimum number of private offices. We will assign private offices only where quiet is deemed essential or confidential conferences are required."*
The one of the following which is usually the MOST valid reason for this rule is that it
    A. permits proper placing of employees who deal with the public
    B. makes it easier to locate supervisors near the units they control
    C. tends to ensure that the work of each unit will flow continually forward within itself
    D. allows placing complementary units close together
    E. makes clerical supervision easier

KEY (CORRECT ANSWERS)

1.	D	11.	A
2.	C	12.	D
3.	E	13.	A
4.	A	14.	C
5.	C	15.	D
6.	E	16.	C
7.	D	17.	E
8.	D	18.	D
9.	E	19.	D
10.	A	20.	C

21.	D
22.	D
23.	D
24.	A
25.	E

EXAMINATION SECTION

TEST 1

DIRECTIONS: Each question or incomplete statement is followed by several suggested answers or completions. Select the one that BEST answers the question or completes the statement. *PRINT THE LETTER OF THE CORRECT ANSWER IN THE SPACE AT THE RIGHT.*

1. An administrator in a department should be thoroughly familiar with modern methods of personnel administration.
   This statement is
   A. *true*, because this familiarity will help him in performing the normal functions of his office
   B. *false*, because personnel administration is not a departmental matter, but is centralized in the Civil Service Commission
   C. *true*, because this knowledge will insure the elimination of personnel problems in the department
   D. *false*, because departmental problems of a minor character are handled by the personnel representative, while major problems are the responsibility of the commissioner

2. The LEAST true of the following is that an administrative assistant in a department
   A. executes the policy laid down by the commissioner or his deputies
   B. in the main, carries out the policies of the commissioner but with some leeway where his own frame of reference is determinative
   C. is never required to formulate policy
   D. is responsible for the successful accomplishment of a section of the department's program

3. If a representative committee of employees in a large department is to meet with an administrative officer for the purpose of improve staff relations and of handling grievances, it is BEST that these meetings be held
   A. at regular intervals
   B. whenever requested by an aggrieved employee
   C. at the discretion of the administrative officer
   D. whenever the need arises

4. In the theory and practice of public administration, the one of the following which is LEAST generally regarded as a staff function is
   A. budgeting
   B. firefighting
   C. purchasing
   D. research and information

5. The LEAST essential factor in the successful application of a service rating system is
   A. careful training of reporting officers
   B. provision for self-rating
   C. statistical analysis to check reliability
   D. utilization of objective standards of performance

6. Of the following, the one which is NOT an aim of service rating plans is
   A. establishment of a fair method of measuring employee value to the employer
   B. application of a uniform measurement to employees of the same class and grade performing similar functions
   C. application of a uniform measurement to employees of the same class and grade however different their assignments may be
   D. establishment of a scientific duties plan

7. A rule or regulation relating to the internal management of a department becomes effective
   A. only after it is filed in the office of the clerk
   B. as soon as issued by the department head
   C. only after it has been published officially
   D. when approved by the mayor

8. Of the following, the one MOST generally regarded as an *administrative* power is the
   A. veto power
   B. message power
   C. power of pardon
   D. rule making power

9. In public administration functional allocation involves
   A. integration and the assignment of administrative power
   B. the assignment of a single power to a single administrative level
   C. the distribution of a number of subsidiary responsibilities among all levels of government
   D. decentralization of administrative responsibilities

10. In the field of public administration, the LEAST general result of coordination is the
    A. performance of a well-rounded job
    B. elimination of jurisdictional overlapping
    C. performance of functions otherwise neglected
    D. elimination of duplication of work

11. Of the following, the MOST complicated and difficult problem confronting the reorganizer in the field of public administration is
    A. ridding the government of graft
    B. ridding the government of crude incompetence
    C. ridding the government of excessive decentralization
    D. conditioning organization to modern social and economic life

12. The MOST accurate description of the process of integration in the field of public administration is
    A. transfer of administrative authority from a lower to a higher level of government
    B. transfer of administrative authority from a higher to a lower level of government
    C. concentration of administrative authority within one level of government
    D. formal cooperation between city and state governments to administer a function

13. The one of the following who was MOST closely allied with *scientific management* is
    A. Mosher   B. Probst   C. Taylor   D. White

14. Of the following wall colors, the one which will reflect the GREATEST amount of light, other things being equal, is
    A. buff   B. light gray   C. light blue   D. brown

15. Natural illumination is LEAST necessary in a(n)
    A. executive office
    B. reception room
    C. central stenographic bureau
    D. conference room

16. The MOST desirable relative humidity in an office is
    A. 30%   B. 50%   c. 70%   D. 90%

17. When several pieces of correspondence are filed in the same folder, they are USUALLY arranged
    A. according to subject
    B. numerically
    C. in the order in which they are received
    D. alphabetically

18. Eliminating slack in work assignment is
    A. speed-up
    B. time study
    C. motion study
    D. efficient management

19. *Time studies* examine and measure
    A. past performance
    B. present performance
    C. long-run effect
    D. influence of change

20. In making a position analysis for a duties classification, the one of the following factors which must be considered is the _____ the incumbent.
    A. capabilities of
    B. qualifications of
    C. efficiency attained by
    D. responsibility assigned to

4 (#1)

21. The MAXIMUM number of subordinates who can be effectively supervised by one administrative assistant is BEST considered as
    A. determined by the law of *span of control*
    B. determined by the law of *span of attention*
    C. determined by the type of work supervised
    D. fixed at not more than six

22. Of the following devices used in personnel administration, the MOST basic is
    A. classification
    B. service rating
    C. appeals
    D. in-service training

23. Of the following, the LEAST important factor for sound organization is the
    A. individual and his position
    B. hierarchical form of organization
    C. location and delegation of authority
    D. standardization of salary schedules

24. *Stretch-out* is a term that originated with the
    A. imposition of a furlough
    B. system of semi-monthly relief payments
    C. development of labor technology
    D. irregular development of low-cost housing projects

25. The one of the following which is LEAST generally true of a personnel division in a large department is that it is
    A. concerned with having a certain point of view on personnel permeate the executive staff
    B. charged with aiding operating executives with auxiliary staff service, assistance and advice
    C. charged to administer a certain few operating duties of its own
    D. charged with the basic responsibility for the efficient operation of the entire department

KEY (CORRECT ANSWERS)

1.	A	11.	D
2.	C	12.	C
3.	A	13.	C
4.	B	14.	A
5.	B	15.	B
6.	D	16.	A
7.	B	17.	C
8.	D	18.	D
9.	C	19.	B
10.	C	20.	D

21.	C
22.	A
23.	D
24.	C
25.	D

TEST 2

DIRECTIONS: Each question or incomplete statement is followed by several suggested answers or completions. Select the one that BEST answers the question or completes the statement. *PRINT THE LETTER OF THE CORRECT ANSWER IN THE SPACE AT THE RIGHT.*

Questions 1-10.

DIRECTIONS: Below are ten words numbered 1 through 10 and twenty other words divided into four groups—Group A, Group B, Group C, and Group D. For each of the ten numbered words, select the word in one of the four groups which is MOST NEARLY the same in meaning. The letter of that group is the answer for the item.

GROUP A	GROUP B	GROUP C	GROUP D
articulation	bituminous	assumption	scope
fusion	deductive	forecast	vindication
catastrophic	repudiation	terse	amortization
inductive	doleful	insolence	productive
leadership	prolonged	panorama	slanderous

1. abnegation   1._____

2. calumnious   2._____

3. purview   3._____

4. lugubrious   4._____

5. hegemony   5._____

6. arrogation   6._____

7. coalescence   7._____

8. prolix   8._____

9. syllogistic   9._____

10. contumely   10._____

11. In large cities the total cost of government is of course GREATER than in small cities but   11._____
    A. this is accompanied by a decrease in per capita cost
    B. the per capita cost is also greater
    C. the per capita cost is approximately the same
    D. the per capita cost is considerably less in approximately 50% of the cases

12. The one of the following which is LEAST characteristic of governmental reorganizations is the
    A. saving of large sums of money
    B. problem of morale and personnel
    C. task of logic and management
    D. engineering approach

13. The LEAST accurate of the following statements about graphic presentation is
    A. it is desirable to show as many coordinate lines as possible in a finished diagram
    B. the horizontal scale should read from left to right and the vertical scale from top to bottom
    C. when two or more curves are represented for comparison on the same chart, their zero lines should coincide
    D. a percentage curve should not be used when the purpose is to show the actual amounts of increase or decrease

14. Grouping of figures in a frequency distribution results in a *loss* of
    A. linearity   B. significance   C. detail   D. coherence

15. The true financial condition of a city is BEST reflected when its accounting system is placed upon a(n) _____ basis.
    A. cash   B. accrual   C. fiscal   D. warrant

16. When the discrepancy between the totals of a trial balance is $36, the LEAST probable cause of the error is
    A. omission of an item
    B. entering of an item on the wrong side of the ledger
    C. a mistake in addition or subtraction
    D. transposition of digits

17. For the MOST effective administrative management, appropriations should be
    A. itemized
    B. lump sum
    C. annual
    D. bi-annual

18. Of the following types of expenditure control in the practice of fiscal management, the one which is LEAST important is that which relates to
    A. past policy affecting expenditures
    B. future policy affecting expenditures
    C. prevention of improper use of funds
    D. prevention of overdraft

19. The sinking fund method of retiring bonds does NOT
    A. permit investment in a new issue of city bonds when the general market is unsatisfactory
    B. cause irreparable injury to the city's credit when the city is unable to make a scheduled contribution
    C. require periodic actuarial computations
    D. cost as much to administer as the serial bond method

20. Of the following, the statement that is FALSE is:
    A. Non-profit hospitalization plans are based on underlying principles similar to those which underlie mutual insurance.
    B. Federal, state, and local governments pay for more than half of the medical care received by more than half of the population of the country.
    C. In addition to non-profit hospitalization, non-profit organizations providing reimbursement for medical and nursing care are now being organized in this state.
    D. Voluntary health insurance must be depended on since a state system of health insurance is unconstitutional.

21. The MOST accurate of the following statements concerning birth and death rates is:
    A. A high birth rate is usually accompanied by a relatively high death rate.
    B. A high birth rate is usually accompanied by a relatively low death rate.
    C. The rate of increase in population for a given area may be obtained by subtracting the death rate from the birth rate.
    D. The rate of increase in population for a given area may be obtained by subtracting the birth rate from the death rate.

22. Empirical reasoning is based upon
    A. experience and observation
    B. *a priori* propositions
    C. application of an established generalization
    D. logical deduction

23. 45% of the employees of a certain department are enrolled in in-service training courses and 35% are registered in college courses.
    The percentage of employees NOT enrolled in either of these types of courses is
    A. 20%
    B. at least 20% and not more than 55%
    C. approximately 40%
    D. none of the above

24. A typist can address approximately R envelopes in a 7-hour day. A list containing S addresses is submitted with a request that all envelopes be typed within T hours.
    The number of typists needed to complete this task would b
    A. $\frac{7RS}{T}$
    B. $\frac{S}{7RT}$
    C. $\frac{R}{7ST}$
    D. $\frac{7S}{RT}$

4 (#2)

25. Bank X allows a customer to write without charge five checks per month for each $100 on deposit, but a check deposited or a cash deposit counts the same as a check written. Bank Y charges ten cents for every check written, requires no minimum balance and allows deposit of cash or of checks made out to customer free. A man receives two salary checks and, on the average, five other checks each month. He pays, on the average, twelve bills a month, five of which are for amounts between $5 and $10, five for amounts between $10 and $20, two for about $30. Assume that he pays these bills either by check or by Post Office money order (the charges for money orders are: $3.01 to $10-11¢; $10.01 to $20-13¢; $20.01 to $40-15¢) and that he has a savings account paying 2%. Assume also that if he has an account at Bank X, he keeps a balance sufficient to avoid any service charges.

25.____

Of the following statements in relation to this man, the one that is TRUE is that
 A. the monthly cost of an account at Bank Y is approximately as great as the cost of an account at Bank X and also the account is more convenient
 B. to use an account at Bank Y costs more than the use of money orders, but this disadvantage is offset by the fact that cancelled checks act as receipts for bills paid
 C. money orders are cheapest but this advantage is offset by the fact that one must go to the Post Office for each order
 D. an account at Bank X is least expensive and has the advantage that checks endorsed to the customer may be deposited in it

KEY (CORRECT ANSWERS)

1.	B		11.	B
2.	D		12.	A
3.	D		13.	A
4.	B		14.	C
5.	A		15.	B
6.	C		16.	C
7.	A		17.	B
8.	B		18.	A
9.	B		19.	B
10.	C		20.	D

21. A
22. A
23. B
24. D
25. D

EXAMINATION SECTION
TEST 1

DIRECTIONS: Each question or incomplete statement is followed by several suggested answers or completions. Select the one that BEST answers the question or completes the statement. *PRINT THE LETTER OF THE CORRECT ANSWER IN THE SPACE AT THE RIGHT.*

1. Several employees complain informally to their supervisor regarding some new procedures which have been instituted.
   The supervisor should IMMEDIATELY
   A. explain that management is responsible
   B. investigate the complaint
   C. refer the matter to the methods analyst
   D. tell the employees to submit their complaint as a formal grievance

   1.____

2. The PRINCIPAL aim of an administrator is to
   A. act as liaison between employee and management
   B. get the work done
   C. keep up morale
   D. train his subordinates

   2.____

3. Work measurement can be applied to operations where workload can be related to
   A. available personnel for the implementation of assigned tasks
   B. follow-up programs for continued progress
   C. cost abatement and optimum efficiency
   D. man hour utilization on assigned tasks

   3.____

4. The one of the following which is NOT a primary advantage of a work measurement program is
   A. the selection of informed personnel
   B. knowledge of personnel needs
   C. support of personnel requests
   D. setting of approximate unit costs

   4.____

5. A program of work measurement would be LEAST likely to
   A. point up the need for management research
   B. keep workload and personnel on an even keel
   C. measure the performance in exceptional operations
   D. evaluate the status of operations

   5.____

6. Generally speaking, there are two kinds of work measurement: (1) the traditional industrial engineering kind where performance standard are determined by time study or other engineering techniques, and (2) the statistical kind where yardsticks (so-called to distinguish them from engineered standard) are developed from a statistical analysis of past performance data. These data consist essentially of periodic reports in which work performed, expressed in identifiable work units, is related to the time required to perform it, usually expressed in man-hours.
The ESSENTIAL difference between the two kinds of work measurement is that
   A. the statistical type if based on past, current, and future determinants of a divergent nature, while engineered standards are restrictive
   B. yardsticks are less restrictive than engineered standards
   C. time study standards employ a higher ratio of man-hour data than do statistical standards
   D. engineered standards are more costly as well as more accurate than routine time study methods

6._____

7. Government has favored the use of the statistical type of work measurement over the industrial type MAINLY because
   A. government is an institution rarely hampered by money-seeking techniques
   B. as the statistical type of work measurement is broadly based, it is more capable of filling the wide expanse of government's needs
   C. employees might object vehemently against speed-ups, thereby sapping work measurement's force
   D. the former appears to be just as effective and less expensive than the latter

7._____

8. A work measurement program is a system by which a
   A. periodic account is kept of individual and group performance
   B. recurring account is kept of group performance
   C. periodic account is kept of performance by an individual
   D. periodic account is kept of performance by a group

8._____

9. Statistical standards developed during the early stages of a work measurement program are
   A. changed too rapidly and thus are of little value in the final program
   B. subject to change as the program moves forward
   C. incorporated into the final program, ultimately for research studies
   D. abandoned before the effective date of the final program

9._____

10. It is NOT an objective of a work measurement program to
    A. furnish a basis for procedural control
    B. provide a true basis for management control
    C. furnish a genuine basis for budget control
    D. provide a basis for management planning

10._____

11. The MOST valid of the following concepts of management control is that it examines   11.____
    A. the method with which work assignments have been accomplished in accordance with preconceived plans and policies
    B. preconceived plans and policies to determine their ultimate value
    C. results to determine how well work assignments have been accomplished in accordance with preconceived plans and policies
    D. the work of individual employees to get an acceptable, so as not to endanger the entire control program

12. Of the following, the LEAST likely area in which a deficiency in operations would be revealed by a work measurement program is   12.____
    A. improper personnel utilization   B. inadequate equipment
    C. distribution of work   D. personnel rating

13. The MOST accurate of the following statements regarding the standard as used in a work measurement program is: 13.____
    A. Standard rates of performance should not be established until the effectiveness of an operation has been determined.
    B. The measure of effectiveness should be kept separate and distinct from the application of standards to actual performance
    C. standards should not be used as guides in planning
    D. Standard rates of performance must be established before effectiveness of an operation can be determined.

14. The first and most important basic consideration in instituting a program of work measurement is the   14.____
    A. indoctrination of personnel
    B. establishment of a uniform technology
    C. selection of the time unit
    D. selection of a standard

15. A _____ is an item or a group of items, generally physical, which, when taken in the aggregate, serve to measure amounts of work.   15.____
    A. Therblig   B. function   C. operation   D. work unit

16. Which of the following epitomizes the *raison d'etre* of work simplification?   16.____
    A. Waste elimination   B. Empirical costs
    C. Time study speed-ups   D. Charting techniques

17. A process charting analysis is likely to be of little value in the event of   17.____
    A. a major change in the department's activity
    B. a new supervisor from the outside coming in to head the unit
    C. increase in volume of work
    D. sizable personnel turnover

18. Staff or functional supervision in an organization
    A. is least justified at the operational level
    B. is contrary to the principle of Unity of Command
    C. is more effective than authoritative supervision
    D. normally does not give the right to take direct disciplinary action

18.____

19. The correlation between a flow process chart and a flow diagram is BEST described by which of the following statements?
    A. A flow process chart is supportive machinery to the flow diagram.
    B. In essence, the flow process chart exhibits time, distance, and location using standard symbols, whereas the flow diagram exhibits flow lines and uses classification symbols.
    C. Much of the information on the flow process chart is reproduced from the flow diagram.
    D. The flow diagram is complementary to the flow process chart.

19.____

20. Indicate which of the following statements is LEAST apt to clarify the underlying distinction between work simplification and other method of betterment procedures.
    Work simplification
    A. is dependent on supervisory participation
    B. is designed for employee participation
    C. emphasizes group participation
    D. emphasizes the ideas of experts

20.____

21. In describing the process of administrative management, the LEAST valid description is that it
    A. is composed of interdependent functions
    B. is comprised of related parts
    C. is cyclical
    D. consists of independent parts

21.____

22. Work activity, as to type, individual performance, and time expenditure, is BEST illustrated by a _____ chart.
    A. flow process
    B. work flow
    C. work distribution
    D. operations

22.____

23. Neither the work distribution nor the flow process chart furnishes adequate intelligence as to
    A. methods
    B. activities
    C. nature of work activity
    D. unit prices

23.____

24. A graphic presentation of the steps and distribution through which each copy of a multiple copy office form travels is a(n)
    A. work distribution chart
    B. flow process chart
    C. flow diagram
    D. operations chart

24.____

25. A CHIEF target of work simplification is 25.____
    A. the achievement of greater productivity with the same effort
    B. obtaining the same work accomplishment with less effort
    C. employee participation and little resistance to change
    D. all of the above

KEY (CORRECT ANSWERS)

1.	B		11.	C
2.	B		12.	D
3.	D		13.	D
4.	A		14.	B
5.	C		15.	D
6.	B		16.	A
7.	D		17.	B
8.	B		18.	D
9.	B		19.	D
10.	A		20.	D

21. D
22. C
23. D
24. C
25. C

TEST 2

DIRECTIONS: Each question or incomplete statement is followed by several suggested answers or completions. Select the one that BEST answers the question or completes the statement. *PRINT THE LETTER OF THE CORRECT ANSWER IN THE SPACE AT THE RIGHT.*

1. In conducting a work simplification program, which of the following office problems is the MOST likely to be solved by the use of the flow process chart?
   A. Are the employee deluged with unrelated tasks?
   B. What activities are the most costly, in terms of time consumed?
   C. Is the proper sequence of work activity employed?
   D. Is there an even distribution of work among the employees?

   1.____

2. In the matter of procedural analysis, which question should be asked FIRST?
   A. When should the step be performed?
   B. Who should perform the step?
   C. What is the significance of the step?
   D. Where can this be improved upon?

   2.____

3. Storage on a movement diagram is represented by
   A. ◇   B. ▽   C. □   D. all of the above

   3.____

4. The use of a flow process chart is LESS desirable in indicating
   A. the time rate for each step   B. distance traveled
   C. equipment-facilities layout   D. sequence of activities

   4.____

5. Division of work is BEST delineated by means of a _____ chart.
   A. work methods   B. flow process
   C. work distribution   D. flow authority

   5.____

6. In seeking to conduct a work simplification analysis, the MOST appropriate first step would be to
   A. chart the procedures
   B. survey the facilities as to spatial access
   C. make problem area determination
   D. set up composition of forms analysis

   6.____

7. The conception of a standard is BEST denoted as a
   A. hypothetical level   B. circumscribed level of work activity
   C. level of comparing   D. quintessential idea

   7.____

8. With reference to office work simplification, it could be considered expedient to
   A. first simplify the procedure and then the individual methods
   B. simplify the individual methods first, then the procedure
   C. concurrently, simplify the methods and the procedure
   D. none of the above

   8.____

9. The MOST valid precept relative to work analysis is
   A. the volume of work is inversely proportional to the distribution or sequence of work
   B. in meeting production standards, the sequence of work transcends its distribution
   C. work sequence and work distribution should be analyzed in relation to work volume
   D. work sequence and work distribution should be examined for work validation concepts

10. The flow process chart is PRINCIPALLY used
    A. as a useful tool to train new employees
    B. to ascertain the effectiveness of the organization's employees
    C. to pinpoint *bottlenecks* affecting an operation
    D. to determine the visibility of organizational relationships

11. The work distribution chart would generally be of little value in answering which of the following questions?
    A. In what order are the activities being carried out?
    B. Which activities consume the most time?
    C. Is a work balance maintained among the employees?
    D. Are the employees laboring under a plethora of unrelated tasks?

12. A worthwhile analytical tool in work simplification is the flow process chart. The MOST valid description is that
    A. a flow process chart is generally reliable without review for a period of a year
    B. the flow process chart should be reviewed and possibly revised at six-month intervals
    C. the flow process chart is an ad hoc instrument
    D. the value of a flow process chart is not determined by time

13. In the analysis of a method of procedure in a work simplification program, a competent analyst should FIRST focalize on the clearance or diminution of
    A. verifications
    B. transportations
    C. inspections
    D. storages

14. Which one of the following statements BEST distinguishes a method from a procedure?
    A. A method is a consistent sequence of procedures.
    B. A procedure comprises a sequence of related methods, performed in most instances by a single person.
    C. A series of related methods comprise a procedure.
    D. In breadth, a method takes precedence over a procedure.

15. The data provided by the flow process chart in a work simplification program is INADEQUATE to answer which one of the following questions?
   A. What is being performed?
   B. In what manner should the work be performed?
   C. What is the quantity of work performed?
   D. Who should perform the work?

15.____

Questions 16-17.

DIRECTIONS: Questions 16 and 17 are to be answered on the basis of the following passage.

Ideally, then, the process of budget formulation would consist of a flow of directives down the organization, and a reverse flow of recommendations in terms of alternatives among which selection would be made at every level. Ideally, also, a change in the recommendations at any level would require reconsideration and revision at all lower levels. By a process of successive approximation, everything would be taken into account and all points of view harmonized. Such a process, however, would be ideal only if the future could be foreseen clearly and time did not matter. As it is, in a complicated organization like the Federal government, the initial policy objectives established for the budget become out-of-date, before such a procedure could be carried through. While this difficulty does not in any way impugn the principle that the budget should be considered in terms of alternatives, it may call for short-cut methods of estimation rather than long drawn-out ones.

16. According to the above passage,
   A. the ideal method for estimating purposes is a short one
   B. the ideal method is not ideal for use in the Federal government
   C. directive should flow up and down via short methods
   D. the Federal government needs to speed up its reverse flow of recommendations for greater budgetary estimates

16.____

17. A suitable title for the above passage would be:
   A. Formulating the Federal Government's Budgetary Principles
   B. Directives and Recommendations: Budgetary Flow
   C. The Process of Budget Formulation
   D. The Application of the Ideal Estimate to the Federal Government

17.____

Questions 18-19.

DIRECTIONS: Questions 18 and 19 are to be answered on the basis of the following passage.

For purpose of budget formulation, the association of budgeting with accounting is less fortunate. Preparing for the future and recording the past do not necessarily require the same aptitudes or attitudes. The task of the accountant is to record past transactions in meticulous detail. Budgeting involves estimates of an uncertain future. But, because of the influence of accounts, government's budgets are prepared in a degree of detail that is quite unwarranted by the uncertain assumptions on which the estimates are based. A major source of government waste could be eliminated if estimates were prepared in no greater detail than was justified by their accuracy.

18. The author of the above paragraph
    A. is undermining the accounting profession
    B. believes accountants dwell solely in the past and cannot deal with the future efficiently
    C. wants the accountants out of government unless they become more accurate in their findings
    D. wishes to redirect the accountants' handling of budget procedures

18.____

19. The author's attitude appears to be
    A. tongue-in-cheek   B. morose
    C. strident   D. constructive

19.____

20. The idea that classic organizational structure tends to create work situations having requirements counter to those for psychological success and self-esteem, sometimes called the *organizational dilemma*, is MOST closely associated with
    A. Argyris   B. Taylor   C. Gulick   D. Maslow

20.____

Questions 21-25.

DIRECTIONS: Questions 21 through 25 contain incorrectly used words which change the meaning of the statement. Identify the word in the statement that is incorrect and select the choice that would make the sentence correct.

21. Standards of production performance are necessary to reveal the quantities of material, the number of hours of labor, the machine hours, and quantities of service (as, for example, power, steam, etc.) necessary to perform the various production operations. The establishment of such standards is an engineering rather than an accounting task, but it should be emphasized that such standards are needless to the development of the budgetary procedure—at least insofar as the budget is to serve as a tool of control. Such standards serve not only in the development of the budget and in measuring efficiency of production performance, but also in developing purchase requirements and in estimating costs.
    A. Manifest   B. Evaluation   C. Essential   D. Function

21.____

22. Where standard costs are not available or their use is impracticable due to uncertainty of prices, estimates of the costs must be made on the basis of past experience and expected conditions. Ability to use standards largely eliminates the use of the budget for purposes of control of costs but its value remains for purposes of coordination of the program with purchases and finance.
    A. Failure   B. Current   C. Culmination   D. Apparent

22.____

23. While one of the first objectives of the labor budget is to provide the highest practicable degree of regularity of employment, consideration must also be given to the estimating and perdurability of labor cost. Regularity of employment in itself effects some reduction in labor cost, but when carried beyond the point of practicality, it may increase other costs. For example, additional sales effort may be required to expand sales volume or to develop new products for slack periods; the cost of carrying inventories and the dangers of obsolescence and price declines must also be considered. A proper balance must be secured.
    A. Material   B. Control   C. Futures   D. To

23.____

24. The essentials of budgeting perhaps can be summarized in this manner:
    I. Develop a sound business program
    II. Report on the progress in achieving that program
    III. Take necessary action as to all variances which are inevitable
    IV. Revise the program to meet the changing conditions as required

    A. Perfect   B. Plans   C. Controllable   D. Secure

24.____

25. If a planning and control procedure is considered worthwhile, then it is a syllogism that preparation for the installation should be adequate. Time devoted to this educational aspect ordinarily will prove quite rewarding. The management to be involved with the budget, and particularly the middle management, must have a clear understanding of the budgetary procedure.
    A. Acquired   B. Remedial   C. Monetary   D. Truism

25.____

KEY (CORRECT ANSWERS)

1.	D	11.	A
2.	C	12.	D
3.	D	13.	D
4.	C	14.	C
5.	C	15.	C
6.	C	16.	B
7.	C	17.	C
8.	A	18.	D
9.	C	19.	D
10.	C	20.	A
21.	C		
22.	B		
23.	B		
24.	C		
25.	D		

TEST 3

DIRECTIONS: Each question or incomplete statement is followed by several suggested answers or completions. Select the one that BEST answers the question or completes the statement. *PRINT THE LETTER OF THE CORRECT ANSWER IN THE SPACE AT THE RIGHT.*

1. The MOST important element in job satisfaction is
   A. job security
   B. responsibility or recognition
   C. salary
   D. type of supervision

   1.____

2. The point of view that the average person wishes to avoid responsibility, wishes to be directed, as little ambition, and wants security above all, is described by Douglas MacGregor as Theory
   A. X
   B. Y
   C. Z
   D. X and Y combined

   2.____

3. To prepare a work distribution chart, two other types of lists must generally be prepared.
   In usual order of preparation, they are a(n) _____ and a(n) _____ list.
   A. flow chart; activity
   B. skills list; task
   C. task list; activity
   D. activity list; task

   3.____

4. A statistical control program in an office is valuable to direct deterioration in operations.
   It is, however, LEAST likely to reveal
   A. when preventative action is needed
   B. when a variation is due to chance
   C. when an assignable cause is present
   D. what the cause of error or deterioration is

   4.____

5. Which of the following BEST defines an organization chart?
   An organizational chart
   A. depicts informal channels of communication within an organization
   B. depicts the major functions of an organization and the normal work flow between subdivisions of the organization
   C. presents graphically the arrangement and interrelationships of the subdivisions and the functions of the organization as they exist
   D. presents graphically the arrangement and relationships of all the positions authorized in an organization

   5.____

6. In considering an office layout for a unit, which of the following factors should generally receive the LEAST consideration?
   A. Lighting levels in the existing area
   B. Major work flow—the processing of paper
   C. Present and projected growth rate of the unit
   D. Traffic patterns of employees and visitors

   6.____

7. The BEST way to secure effective management is usually to
   A. allow staff to help solve administrative problems of line management
   B. provide a good organization structure
   C. select capable managers
   D. set up conservative spans of control

8. Which of the following is NOT an advantage of oral instruction as compared with written instructions?
   Oral
   A. instructions can be easily changed
   B. instructions are superior in transmitting complex directives
   C. instructions facilitate exchange of information between a supervisor and his subordinate(s)
   D. discussions are possible with oral instructions, making it easier to ascertain understanding

9. Which organization principle is MOST closely related to procedural analysis and improvement?
   A. Duplication, overlapping, and conflict should be eliminated.
   B. The objectives of the organization should be clearly defined.
   C. Managerial authority should be clearly defined.
   D. Top management should be freed of burdensome details.

10. Of the following control techniques, a _____ is MOST useful on large, complex projects.
    A. general work plan   B. Gantt chart
    C. monthly progress report   D. PERT chart

11. Work is organized so that the work is broken down into a series of jobs. Each unit of work moves progressively from position to position until completion.
    This paragraph BEST describes a
    A. parallel plan of work subdivision   B. serial plan
    C. unit assembly plan   D. unit process plan

12. According to the classic studies of Rensis Likert, the GREATEST factor making for good morale and increased productivity was having a
    A. good program of employee benefits and wage scales
    B. supervisor who gave his employees free rein after they were fully trained and did not interfere with them
    C. supervisor who was primarily interested in production
    D. supervisor who, while interested in production, was primarily *employee-centered*

13. The managerial grid shows two concerns and a range of interaction between them.
In this grid, the horizontal axis indicates a concern for _____ and the vertical axis indicates a concern for _____.
    A. production; people
    B. hierarchy; people
    C. organization; people
    D. people; costs

13.____

14. It has been decided to make a few important revisions in the methods and procedures of a particular work unit.
Of the following, which method of implementing these revisions would probably be the MOST desirable in terms of morale and of efficiency?
    A. Give all employees in unit individual instructions in the revised procedures and make sure each employee knows them before instructing the next
    B. Institute all revisions at once, followed by on-the-job training for all members of the work unit
    C. Introduce the revisions one at a time and accompany each revision with an orientation for employees
    D. Set up a training course for the employees which instructs them in all aspects of the revised procedures prior to their implementation

14.____

15. An operations research technique which would be employed to determine the optimum number of window clerks or interviewers to have in an agency serving the public would MOST likely be the use of
    A. line of balance
    B. queueing theory
    C. simulation
    D. work sampling

15.____

16. Douglas MacGregor's theory of human motivation classifies worker behavior into two distinct categories: Theory X and Theory Y. Theory X, the traditional view, states that the average man dislikes working and will avoid work if he can, unless coerced. Theory Y holds essentially the opposite view.
The manager can apply both of these theories to worker behavior BEST if he
    A. follows an *open-door* policy only with respect to his immediate subordinates
    B. recognizes his subordinates' mental and social needs as well as agency needs
    C. recognizes that executive responsibility is primarily limited to fulfillment of agency productivity goals
    D. directs his subordinate managers to follow a policy of close supervision

16.____

17. In interpersonal communications, it is important to ascertain whether oral directions and instruction are understood.
One of the MOST important sources of such information is known as
    A. the *halo* effect
    B. evaluation
    C. feedback
    D. quantitative analysis

17.____

18. The *grapevine* MOST often provides a useful service by 18.____
    A. correcting some of the deficiencies of the formal communication system
    B. rapidly conveying a true picture of events
    C. involving staff in current organizational changes
    D. interfering with the operation of the formal communication system

19. People who are in favor of a leadership style in which the subordinates help 19.____
    make decisions contend that it produces favorable effects in a work unit.
    According to these people, which of the following is NOT likely to be an effect
    of such *participative management*?
    A. Reduced turnover
    B. Accelerated learning of duties
    C. Greater acceptance of change
    D. Reduced appearance of the work unit's goals

20. Employees of a public service agency will be MOST likely to develop 20.____
    meaningful goals for both the agency and the employee and become
    committed to attaining them if supervisors
    A. allow them unilaterally to set their own goals
    B. provide them with a clear understanding of the premises underlying the
       agency's goals
    C. encourage them to concentrate on setting only short-range goals for
       themselves
    D. periodically review the agency's goals in order to suggest changes in
       accordance with current conditions

KEY (CORRECT ANSWERS)

1.	B	11.	B
2.	A	12.	D
3.	C	13.	A
4.	D	14.	D
5.	C	15.	B
6.	A	16.	B
7.	B	17.	C
8.	B	18.	A
9.	A	19.	D
10.	D	20.	B

EXAMINATION SECTION
TEST 1

DIRECTIONS: Each question or incomplete statement is followed by several suggested answers or completions. Select the one that BEST answers the question or completes the statement. *PRINT THE LETTER OF THE CORRECT ANSWER IN THE SPACE AT THE RIGHT.*

1. You are assigned to form a new unit to compile data which is to facilitate an executive in decision-making.
   In planning the organization of this unit, the question to be answered FIRST is:

   A. What interpretations are likely to be made of the data by the executive in making a decision?
   B. At what point in the decision-making process will the data be most usefully introduced?
   C. What type of data is needed by the executive in his area of decision-making?
   D. What criteria will the executive use to evaluate the data?

2. The extent of effective decentralization within an organization is INVERSELY related to the

   A. size of the organization
   B. availability of sufficient competent personnel
   C. physical dispersion of the organization's activities
   D. effectiveness of communication within the organization

3. *The tasks of coordination, supervision, and control are likely to become more complicated as the specialization of an organization increases.*
   This statement is GENERALLY

   A. *false;* better performance of these tasks is likely to follow from the detailed attention given to particular problems
   B. *false;* the proportion of specialized personnel is small in proportion to total personnel
   C. *true;* the increased interrelationships arising from increased specialization are sources of potential friction
   D. *true;* the specialist tends to resent direction from superiors who are not specialists

4. The distinctive feature between a method and a procedure may BEST be illustrated by a

   A. series of procedures comprising a method
   B. series of related methods performed usually by one person constituting a procedure
   C. procedure comprised of a series of related methods
   D. procedure encompassing a range more limited than that of a method

5. As part of your duties to analyze operating practices, you make a tour of a unit during which you talk to the employees about work methods, problems, and other pertinent topics. Such informal data gathering is often incomplete or inaccurate. At a later meeting with the unit supervisor, you question him about the information you have gathered, but he is unable to answer the questions immediately. He asks to accompany you on another tour of his unit and answer the questions on the spot. Explaining that employees will be reluctant to speak up in the presence of a supervisor, you refuse.
The situation you have created may BEST be described as a violation of the principle of organization called

   A. delegation of authority
   B. specialization of work
   C. span of control
   D. unity of command

6. A person desiring greater status and income in municipal government must, with few exceptions, move into the supervisory ranks. When he does, he will encounter certain changes in attitudes and relationships to which he must make satisfactory adjustments. His rise will create a degree of hostility and natural jealousy among his colleagues who have not tried to improve their situation or who have tried and failed. In a sense, too, he is forced upon the group he will supervise because under normal civil service practice, the group has little to say in his appointment.
A subtle change takes place also in his social situation; he must be in contact with his subordinates but he cannot be part of them, otherwise he yields a basic obligation to management, of which he is a part.
The MOST important conclusion to be made from this statement is that

   A. a manager should limit his contacts with subordinates to a minimum
   B. he must plan to advance himself further
   C. he should isolate himself from the work of the supervised group
   D. he must subordinate personnel popularity to the interest of the organization

7. A budget that itemizes expenditure estimates by detailing materials to be purchased, equipment to be maintained, salaries to be paid, etcetera, is known as a _____ budget.

   A. performance
   B. capital
   C. line-item
   D. program

8. Organizational activities for which there are no allocated funds available are financed from the _____ funds.

   A. special revenue
   B. sinking
   C. general
   D. special assessment

9. One of the real revolutions in public administration during the last half-century is the growth in importance of the budget as a planning and control instrument. Several trends account for this growing importance. Which of the following is NOT one of these trends?

   A. Rapid growth of the urban population
   B. The cheapening of the dollar
   C. The improved standards of living
   D. Full employment

10. The position classifying bureau of the personnel agency is normally NOT responsible for   10.____

    A. allocating individuals to classes
    B. assigning titles to classes of positions
    C. establishing minimum qualifications for positions
    D. determining which positions are necessary

11. Which of the following statements concerning a job analysis for position classification is FALSE?   11.____

    A. It is a study of the person who is to occupy the job.
    B. Time and motion studies may be used.
    C. It may be used in establishing rates of compensation.
    D. It is often done by staff authority.

12. Which of the following is considered to be an ESSENTIAL element of classifying a position?   12.____

    A. Number of positions similar to the one being classified
    B. Determination of salary to be paid for position
    C. Comparison of the position with similar and related positions
    D. Evaluation of the skills demanded by the position

13. The LEAST important objective of devising a service rating system is   13.____

    A. validating selection procedures
    B. improving quality of supervision
    C. encouraging the development of employee performance
    D. furnishing the basis of formulating a position classification plan

Questions 14-15.

DIRECTIONS: Questions 14 and 15 are to be answered in accordance with the following statement.

The process of validating a factual proposition is quite distinct from the process of validating a value judgment. The former is validated by its agreement with the facts, the latter by human authority.

14. According to the above statement, the one of the following methods which is MOST acceptable for determining whether or not a proposition is factually correct is to   14.____

    A. prove that a related proposition is factually correct
    B. derive it logically from accepted assumptions
    C. show that it will lead to desired results
    D. compare it with experience

15. Assuming that the above statement is correct, the theory that the correctness of all ethical propositions can be tested empirically is   15.____

    A. *correct;* testing empirically is validating by agreement with facts
    B. *incorrect;* ethical propositions are value judgments
    C. *correct;* ethical propositions are based on rational hypotheses
    D. *incorrect;* a factual proposition is validated by its agreement with facts

16. The rejection of the theory of inverse probability was, for a time, wrongly taken to imply that we cannot draw, from knowledge of a sample, inferences respecting the corresponding population. Such a view would entirely deny validity to all experimental science.
According to the above statement,

    A. the theory of inverse probability cannot be applied to an entire population
    B. making deductions from a sample is consistent with experimental science
    C. making deductions from a sample is inconsistent with experimental science
    D. the theory of Inverse probability is based on the study of samples

17. May I point out that if technical employees are given assignments only in their special fields, there will be an immediate gain in conserving special skills. And, if we are to make optimum use of the abilities of the technical employees, it is necessary that these skills be conserved.
Assuming that this analysis is correct, it follows that

    A. if we are not making optimum use of the abilities of technical employees, we have been giving technical employees assignments outside of their special fields
    B. we are making optimum use of the abilities of technical employees if we conserve special skills
    C. we are making optimum use of the abilities of technical employees if we give them assignments only in their special fields
    D. we are not making optimum use of the abilities of technical employees if we give them assignments outside of their special fields

18. *It is less costly to replace old equipment than to repair it.*
Which of the following statements tends to prove this hypothesis MOST conclusively?

    A. The repair of old equipment is frequently as costly as the purchase of new equipment.
    B. Continuance in service of old equipment is at least as costly as its replacement by new equipment.
    C. The replacement of old equipment is more desirable than its repair.
    D. The cost for repairing old equipment is not a one-time cost, while the cost of new equipment is a one-time cost.

19. *An increasing birth rate will be followed by an increased school registration.*
On the basis of this statement *only*, it would be MOST accurate to state that

    A. school registration does not change during a period with a level birth rate
    B. an increasing school registration is preceded by a period with an increasing birth rate
    C. a period with an increasing birth rate is sometimes followed by a decreasing school registration
    D. a period with a decreasing birth rate is sometimes followed by a decreasing school registration

20. It is generally agreed that the *face-to-face* method of communicating is the most effective from a supervisor's standpoint.
This is true PRIMARILY because

   A. the attitude of the recipient can be accurately appraised
   B. it provides a two-way channel of expression which results in clarification of ideas
   C. it is illustrative of the extremely desirable supervisory technique known as the *democratic approach*
   D. it brings the supervisor closer to the actual level of operation

20.____

Questions 21-25.

DIRECTIONS: Questions 21 through 25 contain incorrectly used words which change the meaning of the statement. Identify the word in the statement that is incorrect and select the choice that would make the sentence correct.

21. Lack of employee input in the case of training often exists, but is frequently dealt with in evaluation of the training effort. Failure to deal with as important a factor as this can be ruinous to the training effort.

   A. Seldom   B. Margin   C. Ancillary   D. Contributory

21.____

22. It is a fallacy that policies generated at the top of the hierarchy are often not acceptable to those on the lower levels, particularly in the case of blue-collar workers among whom the rewards and sanctions of the union or members of the immediate social group are more impelling than the rewards or sanctions available to management.

   A. Parologism   B. Truism
   C. Commands   D. Undetermined

22.____

23. Basically, an organization develops when employees in it have rather free control over their behavior within the organization, when the philosophy of the organization is that maximum interpersonal interplay through a minimum number of hierarchical levels is desirable, and when a person traditionally called a *trainer* performs an integrating function.

   A. Instinctively   B. Total
   C. Flat   D. Strong

23.____

24. In gaining cooperation in human relations, the one who would influence must often foster his own ego and fertilize and feed that of the one who is to be influenced.

   A. Lassitude   B. Emulate   C. Suppress   D. Implant

24.____

25. In the United States, in general, we have been criticized for our emphasis upon physical, materialistic, and economic goals. These are still important, but the trends point toward the more complex, or appreciation of the beautiful, as for example in the architecture of our new factories and colors in the workplaces.

   A. Ephemeral   B. Concrete   C. Prosaic   D. Aesthetic

25.____

KEY (CORRECT ANSWERS)

1.	C	11.	A
2.	D	12.	C
3.	C	13.	D
4.	C	14.	D
5.	D	15.	B
6.	D	16.	B
7.	C	17.	D
8.	C	18.	B
9.	D	19.	B
10.	D	20.	B

21. A
22. B
23. D
24. C
25. D

TEST 2

DIRECTIONS: Each question or incomplete statement is followed by several suggested answers or completions. Select the one that BEST answers the question or completes the statement. *PRINT THE LETTER OF THE CORRECT ANSWER IN THE SPACE AT THE RIGHT.*

1. In the communications process, a formal communication should contain a multiplicity of ideas and several related objectives in order to provide for time-saving economy and to enhance the prospects of eventual compliance by subordinates.
   This statement is GENERALLY

   A. *true*, since it reduces to a minimum the need for issuance of frequent communications from policy-making levels
   B. *false*, since the number of ideas and objectives contained in a single communication operates in inverse ratio to the degree of compliance
   C. *true*, since continuity and cohesiveness of plans are developed by infrequent but elaborate formal communications
   D. *false*, since time-saving devices are not the concern of superiors engaged in developing an effective communications process

   1.____

2. Experts in supervisory practices have been emphasizing the importance of the art of listening on the part of supervisors. A recently published text devotes over three hundred pages to a discussion on how managers and supervisors can improve their ability to listen.
   Which one of the following is NOT considered an important rule to follow in developing the skill of listening?

   A. Be attentive and concentrate on what is being said.
   B. Concentrate on the spoken word without concern for implied meanings.
   C. Ask an occasional question when appropriate to the discussion.
   D. Make sure you understand fully what is being said.

   2.____

3. A supervisor who is to direct a team of senior clerks and clerks in a complex project calls them together beforehand to inform them of the tasks each employee will perform on this job.
   Of the following, the CHIEF value of this action by the supervisor is that each member of this team will be able to

   A. work independently in the absence of the supervisor
   B. understand what he will do and how this will fit into the total picture
   C. share in the process of decision-making as an equal participant
   D. judge how well the plans for this assignment have been made

   3.____

4. A supervisor who has both younger and older employees under his supervision may sometimes find that employee absenteeism seriously interferes with accomplishment of goals.
   Studies of such employee absenteeism have shown that the absences of employees

   A. under 35 years of age are usually unexpected and the absences of employees over 45 years are usually unnecessary
   B. of all age groups show the same characteristics as to length of absence

   4.____

C. under 35 years of age are for frequent, short periods while the absences of employees over 45 years of age are less frequent but of longer duration
D. under 35 years of age are for periods of long duration and the absences of employees over 45 years of age are for periods of short duration

5. A long-standing procedure for getting a certain job done by subordinates is apparently a good procedure. Changes in some steps of the procedure are made from time to time to handle special problems that come up.
Reviewing this procedure periodically is *desirable* MAINLY because

   A. the system is working well
   B. checking routines periodically is a supervisor"s chief responsibility
   C. subordinates may be confused as to how the procedure operates as a result of the changes made
   D. it is necessary to determine whether the procedure has become outdated or is in need of improvement

6. In conducting an interview, the BEST type of questions with which to begin the interview are those which the person interviewed is _____ to answer.

   A. willing and able
   B. willing but unable
   C. able to, but unwilling
   D. unable and unwilling

7. In order to determine accurately a child's age, it is BEST for an interviewer to rely on

   A. the child's grade in school
   B. what the mother says
   C. birth records
   D. a library card

8. In his first interview with a new employee, it would be LEAST appropriate for a unit supervisor to

   A. find out the employee's preference for the several types of jobs to which he is able to assign him
   B. determine whether the employee will make good promotion material
   C. inform the employee of what his basic job responsibilities will be
   D. inquire about the employee's education and previous employment

9. If an interviewer takes care to phrase his questions carefully and precisely, the result will MOST probably be that

   A. he will be able to determine whether the person interviewed is being truthful
   B. the free flow of the interview will be lost
   C. he will get the information he wants
   D. he will ask stereotyped questions and narrow the scope of the interview

10. During an interview, the person interviewed is LEAST likely to be cautious about what he tells the interviewer

    A. shortly after the beginning when the questions normally suggest pleasant associations to the person interviewed
    B. as long as the interviewer keeps the questions to the point

C. at the point where the person interviewed gains a clear insight into the area being discussed
D. when the interview appears formally ended and good-byes are being said

11. In an interview held for the purpose of getting information from the person interviewed, it is sometimes desirable for the interviewer to repeat the answer he has received to a question.
For the interviewer to rephrase such an answer in his own words is good practice MAINLY because it

   A. gives the interviewer time to make up his next question
   B. gives the person interviewed a chance to correct any possible misunderstanding
   C. gives the person interviewed the feeling that the interviewer considers his answer important
   D. prevents the person interviewed from changing his answer

12. There are several methods of formulating questions during an interview. The particular method used should be adapted to the interview problems presented by the person being questioned.
Of the following methods of formulating questions during an interview, the ACCEPTABLE one is for the interviewer to ask questions which

   A. incorporate several items in order to allow a cooperative interviewee freedom to organize his statements
   B. are ambiguous in order to foil a distrustful inter-viewee
   C. suggest the correct answer in order to assist an interviewee who appears confused
   D. would help an otherwise unresponsive interviewee to become more responsive

13. An interviewer permits the person being interviewed to read the data the interviewer writes as he records the person's responses on a routine departmental form. This practice is

   A. *desirable*, because it serves to assure the person interviewed that his responses are being recorded accurately
   B. *undesirable*, because it prevents the interviewer from clarifying uncertain points by asking additional questions
   C. *desirable*, because it makes the time that the person interviewed must wait while the answer is written seem shorter
   D. *undesirable*, because it destroys the confidentiality of the interview

14. Suppose that a stranger enters the office of which you are in charge and asks for the address and telephone number of one of your employees.
The MOST appropriate reaction would be to

   A. find out why he needs the information and release it if his reason is a good one
   B. explain that you are not permitted to release such information to unauthorized persons
   C. give him the information but tell him it must be kept confidential
   D. ask him to leave the office immediately

15. A member of the public approaches an employee who is at work at his desk. The employee cannot interrupt his work in order to take care of this person.
The BEST and MOST courteous way of handling this situation is for the employee to

   A. avoid looking up from his work until he is finished with what he is doing
   B. tell this person that he will not be able to take care of him for quite a while
   C. refer the individual to another employee who can take care of him right away
   D. chat with the individual while he continues with his work

16. Some organizations, as a matter of policy, transfer their administrative staff personnel from one unit to another after stated periods of service in the unit.
The MAIN advantage of such a policy is that it

   A. helps keep the staff members abreast of the technical developments in their fields
   B. impedes the formation of personal cliques among staff members
   C. helps develop wider outlook and loyalty to the organization as a whole rather than to the unit assigned
   D. permits the more effective utilization of the individual talents of staff members

17. Leaders generally are somewhat more intelligent than their followers.
The CHIEF difficulty of the leader who is markedly more intelligent than his followers is that a leader has difficulty in

   A. overcoming the suspicion and distrust of intellectuals on the part of the group
   B. understanding the thought processes of persons who are intellectually inferior
   C. accepting the irrational and emotional basis of much of human conduct
   D. making himself understood by the group

18. A psychological study of leadership found that it is possible to predict the behavior of a new man in a leadership position more accurately on the basis of the behavior of his predecessor in the position than on the behavior of the man himself in his previous job.
The BEST explanation of this observation is that there is a tendency

   A. to select similar types of personalities to fill the same type of position
   B. for a newly appointed man to avoid instituting basic changes in operational procedures
   C. for a given organizational structure and set of duties to produce similar patterns of behavior
   D. for increased responsibility to impose more mature patterns of behavior on an incumbent

19. An administrative official finds that the reports reaching him from his subordinates tend to exaggerate the favorable and minimize the unfavorable aspects of situations existing within the unit.
The MOST valid conclusion to draw is that

   A. the administrative official has been overly severe with subordinates and has instilled fear in them
   B. there is a normal tendency for persons to represent themselves and their actions in the best possible light
   C. members of the department tend to be optimists
   D. the administrative official has not been sufficiently critical of previous reports and has not been alert to conditions in the unit

20. A special unit of a department is rife with rumors concerning plans for its future and the possibility of its abolition. As a result, morale and productivity of members assigned to it have suffered. To handle this situation, the administrative official in charge of the unit adopts a policy of promptly corroborating factual rumors and denying false ones.
This method of dealing with the problem will achieve some good results, but its CHIEF weakness is that

    A. it gives status to the rumors by the attention paid to them
    B. the administrative official may not have the necessary information at hand to dispose promptly of all rumors
    C. it *chases* the rumors rather than forestalling them by giving information concerning the unit's future
    D. the administrative official may have confidential information which he should not divulge

21. An administrative official, realizing the importance of harmonious relationships within his unit, made a practice of unobtrusively intervening in any conflict situation between subordinates. Whenever friction seemed to be developing, he would attempt to soothe ruffled feelings, remove the source of difficulty by rescheduling activities or reassigning personnel, et cetera. His efforts were always behind-the-scenes and unknown to the employees involved. Although this method of operation produces some good results, its CHIEF drawback is that it

    A. violates the chain of command principle
    B. involves the administrative official in personal relationships which are not properly his concern
    C. requires confidential sources of information about relationships within the unit, which borders on spying
    D. permits subordinates to engage in unacceptable practices without correction

22. At a division conference at which a basic change in the department's procedure was to be announced, the conference leader started the discussion by asking the group for criticisms of the existing procedures. He then described the new procedures to be employed and explained the improvements in operations that were anticipated.
The conference leader's method of introducing the change was

    A. *good,* mainly because the conference members would be more receptive to the new procedure if they understood the inadequacies of the old
    B. *bad,* mainly because the conference members would realize that the decision for change had been made before the discussion and without consideration of their comments
    C. *good,* mainly because the comments and criticisms of the old procedure would provide the basis for evaluating the feasibility of the new method
    D. *bad,* mainly because the focus of the discussion was on the procedure being replaced rather than on the procedure being introduced

23. A section chief in charge of a specialized unit calls a staff conference to discuss a proposed modification of some procedures. After making some introductory remarks, the chief wants the comments of the members of the staff. The staff consists of eight subordinates ranging in rank from office aide to principal administrative assistant III, each subordinate having responsibility for a different aspect of the program. Of the following, the BEST procedure for the chief to follow is to call upon each subordinate in

A. descending order of rank, mainly because the employees with the highest rank are likely to have the most experience and ability
B. ascending order of rank, mainly because the junior employees are more likely to be freer in their comments if they give their views before the senior employees speak
C. order of their specialized knowledge and competence in the subjects under discussion mainly because those with most knowledge and competence can best lead the discussion
D. order of seating around the table, mainly because informality of procedure and democrative leadership is obtained

24. As a supervisor assigned to a public relations unit in a city agency, you find a certain program under severe attack by a citizen's, group.
To be of GREATEST value to your supervisor, you should

   A. present the department side of the story to all meetings or to all groups whether hostile or not
   B. attempt to get another citizen's group to defend the department program
   C. get greater support from the general public and the press to effectuate the program
   D. ignore group opinions; rather, strive to affect individuals and let them persuade their groups

25. The commission has assigned you to present the department side to a group of citizens well-disposed to government programs.
You should present

   A. *only* the department side
   B. both sides of the story, but present the department side last
   C. both sides of the story, but present the department side first
   D. the facts and let the audience draw its own conclusion

KEY (CORRECT ANSWERS)

1.	B	11.	B
2.	B	12.	D
3.	B	13.	A
4.	C	14.	B
5.	D	15.	C
6.	A	16.	C
7.	C	17.	D
8.	B	18.	C
9.	C	19.	B
10.	D	20.	C

21. D
22. B
23. C
24. B
25. A

TEST 3

DIRECTIONS: Each question or incomplete statement is followed by several suggested answers or completions. Select the one that BEST answers the question or completes the statement. *PRINT THE LETTER OF THE CORRECT ANSWER IN THE SPACE AT THE RIGHT.*

1. Supervisor X, as a representative of the Commissioner, has been ordered to present the department arguments in reference to a new program of inspections and to emphasize such presentation by stressing the enforcement that will follow.
   In this instance,

   A. a mild threat is less of a deterrent than a strong threat
   B. any form of threat should be avoided since you are seeking cooperation
   C. an overly strong threat is less of a deterrent than a mild threat
   D. the mere statement that enforcement will follow is sufficient to effect cooperation

   1.___

2. If, after an investigation and further consultation with central authorities, wholesale bribe-taking has been confirmed within a certain unit, the agency involved should

   A. withhold information from the public until a more secure image can be created
   B. break the story since such agency can present the least damaging picture
   C. arrange a compromise solution and present it to the public as an accomplished fact
   D. permit the central authorities to break the story since it presents a more efficient picture

   2.___

3. The characteristic of flexibility versus stability of a policy seems contradictory to subordinate A.
   The difference can BEST be explained by the administrative manager if he points out that

   A. policies are decision guides and definite formulae for specific actions; therefore, stability must outweigh flexibility
   B. changing events and materials force a change in policy; therefore, flexibility refers to the ability to change policy when it becomes outmoded
   C. policy should be as stable as possible but sufficiently flexible to handle problems that vary from the normal; policy's true purpose must be understood as a guide for decisions, not an inflexible formula for action
   D. most policy at unit level is based on precedent and tradition and, therefore, subject always to the discretion of the supervisor

   3.___

4. When an administrative manager devotes too much time to telling his subordinates how to handle their job problems, then he

   A. is spending too little time in formulating policies for the guidance of his subordinates
   B. is neglecting to delegate sufficient authority to his subordinates
   C. should immediately begin to plan for better use of his time
   D. should evaluate his approach to the administration of his section and establish better controls

   4.___

5. Since the policies of a department are well established, an administrator does not need to formulate section policy. This statement is

   A. *true;* it is difficult for an administrator to establish a policy which will not in some way coincide or contradict established, overall policies
   B. *false;* department policies have to be broad enough to cover the whole organization; they are seldom detailed enough to guide a section in its internal organization
   C. *true;* the administrator's responsibility in this area is to formulate procedure to implement department policy
   D. *false;* uniformity of enforcement is essential, and this is impossible when the administrator does not establish his own section policy

6. Manager X, when giving a decision on a controversial item, reminds the subordinates of the policy under which such a decision was made.
   This reminder is

   A. *good;* the subordinates will be aware that he is not being arbitrary, operating by whim, or playing favorites
   B. *unnecessary;* policies have been explained over and over again to subordinates
   C. a form of buck-passing since the manager is blaming a policy for his unfavorable decision
   D. *bad;* policy commits management to specific decisions and, as such, should not be given unfavorable publicity

7. After objectives and policies have been stated, the next step should be to

   A. develop plans and procedures
   B. make forecasts
   C. examine conditions; gather data
   D. consider a budget

8. After establishing objectives and identifying problems and opportunities, the planning should be

   A. turned over to the controller. You can alter his plan if you do not agree.
   B. assigned to the division heads. Each will work out a plan for his own division
   C. a joint effort of the controller and other division heads. You and any staff experts available will cooperate and assist as planning progresses.
   D. a joint effort of all supervisors and subordinates

9. The MOST; accurate statement concerning plans and planning is:

   A. In the absence of an agency-wide plan, it is better to avoid planning in the individual work unit
   B. Every manager or supervisor must plan if he is to carry out his managerial functions
   C. Every manager should make a preliminary plan and then await the agency-wide plan
   D. The agency-wide plan should precede the preliminary plan

10. Objectives, programs, policies, budgets, and procedures are all _____ planning.

    A. elements of overall   B. guides for
    C. alternates to   D. methods of

11. Developing and understanding objectives, establishing policies, collecting data, developing alternative action proposals, and deciding on action are all

    A. steps in planning
    B. guidelines to consider in planning
    C. the action motif ascribed to planning
    D. alternatives to planning

12. Work measurement can be applied to operations where workload can be related to

    A. available personnel for the implementation of assigned tasks
    B. follow-up programs for continued progress
    C. cost abatement and optimum efficiency
    D. man-hour utilization on assigned tasks

13. If you ask for additional historical information on costs, caseloads, et cetera, you will be

    A. refining the forecast process
    B. developing the groundwork for forecasting
    C. estimating the future
    D. evaluating your research department's efficiency

14. Suppose that the majority of mathematical projections predicts a serious downturn in new cases, while you and your advisors believe that a mild upturn is approaching. In this situation, the BEST procedure is to

    A. follow the course dictated by the mathematical projections because that is what they are there for
    B. follow your own ideas and those of your advisors; management is an art, not a science
    C. modify the course dictated by the mathematical projections so as to reflect both management and specialist judgment
    D. consult another advisor

15. The director of a personnel bureau with 100 employees would probably operate MOST efficiently if he had under his immediate supervision approximately _____ subordinates.

    A. 5　　　　B. 25　　　　C. 50　　　　D. 100

16. A worker is *usually* MOST productive when he is assigned to work which

    A. he is able to do best
    B. involves a variety of skills
    C. is under close supervision
    D. requires little skill

17. It is desirable for all staff specialists to have some knowledge of line activities PRIMARILY in order that they may

    A. direct line activities when necessary
    B. have a proper framework for research
    C. know how to deal with all types of personnel
    D. take cognizance of the agency's needs and problems

18. When a supervisor delegates an assignment, he should

    A. delegate his responsibility for the assignment
    B. make certain that the assignment is properly performed
    C. participate in the beginning and final stages of the assignment
    D. retain all authority needed to complete the assignment

19. Which one of the following is LEAST important in the management of a suggestion program?

    A. Giving awards which are of sufficient value to encourage competition
    B. Securing full support from the department's officers and executives
    C. Publicizing the program and the awards given
    D. Providing suggestion boxes in numerous locations

20. The MOST certain means to *decrease* morale is to

    A. insist on strict adherence to safety rules
    B. make each employee responsible for the tidiness of his work area
    C. overlook evidence of hostility between groups of employees
    D. provide strong, aggressive leadership

KEY (CORRECT ANSWERS)

1.	C	11.	A
2.	B	12.	D
3.	C	13.	B
4.	A	14.	C
5.	B	15.	A
6.	A	16.	A
7.	C	17.	D
8.	C	18.	B
9.	B	19.	D
10.	A	20.	C

EXAMINATION SECTION

TEST 1

DIRECTIONS: Each question or incomplete statement is followed by several suggested answers or completions. Select the one that BEST answers the question or completes the statement. *PRINT THE LETTER OF THE CORRECT ANSWER IN THE SPACE AT THE RIGHT.*

1. In almost every organization there is a nucleus of highly important functions commonly designated as *management*.
   Which of the following statements BEST characterizes *management*?
   A. Getting things done through others
   B. The highest level of intelligence in any organization
   C. The process whereby democratic and participative activities are maximized
   D. The *first among equals*

2. Strategies in problem-solving are important to anyone aspiring to advancement in the field of administration.
   Which of the following is BEST classified as the first step in the process of problem-solving?
   A. Collection and organization of data
   B. The formulation of a plan
   C. The definition of the problem
   D. The development of a method and methodology

3. One of the objectives of preparing a budget is to
   A. create optimistic goals which each department can attempt to meet
   B. create an overall company goals by combining the budgets of the various departments
   C. be able to compare planned expenditures against actual expenditures
   D. be able to identify accounting errors

4. The rise in demand for *systems* personnel in industrial and governmental organizations over the past five years has been extraordinary.
   In which of the following areas would a *systems* specialist assigned to an agency be LEAST likely to be of assistance?
   A. Developing, recommending, and establishing an effective cost and inventory system
   B. Development and maintenance of training manuals
   C. Reviewing existing work procedures and recommending improvements
   D. Development of aptitude tests for new employees

5. Management experts have come to the conclusion that the traditional forms of motivation used in industry and government, which emphasize authority over and economic rewards for the employee, are no longer appropriate.

101

To which of the following factors do such experts attribute the GREATEST importance in producing this change?
A. The desire of employees to satisfy material needs has become greater and more complex.
B. The desire for social satisfaction has become the most important aspect of the job for the average worker.
C. With greater standardization of work processes, there has been an increase in the willingness of workers to accept discipline.
D. In general, employee organizations have made it more difficult for management to fire an employee.

6. In preparing a budget, it is usually considered advisable to start the initial phases of preparation at the operational level of management.
Of the following, the justification that management experts usually advance as MOST reasonable for this practice is that operating managers, as a consequence of their involvement, will
A. develop a background in finance or accounting
B. have an understanding of the organizational structure
C. tend to feel responsible for carrying out budget activities
D. have the ability to see the overall financial picture

6.____

7. An administrative officer has been asked by his superior to write a concise, factual report with objective conclusions and recommendations based on facts assembled by other researchers.
Of the following factors, the administrative officer should give LEAST consideration to
A. the educational level of the person or persons for whom the report is being prepared
B. the use to be made of the report
C. the complexity of the problem
D. his own feelings about the importance of the problem

7.____

8. In an agency, upon which of the following is a supervisor's effectiveness MOST likely to depend?
The
A. degree to which a supervisor allows subordinates to participate in the decision-making process and the setting of objectives
B. degree to which a supervisor's style meets management's objectives and subordinates' needs
C. strength and forcefulness of the supervisor in pursuing his objectives
D. expertise and knowledge of the supervisor has about the specific work to be done

8.____

9. For authority to be effective, which of the following is the MOST basic requirement?
Authority must be
A. absolute   B. formalized   C. accepted   D. delegated

9.____

10. Management no longer abhors the idea of employees taking daily work breaks, but prefers to schedule such breaks rather than to allot to each employee a standard amount of free time to be taken off during the day as he wishes. Which of the following BEST expresses the reason management theorists give for the practice of scheduling such breaks?
    A. Many jobs fall into natural work units which are scheduled, and the natural time to take a break is at the end of the unit
    B. Taking a scheduled break permits socialization and a feeling of accomplishment
    C. Managers have concluded that scheduling rest periods seems to reduce the incidence of unscheduled ones
    D. Many office workers who really need such breaks are hesitant about taking them unless they are scheduled

10.____

11. The computer represents one of the major developments of modern technology. It is widely used in both scientific and managerial activities because of its many advantages.
    Which of the following is NOT an advantage gained by management in the use of the computer?
    A computer
    A. provides the manager with a greatly enlarged memory so that he can easily be provided with data for decision making
    B. relieves the manager of basic decision-making responsibility, thereby giving him more time for directing and controlling
    C. performs routine, repetitive calculations with greater precision and reliability than employees
    D. provides a capacity for rapid simulations of alternative solutions to problem solving

11.____

12. A supervisor of a unit in a division is usually responsible for all of the following EXCEPT
    A. the conduct of subordinates in the achievement of division objectives
    B. maintaining quality standards in the unit
    C. the protection and care of materials and equipment in the unit
    D. performing the most detailed tasks in the unit himself

12.____

13. You have been assigned to teach a new employee the functions and procedures of your office.
    In your introductory talk, which of the following approaches is PREFERABLE?
    A. Advise the new employee of the employee benefits and services available to him, over and above his salary
    B. Discuss honestly the negative aspects of departmental procedures and indicate methods available to overcome them
    C. Give the new employee an understanding of the general purpose of office procedures and functions and of their relevance to departmental objectives
    D. Give a basic and detailed explanation of the operations of your office, covering all functions and procedures

13.____

14. It is your responsibility to assign work to several clerks under your supervision. One of the clerks indignantly refuses to accept an assignment and asks to be given something else. He has not yet indicated why he does not want the assignment, but is sitting there glaring at you, awaiting your reaction.
Of the following, which is the FIRST action you should take?
    A. Ask the employee into your office in order to reprimand him and tell him emphatically that he must accept the assignment
    B. Talk to the employee privately in an effort to find the reason for his indignation and refusal, and then base your action upon your findings
    C. Let the matter drop for a day or two to allow the employee to cool off before you insist that he accept the assignment
    D. Inform the employee quietly and calmly that as his supervisor you have selected him for this assignment and that you fully expect him to accept it

15. Administrative officers are expected to be able to handle duties delegated to them by their supervisors and to be able, as they advance in status, to delegate tasks to assistants.
When considering whether to delegate tasks to a subordinate, which of the following questions should be LEAST important to an administrative officer?
In the delegated tasks,
    A. how significant are the decisions to be made, and how much consultation will be involved?
    B. to what extent is uniformity and close coordination of activity required?
    C. to what extent must speedy-on-the-spot decisions be made?
    D. to what extent will delegation relieve the administrative officer of his burden of responsibility?

16. A functional forms file is a collection of forms which are grouped by
    A. purpose   B. department   C. title   D. subject

17. All of the following are reasons to consult a records retention schedule except one.
Which one is that?
To determine
    A. whether something should be filed
    B. how long something should stay in file
    C. who should be assigned to filing
    D. when something on file should be destroyed

18. Listed below are four of the steps in the process of preparing correspondence for filing.
If they were to be put in logical sequence, the SECOND step would be
    A. preparing cross-reference sheets or cards
    B. coding the correspondence using a classification system
    C. sorting the correspondence in the order to be filed
    D. checking for follow-up action required and preparing a follow-up slip

19. New material added to a file folder should USUALLY be inserted
    A. in the order of importance (the most important in front)
    B. in the order of importance (the most important in back)
    C. chronologically (most recent in front)
    D. chronologically (most recent in back)

19.____

20. An individual is looking for a name in the white pages of a telephone directory. Which of the following BEST describes the system of filing found there?
    A(n) _____ file
    A. alphabetic   B. sequential   C. locator   D. index

20.____

21. The MAIN purpose of a tickler file is to
    A. help prevent overlooking matters that require future attention
    B. check on adequacy of past performance
    C. pinpoint responsibility for recurring daily tasks
    D. reduce the volume of material kept in general files

21.____

22. Which of the following BEST describes the process of reconciling a bank statement?
    A. Analyzing the nature of the expenditures made by the office during the preceding month
    B. Comparing the statement of the bank with the banking records maintained in the office
    C. Determining the liquidity position by reading the bank statement carefully
    D. Checking the service charges noted on the bank statement

22.____

23. From the viewpoint of preserving agency or institutional funds, which of the following is the LEAST acceptable method for making a payment?
    A check made out to
    A. cash   B. a company
    C. an individual   D. a partnership

23.____

24. In general, the CHIEF economy of using multicopy forms is in
    A. the paper on which the form is printed
    B. printing the form
    C. employee time
    D. carbon paper

24.____

25. Suppose your supervisor has asked you to develop a form to record certain information needed.
    The FIRST thing you should do is to
    A. determine the type of data that will be recorded repeatedly so that it can be preprinted
    B. study the relationship of the form to the job to be accomplished so that the form can be planned
    C. determine the information that will be recorded in the same place on each copy of the form so that it can be used as a check
    D. find out who will be responsible for supplying the information so that space can be provided for their signatures

25.____

26. An administrative officer in charge of a small fund for buying office supplies has just written a check to Charles Laird, a supplier, and has sent the check by messenger to him. A half-hour later, the messenger telephones the administrative officer. He has lost the check.
Which of the following is the MOST important action for the administrative officer to take under these circumstances?
   A. Ask the messenger to return and write a report describing the loss of the check
   B. Make a note on the performance record of the messenger who lost the check
   C. Take the necessary steps to have payment stopped on the check
   D. Refrain from doing anything since the check may be found shortly

26._____

27. A petty cash fund is set up PRIMARILY to
   A. take care of small investments that must be made from time to time
   B. take care of small expenses that arise from time to time
   C. provide a fund to be used as the office wants to use it with little need to maintain records
   D. take care of expenses that develop during emergencies, such as machine breakdowns and fires

27._____

28. Of the following, which is usually the MOST important guideline in writing business letters?
A letter should be
   A. neat
   B. written in a formalized style
   C. written in clear language intelligible to the reader
   D. written in the past tense

28._____

29. Suppose you are asked to edit a policy statement. You note that personal pronouns like *you*, *we*, and *I* are used freely.
Which of the following statements BEST applies to this use of personal pronouns?
It
   A. is proper usage because written business language should not be different from carefully spoken business language
   B. requires correction because is it ungrammatical
   C. is proper because it is clearer and has a warmer tone
   D. requires correction because policies should be expressed in an impersonal manner

29._____

30. Good business letters are coherent.
To be coherent means to
   A. keep only one unifying idea in the message
   B. present the total message
   C. use simple, direct words for the message
   D. tie together the various ideas in the message

30._____

31. Proper division of a letter into paragraphs requires that the writer of business letters should, as much as possible, be sure that
    A. each paragraph is short
    B. each paragraph develops discussion of just one topic
    C. each paragraph repeats the theme of the total message
    D. there are at least two paragraphs for every message

31.____

32. An editor is given a letter with this initial paragraph:
    We have received your letter, which we read with interest, and we are happy to respond to your question. In fact, we talked with several people in our office to get ideas to send to you.
    Which of the following is MOST reasonable for the editor to conclude?
    The paragraph is
    A. concise
    B. communicating something of value
    C. unnecessary
    D. coherent

32.____

33. As soon as you pick up the phone, a very angry caller begins immediately to complain about city agencies and *red tape*. He says that he has been shifted to two or three different offices. It turns out that he is seeking information which is not immediately available to you. You believe you know, however, where it can be found.
    Which of the following actions is the BEST one for you to take?
    A. To eliminate all confusion, suggest that the caller write the mayor stating explicitly what he wants
    B. Apologize by telling the caller how busy city agencies now are, but also tell him directly that you do not have the information he needs
    C. Ask for the caller's telephone number and assure him you will call back after you have checked further
    D. Give the caller the name and telephone number of the person who might be able to help, but explain that you are not positive he will get results

33.____

34. Suppose that one of your duties is to dictate responses to routine requests from the public for information. A letter writer asks for information which, as expressed in a one-sentence, explicit agency rule, cannot be given out to the public.
    Of the following ways of answering the letter, which is the MOST efficient?
    A. Quote verbatim that section of the agency rules which prohibit giving this information to the public
    B. Without quoting the rule, explain why you cannot accede to the request and suggest alternative sources
    C. Describe how carefully the request was considered before classifying it as subject to the rule forbidding the issuance of such information
    D. Acknowledge receipt of the letter and advise that the requested information is not released to the public

34.____

35. Suppose you assist in supervising a staff which has rather high morale, and your own supervisor asks you to poll the staff to find out who will be able to work overtime this particular evening to help complete emergency work.
Which of the following approaches would be MOST likely to win their cooperation while maintaining their morale?
    A. Tell them that the better assignments will be given only to those who work overtime
    B. Tell them that occasional overtime is a job requirement
    C. Assure them they'll be doing you a personal favor
    D. Let them know clearly why the overtime is needed

36. Suppose that you have been asked to write and to prepare for reproduction new departmental vacation leave regulations.
After you have written the new regulations, all of which fit on one page, which one of the following would be the BESST method of reproducing 1,000 copies?
    A. An outside private printer, because you can best maintain confidentiality using this technique
    B. Xeroxing, because the copies will have the best possible appearance
    C. Typing copies, because you will be certain that there are the fewest possible errors
    D. Including it in the next company newsletter

37. Administration is the center, but not necessarily the source, of all ideas for procedural improvement.
The MOST significant implication that this principle bears for the administrative officer is that
    A. before procedural improvements are introduced, they should be approved by a majority of the staff
    B. it is the unique function of the administrative officer to derive and introduce procedural improvements
    C. the administrative officer should derive ideas and suggestions for procedural improvement from all possible sources, introducing any that promise to be effective
    D. the administrative officer should view employee grievances as the chief source of procedural improvements

38. Your bureau is assigned an important task.
Of the following, the function that you, as an administrative officer, can LEAST reasonably be expected to perform under these circumstances is
    A. division of the large job into individual tasks
    B. establishment of *production lines* within the bureau
    C. performance personally of a substantial share of all the work
    D. check up to see that the work has been done well

39. Suppose that you have broken a complex job into its smaller components before making assignments to the employees under your jurisdiction.
Of the following, the LEAST advisable procedure to follow from that point is to
   A. give each employee a picture of the importance of his work for the success of the total job
   B. establish a definite line of work flow and responsibility
   C. post a written memorandum of the best method for performing each job
   D. teach a number of alternative methods for doing each job

40. As an administrative officer, you are requested to draw up an organization chart of the whole department.
Of the following, the MOST important characteristic of such a chart is that it will
   A. include all peculiarities and details of the organization which distinguish it from any other
   B. be a schematic representation of purely administrative functions within the department
   C. present a modification of the actual departmental organization in the light of principles of scientific management
   D. present an accurate picture of the lines of authority and responsibility

KEY (CORRECT ANSWERS)

1.	A	11.	B	21.	A	31.	B
2.	C	12.	D	22.	B	32.	C
3.	C	13.	C	23.	A	33.	C
4.	D	14.	B	24.	C	34.	A
5.	D	15.	D	25.	B	35.	D
6.	C	16.	A	26.	C	36.	B
7.	D	17.	C	27.	B	37.	C
8.	B	18.	A	28.	C	38.	C
9.	C	19.	C	29.	D	39.	D
10.	C	20.	A	30.	D	40.	D

TEST 2

DIRECTIONS: Each question or incomplete statement is followed by several suggested answers or completions. Select the one that BEST answers the question or completes the statement. *PRINT THE LETTER OF THE CORRECT ANSWER IN THE SPACE AT THE RIGHT.*

Questions 1-10.

DIRECTIONS: In each of Questions 1 through 10, a pair of related words written in capital letters is followed by four other pairs of words. For each question, select the pair of words which MOST closely expresses a relationship similar to that of the pair in capital letters.

    SAMPLE QUESTION:
        BOAT – DOCK

    A. air plane – hangar   B. rain – snow
    C. cloth – cotton   D. hunger - food

Choice A is the answer to this sample question since, of the choices given, the relationship between airplane and hangar is most similar to the relationship between boat and dock.

1. AUTOMOBILE – FACTORY
 A. tea – lemon
 B. wheel – engine
 C. pot – flower
 D. paper – mill

2. GIRDER – BRIDGE
 A. petal – flower
 B. street – sidewalk
 C. meat – vegetable
 D. sun – storm

3. RADIUS – CIRCLE
 A. brick – building
 B. tie – tracks
 C. spoke – wheel
 D. axle – tire

4. DISEASE – RESEARCH
 A. death – poverty
 B. speech – audience
 C. problem – conference
 D. invalid – justice

5. CONCLUSION – INTRODUCTION
 A. commencement – beginning
 B. housing – motor
 C. caboose – engine
 D. train – cabin

6. SOCIETY – LAW
 A. baseball – rules
 B. jury – law
 C. cell – prisoner
 D. sentence – jury

7. PLAN – ACCOMPLISHMENT
   A. deed – fact
   B. method – success
   C. graph – chart
   D. rules – manual

7.____

8. ORDER – GOVERNMENT
   A. chaos – administration
   B. confusion – pandemonium
   C. rule – stability
   D. despair – hope

8.____

9. TYRANNY – FREEDOM
   A. despot – mob
   B. wealth – poverty
   C. nobility – commoners
   D. dictatorship – democracy

9.____

10. FAX – LETTER
    A. hare – tortoise
    B. lie – truth
    C. number – word
    D. report – research

10.____

Questions 11-16.

DIRECTIONS: Questions 11 through 16 are to be answered SOLELY on the basis of the information given in the passage below.

Inherent in all organized endeavors is the need to resolve the individual differences involved in conflict. Conflict may be either a positive or negative factor, since it may lead to creativity, innovation, and progress, on the one hand, or it may result, on the other hand, in a deterioration or even destruction of the organization. Thus, some forms of conflict are desirable, whereas others are undesirable and ethically wrong.

There are three management strategies which deal with interpersonal conflict. In the "divide-and-rule strategy," management attempts to maintain control by limiting the conflict to those directly involved and preventing their disagreement from spreading to the larger group. The "suppression –of-differences strategy" entails ignoring conflicts or pretending they are irrelevant. In the "working-through-differences strategy," management actively attempts to solve or resolve intergroup or interpersonal conflicts. Of the three strategies, only the last directly attacks and has the potential for eliminating the causes of conflict. An essential part of this strategy, however, is its employment by a committed and relatively mature management team.

11. According to the above passage, the *divide-and-rule strategy* for dealing with conflict is the attempt to
    A. involve other people in the conflict
    B. restrict the conflict to those participating in it
    C. divide the conflict into positive and negative factors
    D. divide the conflict into a number of smaller ones

11.____

12. The word *conflict* is used in relation to both positive and negative factors in this passage.
    Which one of the following words is MOST likely to describe the activity which the word *conflict*, in the sense of the passage, implies?
    A. Competition   B. Cooperation   C. Confusion   D. Aggression

12.____

13. According to the above passage, which one of the following characteristics is shared by both the *suppression-of-difference strategy* and the *divide-and-rule strategy*?
    A. Pretending that conflicts are irrelevant
    B. Preventing conflicts from spreading to the group situation
    C. Failure to directly attack the causes of conflict
    D. Actively attempting to resolve interpersonal conflict

13._____

14. According to the above passage, the successful resolution of interpersonal conflict requires
    A. allowing the group to mediate conflicts between two individuals
    B. division of the conflict into positive and negative factors
    C. involvement of a committed, mature management team
    D. ignoring minor conflicts until they threaten the organization

14._____

15. Which can be MOST reasonably inferred from the above passage? A conflict between two individuals is LEAST likely to continue when management uses
    A. the *working-through-differences strategy*
    B. the *suppression-of-differences strategy*
    C. the *divide-and-rule strategy*
    D. a combination of all three strategies

15._____

16. According to the above passage, a DESIRABLE result of conflict in an organization is when conflict
    A. exposes production problems in the organization
    B. can be easily ignored by management
    C. results in advancement of more efficient managers
    D. leads to development of new methods

16._____

Questions 17-23.

DIRECTIONS: Questions 17 through 23 are to be answered SOLELY on the basis of the information given in the passage below.

Modern management places great emphasis on the concept of communication. The communication process consists of the steps through which an idea or concept passes from its inception by one person, the sender, until it is acted upon by another person, the receiver. Through an understanding of these steps and some of the possible barriers that may occur, more effective communication may be achieved. The first step in the communication process is ideation by the sender. This is the formation of the intended content of the message he wants to transmit. In the next step, encoding, the sender organizes his ideas into a series of symbols designed to communicate his message to his intended receiver. He selects suitable words or phrases that can be understood by the receiver, and he also selects the appropriate media to be used—for example, memorandum, conference, etc. The third step is transmission of the encoded message through selected channels in the organizational structure. In the fourth step, the receiver enters the process by tuning in to receive the message. If the receiver does not function, however, the message is lost. For example, if the message is oral, the receiver must be a good listener. The fifth step is decoding of the message by the receiver, as for example, by changing words into ideas. At this step, the decoded message may not be the same idea that the sender originally encoded because the sender and receiver have different perceptions regarding the meaning of certain words.

Finally, the receiver acts or responds. He may file the information, ask for more information, or take other action. There can be no assurance, however, that communication has taken place unless there is some type of feedback to the sender in the form of an acknowledgement that the message was received.

17. According to the above passage, *ideation* is the process by which the 17.____
    A. sender develops the intended content of the message
    B. sender organizes his ideas into a series of symbols
    C. receiver tunes in to receive the message
    D. receiver decodes the message

18. In the last sentence of the passage, the word *feedback* refers to the process by which the sender is assured that the 18.____
    A. receiver filed the information
    B. receiver's perception is the same as his own
    C. message was received
    D. message was poorly interpreted

19. Which one of the following BEST shows the order of the steps in the communication process as described in the passage? 19.____
    A. 1 – ideation   2 – encoding
       3 – decoding   4 – transmission
       5 – receiving   6 – action
       7 – feedback to the sender
    B. 1 – ideation   2 – encoding
       3 – transmission   4 – decoding
       5 – receiving   6 – action
       7 – feedback to the sender
    C. 1 – ideation   2 – decoding
       3 – transmission   4 – receiving
       5 – encoding   6 – action
       7 – feedback to the sender
    D. 1 – ideation   2 – encoding
       3 – transmission   4 – receiving
       5 – decoding   6 – action
       7 – feedback to the sender

20. Which one of the following BEST expresses the main theme of the passage? 20.____
    A. Different individuals have the same perceptions regarding the meaning of words.
    B. An understanding of the steps in the communication process may achieve better communication.
    C. Receivers play a passive role in the communication process.
    D. Senders should not communicate with receivers who transmit feedback.

21. The above passage implies that a receiver does NOT function properly when he 21._____
    A. transmits feedback   B. files the information
    C. is a poor listener   D. asks for more information

22. Which of the following, according to the above passage, is included in the 22._____
    SECOND step of the communication process?
    A. Selecting the appropriate media to be used in transmission
    B. Formulation of the intended content of the message
    C. Using appropriate media to respond to the receiver's feedback
    D. Transmitting the message through selected channels in the organization

23. The above passage implies that the *decoding* process is MOST NEARLY the 23._____
    reverse of the _____ process.
    A. transmission   B. receiving   C. feedback   D. encoding

Questions 24-27.

DIRECTIONS: Questions 24 through 27 are to be answered SOLELY on the basis of the information given in the passage below.

A personnel researcher has at his disposal various approaches for obtaining information, analyzing it, and arriving at conclusions that have value in predicting and affecting the behavior of people at work. The type of method to be used depends on such factors as the nature of the research problem, the available data, and the attitude of those people being studied to the various kinds of approaches. While the experimental approach, with its use of control groups, is the most refined type of study, there are others that are often found useful in personnel research. Surveys, in which the researcher obtains facts on a problem from a variety of sources, are employed in research on wages, fringe benefits, and labor relations. Historical studies are used to trace the development of problems in order to understand them better and to isolate possible causative factors. Case studies are generally developed to explore all the details of a particular problem that is representative of other similar problems. A researcher chooses the most appropriate form of study for the problem he is investigating. He should recognize, however, that the experimental method, commonly referred to as the scientific method, if used validly and reliably, gives the most conclusive results.

24. The above statement discusses several approaches used to obtain information 24._____
    on particular problems.
    Which of the following may be MOST reasonably concluded from the passage?
    A(n)
    A. historical study cannot determine causative factors
    B. survey is often used in research on fringe benefits
    C. case study is usually used to explore a problem that is unique and unrelated to other problems
    D. experimental study is used when the scientific approach to a problem fails

6 (#2)

25. According to the above passage, all of the following are factors that may determine the type of approach a researcher uses EXCEPT
    A. the attitudes of people toward being used in control groups
    B. the number of available sources
    C. his desire to isolate possible causative factors
    D. the degree of accuracy he requires

25.____

26. The words *scientific method*, used in the last sentence of the paragraph, refer to a type of study which, according to the paragraph,
    A. uses a variety of sources
    B. traces the development of problems
    C. uses control group
    D. analyzes the details of a representative problem

26.____

27. Which of the following can be MOST reasonably concluded from the above passage?
    In obtaining and analyzing information on a particular problem, a researcher employs the method which is the
    A. most accurate
    B. most suitable
    C. least expensive
    D. least time-consuming

27.____

Questions 28-31.

DIRECTIONS: Questions 28 through 31 are to be answered according to the information given in the following graph, which indicates at 5-year intervals the number of citations issued for various offenses from the year 2000 to the year 2020.

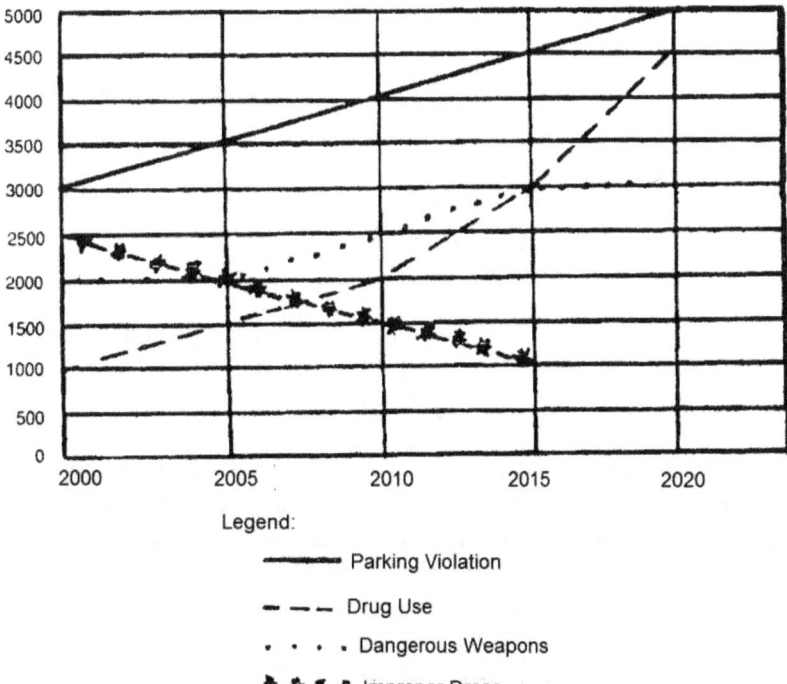

Legend:
⎯⎯⎯ Parking Violation
— — — Drug Use
. . . . Dangerous Weapons
🐛🐛🐛🐛 Improper Dress

115

28. Over the 20-year period, which offense shows an AVERAGE rate of increase of more than 150 citations per year? 28.____
    A. Parking Violations
    B. Dangerous Weapons
    C. Drug Use
    D. None of the above

29. Over the 20-year period, which offense shows a CONSTANT rate of increase or decrease? 29.____
    A. Parking Violations
    B. Drug Use
    C. Dangerous Weapons
    D. Improper Dress

30. Which offense shows a TOTAL INCREASE OR DECREASE of 50% for the full 20-year period? 30.____
    A. Parking Violations
    B. Drug Use
    C. Dangerous Weapons
    D. Improper Dress

31. The percentage increase in total citations issued from 2005 to 2010 is MOST NEARLY 31.____
    A. 7%   B. 11%   C. 21%   D. 41%

Questions 32-35.

DIRECTIONS: Questions 32 through 35 are to be answered SOLELY on the basis of the information given in the following chart, which shows the annual number of administrative actions completed for the four divisions of a bureau. Assume that the figures remain stable from year to year.

	DIVISIONS				
Administrative Actions	W	X	Y	Z	TOTALS
Telephone Inquiries Answered	8,000	6,800	7,500	4,800	27,100
Interviews Conducted	500	630	550	500	2,180
Applications Processed	15,000	18,000	14,500	9,500	57,000
Letters Typed	2,500	4,400	4,350	3,250	14,500
Reports Completed	200	250	100	50	600
Totals	26,200	30,080	27,000	18,100	101,380

32. In which division is the number of Applications Processed the GREATEST percentage of the total Administrative Action for that division? 32.____
    A. W   B. X   C. Y   D. Z

33. The bureau chief is considering a plant that would consolidate the typing of letters in a separate unit. This unit would be responsible for the typing of letters for all divisions in which the number of letters typed exceeds 15% of the total number of Administrative Actions. 33.____
    Under this plan, which of the following divisions would CONTINUE to type its own letters?
    A. W and X   B. W, X, and Y   C. X and Y   D. X and Z

34. The setting up of a central information service that would be capable of answering 25% of the whole bureau's telephone inquiries is under consideration. Under such a plan, the divisions would gain for other activities that time previously spent on telephone inquiries.
Approximately how much total time would such a service gain for all four divisions if it requires 5 minutes to answer the average telephone inquiry?
_____ hours.
   A. 500   B. 515   C. 565   D. 585

35. Assume that the rate of production shown in the table can be projected as accurate for the coming year and that monthly output is constant for each type of administrative action within a division. Division Y is scheduled to work exclusively on a 4-month long special project during that year. During the period of the project, Division Y's regular workload will be divided evenly among the remaining divisions.
Using the figures in the table, what would be MOST NEARLY the percentage increase in the total Administrative Actions completed by Division Z for the year?
   A. 8%   B. 16%   C. 25%   D. 50%

36. You have conducted a traffic survey a 10 two-lane bridges and find the traffic between 4:30 and 5:30 P.M. average 665 cars per bridge that hour. You can't find the tabulation sheet for Bridge #7, but you know that 6066 cars were counted at the other 9 bridges.
Determine from this how many must have been counted at Bridge #7.
   A. 584   B. 674   C. 665   D. 607

37. You pay temporary help $11.20 per hour and regular employees $12.00 per hour. Your workload is temporarily heavy, so you need 20 hours of extra regular employees' time to catch up. If you do this on overtime, you must pay time-and-a-half. If you use temporary help, it takes 25% more time to do the job.
What is the difference in cost between the two alternatives?
   A. $20 more for temporary   B. $40 more for temporary
   C. $80 more for regular   D. $136 more for regular

38. An experienced clerk can process the mailing of annual forms in 9 day. A new clerk takes 14 days to process them.
If they work together, how many days MOST NEARLY will it take to do the processing?
   A. 4½   B. 5½   C. 6½   D. 7

39. A certain administrative aide is usually able to successfully handle 27% of all telephone inquiries without assistance. In a particular month, he receives 1,200 inquiries and handles 340 of them successfully on his own.
How many more inquiries has he handled successfully in that month than would have been expected of him based on his usual rate?
   A. 10   B. 16   C. 24   D. 44

9 (#2)

40. Suppose that on a scaled drawing of an office building floor, ½ inch represents three feet of actual floor dimensions.
A floor which is, in fact, 75 feet wide and 132 feet long has which of the following dimensions on this scaled drawing? _____ inches wide and _____ inches long.
   A. 9.5; 20.5   B. 12.5; 22   C. 17;32   D. 25; 44

40.____

41. In a division of clerks and stenographers, 15 people are currently employed, 20% of whom are stenographers.
If management plans are to maintain the current number of stenographers, but to increase the clerical staff to the point where 12% of the total staff are stenographers, what is the MAXIMUM number of additional clerks that should be hired to meet these plans?
   A. 3   B. 8   C. 10   D. 12

41.____

42. Suppose that a certain agency had a 2018 budget of $1,200,500. The 2019 budget was 7% higher than that of 2018, and the 2020 budget was 8% higher than that of 2019.
Of the following, which one is MOST NEARLY that agency's budget for 2020?
   A. $1,177,624   B. $1,261,737   C. $1,265,575   D. $1,271,738

42.____

Questions 43-50.

DIRECTIONS: Your office keeps a file card record of the work assignments for all the employees in a certain bureau. On each card is the employee's name, a work assignment code number, and the date of this assignment. In this filing system, the employee's name is filed alphabetically, the work assignment code is filed numerically, and the date of assignment is filed chronologically (earliest date first).

Each of Questions 43 through 50 represents five cards to be filed, numbered (1) through (5) shown in Column I. Each card is made up of the employee's name, a work assignment code number shown in parentheses, and the date of this assignment. The cards are to be filed according to the following rules:

First: File in alphabetical order.
Second: When two or more cards have the same employee's name, file according to the work assignment number, beginning with the lowest number.
Third: When two or more cards have the same employee's name and same assignment number, file according to the assignment date beginning with earliest date.

Column II shows the cards arranged in four different orders. Pick the answer (A, B, C, or D) in Column II which shows the cards arranged correctly according to the above filing rules.

SAMPLE QUESTION:
		Column I		Column II
(1)	Cluney	(486503)	6/17/07	A. 2, 3, 4, 1, 5
(2)	Roster	(246611)	5/10/06	B. 2, 5, 1, 3, 4
(3)	Altool	(711433)	10/15/07	C. 3, 2, 1, 4, 5
(4)	Cluney	(527610)	12/18/06	D. 3, 5, 1, 4, 2
(5)	Cluney	(486500)	4/8/07	

The CORRECT way to file the cards is:
(3)	Altool	(711433)	10/15/07
(5)	Cluney	(486500)	4/8/07
(1)	Cluney	(486503)	6/17/07
(4)	Cluney	(527610)	12/18/06
(2)	Roster	(246611)	5/10/06

The correct filing order is shown by the numbers in front of each name (3, 5, 1, 4, 2). The answer to the sample question is the letter in Column II in front of the numbers 3, 5, 1, 4, 2. This answer is D.

			Column I		Column II
43.	(1)	Prichard	(013469)	4/6/06	A. 5, 4, 3, 2, 1
	(2)	Parks	(678941)	2/7/06	B. 1, 2, 5, 3, 4
	(3)	Williams	(551467)	3/6/05	C. 2, 1, 5, 3, 4
	(4)	Wilson	(551466)	8/9/02	D. 1, 5, 4, 3, 2
	(5)	Stanhope	(300014)	8/9/02	
44.	(1)	Ridgeway	(623809)	8/11/06	A. 5, 1, 3, 4, 2
	(2)	Travers	(305439)	4/5/02	B. 5, 1, 3, 2, 4
	(3)	Tayler	(818134)	7/5/03	C. 1, 5, 3, 2, 4
	(4)	Travers	(305349)	5/6/05	D. 1, 5, 4, 2, 3
	(5)	Ridgeway	(62309)	10/9/06	
45.	(1)	Jaffe	(384737)	2/19/06	A. 3, 5, 2, 4, 1
	(2)	Inez	(859176)	8/8/07	B. 3, 5, 2, 1, 4
	(3)	Ingrahm	(946460)	8/6/04	C. 2, 3, 5, 1, 4
	(4)	Karp	(256146)	5/5/05	D. 2, 3, 5, 4, 1
	(5)	Ingrahm	(946460)	6/4/05	
46.	(1)	Marrano	(369421)	7/24/04	A. 1, 5, 3, 4, 2
	(2)	Marks	(652910)	2/23/06	B. 3, 5, 4, 2, 1
	(3)	Netto	(556772)	3/10/07	C. 2, 4, 1, 5, 3
	(4)	Marks	(652901)	2/17/07	D. 4, 2, 1, 5, 3
	(5)	Netto	(556772)	6/17/05	
47.	(1)	Abernathy	(712467)	6/23/05	A. 5, 3, 1, 2, 4
	(2)	Acevedo	(680262)	6/23/03	B. 5, 4, 2, 3, 1
	(3)	Aaron	(967647)	1/17/04	C. 1, 3, 5, 2, 4
	(4)	Acevedo	(680622)	5/14/02	D. 2, 4, 1, 5, 3
	(5)	Aaron	(967647)	4/1/00	

48. (1) Simon   (645219) 8/19/05   A. 4, 1, 2, 5, 3   48.____
    (2) Simon   (645219) 9/2/03   B. 4, 5, 2, 1, 3
    (3) Simons   (645218) 7/7/05   C. 3, 5, 2, 1, 4
    (4) Simms   (646439) 10/12/06   D. 5, 1, 2, 3, 4
    (5) Simon   (645219) 10/16/02

49. (1) Rappaport (312230) 6/11/06   A. 4, 3, 1, 2, 5   49.____
    (2) Rascio   (777510) 2/9/05   B. 4, 3, 1, 5, 2
    (3) Rappaport (312230) 7/3/02   C. 3, 4, 1, 5, 2
    (4) Rapaport (312330) 9/6/05   D. 5, 2, 4, 3, 1
    (5) Rascio   (777501) 7/7/05

50. (1) Johnson   (843250) 6/8/02   A. 1, 3, 2, 4, 5   50.____
    (2) Johnson   (843205) 4/3/05   B. 1, 3, 2, 5, 4
    (3) Johnson   (843205) 8/6/02   C. 3, 2, 1, 4, 5
    (4) Johnson   (843602) 3/8/06   D. 3, 2, 1, 5, 4
    (5) Johnson   (843602) 8/3/05

KEY (CORRECT ANSWERS)

1.	D	11.	B	21.	C	31.	B	41.	C
2.	A	12.	A	22.	A	32.	B	42.	D
3.	C	13.	C	23.	D	33.	A	43.	C
4.	C	14.	C	24.	B	34.	C	44.	A
5.	C	15.	A	25.	D	35.	B	45.	C
6.	A	16.	D	26.	C	36.	A	46.	D
7.	B	17.	A	27.	B	37.	C	47.	A
8.	C	18.	C	28.	C	38.	B	48.	B
9.	D	19.	D	29.	A	39.	B	49.	B
10.	A	20.	B	30.	C	40.	B	50.	D

EXAMINATION SECTION

TEST 1

DIRECTIONS: Each question or incomplete statement is followed by several suggested answers or completions. Select the one that BEST answers the question or completes the statement. *PRINT THE LETTER OF THE CORRECT ANSWER IN THE SPACE AT THE RIGHT.*

1. The PRIMARY purpose of program analysis as it is used in government is to
   A. replace political judgments with rational programs and policies
   B. help decision-makers to sharpen their judgments about program choices
   C. analyze the impact of past programs on the quality of public services
   D. reduce costs by eliminating waste in public programs and services

   1.____

2. While there is no complete method for program analysis that is agreed to by all the experts and is relevant to all types of problems, the MOST important element in program analysis involves the
   A. development of alternatives and the definition of objectives or criteria
   B. collection of information and the construction of a mathematical model
   C. design of experiments and procedures to validate results
   D. collection of expert opinion and the combination of their views

   2.____

3. Electronic data processing is a particularly valuable tool of analysis in situations where the analyst has a processing problem involving
   A. *small* input, *few* operations, and *small* output
   B. *large* input, *many* operations, and *small* output
   C. *large* input, *few* operations, and *large* output
   D. *small* input, *many* operations, and *small* output

   3.____

4. In order for an analyst to use electronic data processing to solve an analytic problem, the problem must be clearly defined.
   The BEST way to prepare material for such definition in electronic data processing is to
   A. discuss the problem with computer programmers in a meeting
   B. prepare a flow diagram outlining the steps in the analysis
   C. write a memorandum with a list of the relevant program issues
   D. write a computer program using FORTRAN, BASIC, or another language

   4.____

5. The "growth rate" referred to in current political and economic discussion refers to change from year to year in a country's
   A. investments   B. population
   C. gross national product   D. sale of goods

   5.____

6. Interactive or conversational programming is important to the program analyst ESPECIALLY for
   A. preparing analyses leading to management information systems
   B. communicating among analysts in different places
   C. using canned programs in statistical analysis
   D. testing trial solutions in rapid sequence

6.____

7. Program analysts often calls for recommendation of a choice between competing program possibilities that differ in the timing of major costs. Analysts using the present value technique by setting an interest or discount rate are in effect arguing that, other things being equal,
   A. it is inadvisable to defer the start of projects because of rising costs
   B. projects should be completed within a short time period to save money
   C. expenditures should be made out of tax revenues to avoid payment of interest
   D. postponing expenditures is advantageous at some measurable rate

7.____

8. Of the following, the formula which is MOST appropriately used to estimate the net need for a given type of service is that net need equals
   A. current clients – anticipate losses + anticipated gains
   B. $\dfrac{\text{current supply}}{\text{standard}}$ + current clients
   C. (client population x standard) – current supply
   D. current supply – anticipated losses + anticipated gains

8.____

9. The purpose of feasibility analysis is to protect the analyst from naïve alternatives and, MOST generally, to
   A. identify and quantify technological constraints
   B. carry out a preliminary stage of analysis
   C. anticipate potential blocks to implementation
   D. line up the support of political leadership

9.____

Questions 10-11.

DIRECTIONS: Questions 10 and 11 are to be answered on the basis of the following chart. In a hypothetical problem involving four criteria and four alternatives, the following data have been assembled.

Cost Criterion	Effectiveness Criterion	Timing Criterion	Feasibility Criterion
Alternative A $500,000	50 units	3 months	probably feasible
Alternative B $300,000	100 units	6 months	probably feasible
Alternative C $400,000	50 units	12 months	probably infeasible
Alternative D $200,000	75 units	3 months	probably infeasible

10. On the basis of the above data, it appears that the one alternative which is dominated by another alternative is Alternative
    A. A B. B C. C D. D

10.____

11. If the feasibility constraint is absolute and fixed, then the critical trade-off is between lower cost
    A. on the one hand and faster timing and higher effectiveness on the other
    B. and higher effectiveness on one hand and faster timing on the other
    C. and faster timing on the one hand and higher effectiveness on the other
    D. on the one hand and higher effectiveness on the other

12. A classification of an agency's activities in a program structure is MOST useful if it highlights
    A. trade-offs that might not otherwise be considered
    B. ways to improve the efficiency of each activity
    C. the true organizational structure of an agency
    D. bases for insuring that expenditures stay within limits

13. CPM, like PERT, is a useful tool for scheduling large-scale, complex processes. In CPM, the critical path is the
    A. path composed of important links
    B. path composed of uncertain links
    C. longest path through the network
    D. shortest path through the network

14. Classical evaluative research calls for the use of control groups. However, there are practical difficulties in collecting data on individuals to be used as "controls" in program evaluations.
    Researchers may attempt to overcome these difficulties by
    A. using control groups that have no choice such as prison inmates or inmates of other public institutions or facilities
    B. developing better measures of the inputs, processes, and outputs relevant to public programs and services
    C. using experimental demonstration projects with participants in the different projects serving as comparison groups for one another
    D. abandoning attempts at formal evaluation in favor of more qualitative approaches employing a journalistic style of analysis

15. During the course of an analysis of the remaining "life" of a certain city's landfill for refuse disposal, there was a great deal of debate about the impact of changing rates of garbage generation on the amount of landfill needed and about what rates of garbage generation to expect over the next decade. Faced with the need to attempt to resolve this debate, an analyst would construct a simple model of the refuse disposal system and
    A. project landfill needs without considering refuse generation in the future
    B. conduct a detailed household survey in order to estimate future garbage generation rates
    C. ask the experts to continue to debate the issue until the argument is won by one view
    D. do a sensitivity analysis to test the impact of alternative assumptions about refuse generation

16. The limitations of traditional surveys have fostered the development and use of panels.
A panel is a
   A. group of respondents that serves as a continuous source of survey information
   B. group of advisors expert in the design and implementation of surveys
   C. representative sample of respondents at a single point in time
   D. post-survey discussion group composed of former respondents

16._____

17. The difference between sensitivity analysis and risk analysis is that risk analysis
   A. is applicable only to profit and loss situations where the concept of risk is operable
   B. includes an estimate of probabilities of different values of input factors
   C. is applicable to physical problems while sensitivity analysis is applicable to social ones
   D. requires a computer simulation while sensitivity analysis does not

17._____

18. A decision tree, although initially applied to business problems, is a graphic device which is useful to public analysts in
   A. scheduling complex processes
   B. doing long-range forecasting
   C. formulating the structure of alternatives
   D. solving production-inventory problems

18._____

19. The purpose of a management information system in an agency is to
   A. structure data relevant to managerial decision-making
   B. put all of an agency's data in machine-processing form
   C. simplify the record-keeping operations in an agency
   D. keep an ongoing record of management's activities

19._____

20.

[Chart: Number of responses to alarms (y-axis) vs. Time (x-axis), showing "total alarms" line above "false alarms" line, both trending upward slightly]

Assume that an analyst is presented with the above chart for a fire department and supplied also with information indicating a stable size firefighting staff over this time.
The analyst could REASONABLY conclude regarding productivity that
   A. productivity over this time period was essentially stable for this firefighting force because the number of responses to real fires during this period was stable, as was the work force
   B. productivity was essentially increasing for this force because the number of total responses was increasing relative to a stable force

20._____

C. productivity was declining because a greater proportion of the total work effort was wasted effort in responding to false alarms
D. it is impossible to make a judgment about the productivity of the firefighting staff without a judgment about the value of a response to a false alarm

21. In the design of a productivity program for the sanitary department, the BEST measure of productivity would be
    A. tons of refuse collected annually
    B. number of collections made per week
    C. tons of refuse collected per truck shift
    D. number of trucks used per shift

21.____

22. The cohort-survival method for estimating future population has been widely employed.
    In this method,
    A. migration is assumed to be constant over time
    B. net migration within cohorts is assumed to be zero
    C. migration is included as a multiplier factor
    D. net migration within cohorts is assumed to be constant

22.____

23. Cost-effectiveness and cost-benefit analysis represent a systematic approach to balancing potential losses against potential gains as a prelude to public action.
    In addition to limitations based on difficulties of measurement and inadequacies in data that are typical of systematic program analysis, cost-benefit analysis suffers from a serious conceptual flaw in that
    A. the definition of benefit or cost does not typically distinguish to whom benefits or costs accrue
    B. a full-scale cost benefit analysis takes too long to do, is too expensive, and needs too much data
    C. it has been shown that such analyses are more suitable for defense or water resources problems
    D. such analyses are not useful in any problem involving capital and operating costs or benefits

23.____

24. If you were asked to develop a total cost estimate for one year for a program involving both a capital improvement and operating costs, the BEST way to estimate the capital cost component would be to
    A. divide the estimated cost of the capital improvement by the projected operating costs over the life of the improvement
    B. multiply the annual operating cost by the projected life of the capital improvement
    C. divide the amortized cost of the capital improvement by the projected life of the improvement
    D. multiply the portion of the capital improvement to be completed within the year by the cost of the improvement

24.____

25. In comparing the costs of two or more alternative programs, it is important to consider all relevant costs.
    The MOST important principle in defining "relevant cost" is that
    A. only marginal or incremental cost should be considered in the estimate
    B. only recurring costs should be considered for each alternative
    C. estimates should include the sunk costs for each alternative
    D. cost estimates need to be as precise as in budget preparation

25.____

26. Different techniques for projecting future costs may be suitable in different situations. Assume that it is necessary to estimate the future costs of maintaining garbage collection vehicles.
    Under which of the following conditions would it be advisable to develop a cost-estimating equation rather than to use unadjusted current data?
    A. When it is expected that more complex equipment will replace simpler equipment
    B. Whether or not it is expected that the nature of future garbage collection will change
    C. When the current unadjusted data still has to be verified
    D. When the nature of future garbage collection equipment is unknown

26.____

27. The following data has been collected on the costs of two pilot programs, each representing a different approach to the same problem.

	Total Cost	Fixed Cost	Variable Cost	Average Unit Cost	Number of Users
Program A	$45,000	$20,000	$50 per user	$90 Per User	500
Program B	$42,000	$7,000	$100 Per User	$120 Per User	350

Assume that the pilot programs are extended city-wide and other factors are constant.
Using the above data, what would a cost analysis conclude about the relative costs of the two programs?
Program
A. B would be less costly with fewer than 300 users and Program A would be less costly with more than 300 users
B. B would be less costly with fewer than 260 users and Program A would be less costly with more than 260 users
C. A would be less costly without regard to the size of the program
D. B would be less costly without regard to the size of the program

27.____

Questions 28-30.

DIRECTIONS: Questions 28 through 30 are to be answered on the basis of the following data assembled for a cost-benefit analysis.

	Cost	Benefit
No program	0	0
Alternative W	$3,000	$6,000
Alternative X	$10,000	$17,000
Alternative Y	$17,000	$25,000
Alternative Z	$30,000	$32,000

28. From the point of view of pushing public expenditure to the point where marginal benefit equals or exceeds marginal cost, the BEST alternative is Alternative   28._____
   A. W   B. X   C. Y   D. Z

29. From the point of view of selecting the alternative with the best cost-benefit ratio, the BEST alternative is Alternative   29._____
   A. W   B. X   C. Y   D. Z

30. From the point of view of selecting the alternative with the best measure of net benefit, the BEST alternative is Alternative   30._____
   A. W   B. X   C. Y   D. Z

Questions 31-35.

DIRECTIONS: The set of answers listed below applies to Questions 31 through 35. Each answer is a type of statistical test.

   A. Analysis of variance
   B. Pearson Product-Moment Correlation (r)
   C. t-test
   D. x^2 test (Chi-squared)

Pick the test which is MOST appropriate to the situation described. An answer may be used more than once.

31. A comparison between two correlated means obtained from a small sample.   31._____
   The CORRECT answer is:
   A. A   B. B   C. C   D. D

32. A comparison of three or more means.   32._____
   The CORRECT answer is:
   A. A   B. B   C. C   D. D

33. A comparison of the divergence of observed frequencies with those expected on the hypothesis of equal probability of occurrence.   33._____
   The CORRECT answer is:
   A. A   B. B   C. C   D. D

34. A comparison of the divergence of observed frequencies with those expected on the hypothesis of a normal distribution.   34._____
   The CORRECT answer is:
   A. A   B. B   C. C   D. D

35. A comparison between two uncorrelated means obtained from small samples.   35._____
   The CORRECT answer is:
   A. A   B. B   C. C   D. D

36. There are many different models for evaluative research.
A time-series design is an example of a _____ experimental design.
   A. field   B. true   C. quasi-   D. pre-

37. In policy research, as in all kinds of research, it is important to develop research hypotheses early.
The MAIN purpose of a research hypothesis is to
   A. include the kind of statistical procedures to be used in the research
   B. provide a ready answer in case data is not available for doing research
   C. serve as a guide to the kind of data that must be collected in order to answer the research question
   D. clarify what is known and what is not known in the research problem

38. While descriptive and causal research are not completely separable, there has been a distinct effort to move in the direction of causal research.
Such an effort is epitomized by the use of
   A. predictive models and measures of deviation from predictions
   B. option and attitudinal surveys in local neighborhoods
   C. community studies and area profiles of localities
   D. individual case histories and group case studies

39. The one of the following which BEST describes a periodic report is that it
   A. provides a record of accomplishments for a given time span and a comparison with similar time spans in the past
   B. covers the progress made in a project that has been postponed
   C. integrates, summarizes, and perhaps interprets published data on technical or scientific material
   D. describes a decision, advocates a policy or action, and presents facts in support of the writer's position

40. The PRIMARY purpose of including pictorial illustrations in a formal report is usually to
   A. amplify information which has been adequately treated verbally
   B. present detail that are difficult to describe verbally
   C. provide the reader with a pleasant, momentary distraction
   D. present supplementary information incidental to the main ideas developed in the report

KEY (CORRECT ANSWERS)

1.	B	11.	B	21.	C	31.	C
2.	A	12.	A	22.	B	32.	A
3.	B	13.	C	23.	A	33.	D
4.	B	14.	C	24.	C	34.	D
5.	C	15.	D	25.	A	35.	C
6.	D	16.	A	26.	A	36.	C
7.	D	17.	B	27.	B	37.	C
8.	C	18.	C	28.	C	38.	A
9.	C	19.	A	29.	A	39.	A
10.	C	20.	D	30.	C	40.	B

TEST 2

DIRECTIONS: Each question or incomplete statement is followed by several suggested answers or completions. Select the one that BEST answers the question or completes the statement. *PRINT THE LETTER OF THE CORRECT ANSWER IN THE SPACE AT THE RIGHT.*

1. A measurement procedure is considered to be RELIABLE to the extent that 1.____
   A. independent applications under similar conditions yield consistent results
   B. independent applications under different conditions yield similar results
   C. scores reflect true differences among individuals or situations
   D. scores reflect true differences in the same individual over time

2. Different scales of measurement are distinguished by the feasibility of various empirical operations. 2.____
   An ordinal scale of measurement
   A. is not as useful as a ratio or interval scale
   B. is useful in rank-ordering or priority setting
   C. provides the data for addition or subtraction
   D. provides the data for computation of means

3. A widely used approach to sampling is systematic sampling, i.e., selecting every Kth element in a listing. 3.____
   Even with a random start, a DISADVANTAGE in this approach is that
   A. the listing used may contain a cyclical pattern
   B. it is too similar to a simple random sample
   C. the system does not insure a probability sample
   D. it yield an unpredictable sample size

4. A rule of thumb sometimes used in sample size selection it to set sample size equal to five percent of the population size. 4.____
   Other things being equal, this rule
   A. tends to oversample small populations
   B. tends to oversample large populations
   C. provides an accurate rule for sampling
   D. is a relatively inexpensive basis for sampling

5. With regard to a stratified random sample, it may be APPROPRIATE to sample the various strata in different proportions in order to 5.____
   A. approximate the characteristics of a true random sample
   B. establish classes that are internally heterogenous in each case
   C. avoid the necessity of subdividing the cases within each stratum
   D. adequately cover important strata that have small numbers of cases

6. One possible response to the "unknown" or "no answer" category in a tabulation of survey information is to "allocate" the unknown responses, i.e., to estimate the missing data on the basis of other known information about the respondents. 6.____

This technique is APPROPRIATE when the unknown category
- A. is very small and is randomly distributed within all subgroups of respondents
- B. is very large and is randomly distributed within all subgroups of respondents
- C. reflects an interviewing failure and a subgroup in the sample ends to produce more unknowns
- D. is a legitimate category and a subgroup in the sample tends to produce more unknowns

7. In presenting cross-tabulated data showing the relationship between two variables, it is MOST meaningful to compute percentages
   - A. in both directions in all instances
   - B. of each cell in relation to the grand total
   - C. in the direction of the smaller number of cells
   - D. in the direction of the causal factor

8. In portraying data based on a sampling operation, it is MOST meaningful and comprehensible to the reader to present
   - A. percentages for the sample and the universe
   - B. percentages by themselves
   - C. percentages and the base figures
   - D. numbers by themselves

9. A new bridge spanning a river is expected to carry 60,000 cars a day on a rainy day and 80,000 cars a day on other kinds of days.
   If there is a $5 toll and one chance in four of a rainy day, the expected value of a day's revenue is
   A. $175,000   B. $375,000   C. $475,000   D. $700,000

10. The analyst who is asked to estimate the probability of a relatively rare event occurring cannot use the classical frequency measures of probability but rather should
    - A. use a random-numbers table to pick a probability
    - B. project historical data into the future
    - C. indicate that no probabilistic judgment is possible
    - D. make the best possible judgment as to the subjective probability

11. A useful source of census data for computing annual indicators is the
    - A. Public Use Sample
    - B. Continuing Population Survey
    - C. Census of Population
    - D. Census of Governments

12. An analyst presented with a set of household records showing age, ethnicity, income, and family status and wishing to study the inter-relationship of all of these variables simultaneously will probably equal
    - A. one four-way cross-tabulation
    - B. four three-way cross-tabulation
    - C. six two-way cross-tabulations
    - D. four single tabulations

13. Downward communication, from high management to lower levels in an organization, will often not be fully accepted at the lowest levels of an organization unless high-level management
    A. communicates through several levels of mid-level management, where the message can be properly modified and interpreted
    B. communicates directly with the level of the organization it wishes to reach, bypassing any intermediate levels
    C. first establishes an atmosphere in which upward communication is encouraged and listened to
    D. establishes penalties for non-compliance with its communications

13.____

14. A top-level manager sometimes has an inaccurate view of the actual lower-level operations of his agency, particularly of those operations which are not running well.
    Of the following, the MOST frequent cause of this is the
    A. general unconcern of top-level management with the way an agency actually operates
    B. tendency of the people at the lowest level in an agency to lie about their actual performance
    C. unwillingness of top-level management to deal with unfavorable information when it is presented
    D. tendency of mid-level management to edit bad news and unpleasant information from reports directed to top management

14.____

15. In the conduct of productivity analyses, work measurement is a USEFUL technique for
    A. substantiating executive decisions
    B. designing a research study
    C. developing performance yardsticks
    D. preparing a manual of procedure

15.____

16. Issue analysis is closely identified with the "fire-fighting" function of management. As such, issue analysis is a(n)
    A. systematic assessment over time of an agency's strategic options
    B. annual review of the issues that have come up during the past year
    C. basis for a set of procedures to be followed in an emergency
    D. analysis of a specific policy question often performed in a crisis environment

16.____

17. The transportation agency in a large city wishes to study the impact of fare increases on ridership in buses. Ridership data for peak hours has been assembled for the same time period for three geographic subareas (A, B, and C) with approximately the same socio-economic characteristics, residential density, and distance from the central business district (CBD). Subarea A had experienced a moderate fare increase on its bus line; Subarea B had had no fare increase; and Subarea C had experienced a major fare increase during the time period

17.____

In the design of this study, the analysis should be framed:
A. Ridership = f (fare level)
B. Ridership = f (fare level), distance from CBD)
C. Fare level = f (ridership)
D. Ridership = f (fare level, socio-economic characteristics, residential density)

18. What organizational concept is illustrated when a group is organized on an *ad hoc* basis to accomplish a specific goal?
    A. Functional Teamwork
    B. Line/staff
    C. Task Force
    D. Command

18.____

19. The concept of "demand" provides an appropriate theoretical basis for estimating the needs for public services or programs where the service will be on a _____ basis and _____ life-sustaining necessities.
    A. fee; involves
    B. free; involves
    C. free; does not involve
    D. fee; does not involve

19.____

20. Analysts should be wary of relying exclusively on traditional service standards (e.g., one acre of playground per 1,000 population).
    Such standards are often DEFICIENT because they tend to overstate
    A. the consumer view and understate behavior and values of producers
    B. the producer view and understate behavior and values of users or consumers
    C. local conditions and understate national conditions
    D. behavioral factors and understate practical effects

20.____

21. The BEST measure of the performance of a manpower program would be
    A. percentage reduction in unemployment by impacted population groups
    B. number of trainees placed in jobs at the beginning of the training program
    C. percentage of students completing a training program
    D. cost per student of the training program and the job placement effort

21.____

22. Indices are single figures that measure multi-dimensional concepts.
    The critical judgment in the construction of an index involves
    A. the trade-off between accuracy and simplicity
    B. determination of enough data to do the measurement
    C. avoidance of all possible error
    D. developing a theoretical basis for it

22.____

23. Evaluation of public programs is complicated by the reality that programs tend to reflect negotiated compromises among conflicting objectives.
    The absence of clear, unitary objectives PARTICULARLY complicates the
    A. assessment of program input or effort
    B. development of effectiveness criteria
    C. design of new programs to replace the old
    D. diagnosis of a program's processes

23.____

24. The BASIC purpose of the "Super-Agencies" is to
    A. reduce the number of departments and agencies in the city government
    B. reduce the number of high-level administrators
    C. coordinate agencies reporting to the mayor and supervise agencies in related fields
    D. supervise departments and agencies in unrelated fields

25. In most municipal budgeting systems involving capital and operating budgets, the leasing or renting of facilities is usually shown in
    A. the operating budget
    B. the capital budget
    C. a separate schedule
    D. either budget

26. New York City's budgeting procedure is unusual in that budget appropriations are considered in two parts, as follows:
    A. Capital budget and income budget
    B. Expense budget and income budget
    C. Revenue budget and expense budget
    D. Expense budget and capital budget

27. The "growth rate" referred to in current political and economic discussion refers to change from year to year in a country's
    A. gross national product
    B. population
    C. available labor force
    D. capital goods investment

Questions 28-29.

DIRECTIONS: Questions 28 and 29 are to be answered on the basis of the following illustration. Assume that the figures in the chart are cubes.

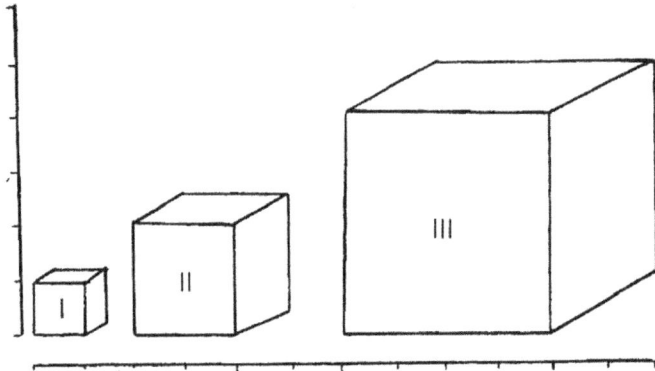

28. In the illustration above, how many times GREATER is the quantity represented by Figure III than the quantity represented by Figure II?
    A. 2   B. 4   C. 8   D. 16

29. The above illustration illustrates a progression in quantity BEST described as
    A. arithmetic   B. geometric   C. discrete   D. linear

Questions 30-35.

DIRECTIONS: Questions 30 through 35 are to be answered on the basis of the following chart.

In a national study of poverty trends, the following data have been assembled by interpretation.

Item	Persons Below Poverty, By Residence			
	Number (millions)		Percent	
	U.S.	Metropolitan Areas	U.S.	Metropolitan Areas
2010				
Total	38.8	17.0	22.0	15.3
Under 25 years	20.0	8.8	25.3	18.1
65 years & over	5.5	2.5	35.2	26.9
Black	9.9	5.0	55.1	42.8
Other	28.3	11.8	18.1	12.0
2020				
Total	24.3	12.3	12.2	9.5
Under 25 years	12.2	6.4	13.2	10.4
65 years & over	4.8	2.3	25.3	20.2
Black	7.2	3.9	32.3	24.4
Other	16.7	8.2	9.5	7.3

30. If no other source of data were available, which of the following groups would you expect to have the HIGHEST rate of poverty?
    A. Others over 65
    B. Others under 65
    C. Blacks over 65
    D. Blacks under 65

31. Between 2010 and 2020, the percentage of poor in the United States who were Black
    A. increased from 25.5% to 29.6%
    B. decreased from 55.1% to 32.3%
    C. decreased from 9.9% to 7.2%
    D. stayed the same

32. The data in the second column of the table indicate that, in the metropolitan areas, the number of poor declined by 4.7 million or 36.2% between 2010 and 2020. Yet, the fourth column shows a corresponding decline from 15.3% to 9.5%, or only 5.8%.
    This apparent discrepancy reflects the fact that
    A. metropolitan areas are growing while the number of poor is contracting
    B. two columns in question are based on different sources of information
    C. difference between two percentages is not the same as the percent change in total numbers
    D. tables have inherent errors and must be carefully checked

33. The percentages in each of the last two columns of the table for 2010 and 2020 don't add up to 100%. This is for the reason that
    A. rounding off each entry to the nearest decimal place caused an error in the total such that the total is not equal to 100%
    B. these columns show the percentage of Blacks, aged, etc. who are poor rather than the percentage of poor who are Black, aged, etc.
    C. there was an error in the construction of the table which was not noticed until the table was already in print
    D. there is double counting in the entries in the table; some people ae counted more than once

34. Data such as that presented in the table on persons below poverty level are shown to a single decimal place because
    A. data in every table should always be shown to a single decimal place
    B. it is the minimal number of decimal places needed to distinguish among table entries
    C. there was no room for more decimal places in the table without crowding
    D. the more accurately a figure is shown the better it is for the user

35. In comparing the poverty of the young (under 25 years) with that of the older population (65 years and over) in 2010 and 2020, one could REASONABLY conclude that
    A. more young people than old people were poor but older people had a higher rate of poverty
    B. more older people than young people were poor but young people had a higher rate of poverty
    C. there is a greater degree of poverty among the younger population than among the older people

Questions 36-37.

DIRECTIONS: Questions 36 and 37 are to be answered ONLY on the basis of the information given in the following passage.

Two approaches are available in developing criteria for the evaluation of plans. One approach, designated <u>Approach A</u>, is a review and analysis of characteristics that differentiate successful plans from unsuccessful plans. These criteria are descriptive in nature and serve as a checklist against which the plan under consideration may be judged. These characteristics have been observed by many different students of planning, and there is considerable agreement concerning the characteristics necessary for a plan to be successful.

A second approach to the development of criteria for judging plans, designated <u>Approach B</u> is the determination of the degree to which the plan under consideration is economic. The word "economic" is used here in its broadest sense, i.e., effective in its utilization of resources. In order to determine the economic worth of a plan, it is necessary to use a technique that permits the description of any plan in economic terms and to utilize this technique to the extent that it becomes a "way of thinking" about plans.

36. According to Approach B, the MOST successful plan is generally one which
    A. costs least to implement
    B. gives most value for resources expended
    C. uses the least expensive resources
    D. utilizes the greatest number of resources

37. According to Approach A, a successful plan is one which is
    A. descriptive in nature
    B. lowest in cost
    C. similar to other successful plans
    D. agreed upon by many students of planning

Questions 38-40.

DIRECTIONS: Questions 38 through 40 are to be answered ONLY on the basis of the information provided in the following passage.

The primary purpose of control reports is to supply information intended to serve as the basis for corrective action if needed. At the same time, the significance of control reports must be kept in proper perspective. Control reports are only a part of the planning-management information system. Control information includes non-financial as well as financial data that measure performance and isolate variances from standard. Control information also provides feedback so that planning information may be updated and corrected. Whenever possible, control reports should be designed so that they provide feedback for the planning process as well as provide information of immediate value to the control process.

Since the culmination of the control process is the taking of necessary corrective action to bring performance in line with standards, it follows that control information must be directed to the person who is organizationally responsible for taking the required action. Usually the same information, though in a somewhat abbreviated form, is given to the responsible manager's superior. A district sales manager needs a complete daily record of the performance of each of his salesmen; yet, the report forwarded to the regional sales manager summarizes only the performance of each sales district in his region. In preparing reports for higher echelons of management, summary statements and recommendations for action should appear on the first page; substantiating data, usually the information presented to the person directly responsible for the operation, may be include if needed.

38. A control report serves its primary purpose as part of the process which leads DIRECTLY to
    A. better planning for future action
    B. increasing the performance of district salesmen
    C. the establishment of proper performance standards
    D. taking corrective action when performance is poor

39. The one of the following which would be the BEST description of a control report is that a control report is a form of
    A. planning
    B. communication
    C. direction
    D. organization

40. If control reports are to be effective, the one of the following which is LEAST essential to the effectiveness of control reporting is a system of
    A. communication
    B. standards
    C. authority
    D. work simplification

KEY (CORRECT ANSWERS)

1. A	11. B	21. A	31. B
2. B	12. A	22. A	32. C
3. A	13. C	23. B	33. B
4. B	14. D	24. C	34. D
5. D	15. C	25. A	35. A
6. C	16. D	26. D	36. B
7. D	17. A	27. A	37. C
8. C	18. C	28. C	38. D
9. B	19. D	29. B	39. B
10. D	20. B	30. C	40. D

EXAMINATION SECTION
TEST 1

DIRECTIONS: Each question or incomplete statement is followed by several suggested answers or completions. Select the one that *BEST* answers the question or completes the statement. *PRINT THE LETTER OF THE CORRECT ANSWER IN THE SPACE AT THE RIGHT.*

1. An analyst is writing a report dealing with the distribution of deaths caused by various types of cardiovascular diseases. He decides to facilitate the reader's grasp of the information presented by including in the report a device that permits comparison of parts to each other, and to the whole at the same time.
   Of the following, the *MOST* appropriate and efficient device he should use for this purpose is the

   A. graph
   B. pie diagram
   C. flow sheet
   D. line chart with one series

   1.____

2. In carrying out a cost-effectiveness analysis, the analyst should follow certain guidelines. The *MOST* important of these guidelines involves the

   A. utilization of both the fixed utility approach and the fixed budget approach
   B. proper structuring of the problem and design of the analysis
   C. necessity of building a model that is highly formal and mathematical
   D. provision for implicit treatment of uncertainty

   2.____

3. In a decision which involves fairness -- such as assigning new office equipment to workers when the agency does not receive enough new office equipment for the entire group -- the *PRIMARY* determinant of the decision's effectiveness will be the

   A. systematic or traditional approach which is emphasized in reaching the decision
   B. random nature of the assignment
   C. feedback a decisionmaker receives concerning the decision
   D. acceptance of the decision by the persons who have to execute it

   3.____

4. In order to give line personnel some insight into staff problems and vice versa it has been suggested that line and staff assignments within a particular city agency be rotated. Which of the following criticisms would be *MOST* valid for opposing such a proposal?

   A. Generally speaking, line and staff personnel have different perspectives on organizational structures which makes rotation in assignments extremely difficult.
   B. Since their educational backgrounds are often quite diverse, staff personnel are often at a disadvantage when serving in line assignments.
   C. Line personnel frequently resent having to perform the more difficult tasks that staff assignments entail.
   D. Serving in a rotating assignment may not necessarily provide the personnel with any significant degree of insight as anticipated.

   4.____

5. Which one of the following approaches to criticism of a subordinate or associate is *generally* the *MOST* appropriate and effective?
   Criticize

   A. by making a comparison with a more exemplary employee

   5.____

B. the act, not the person
C. in a humorous vein
D. in general rather than specific terms

6. Assume that two policy units have been formed to study the impact of Federal programs in the city. The two units operate in an essentially similar manner, except for their communications procedures. In unit A any member may communicate and exchange information with any other member of the unit; in unit B a member may only communicate information with the unit supervisor.
In evaluating the effect that these communications procedures have on the level of productivity, it will *generally* be found that

   A. unit A's level of productivity will be greater than unit B's level of productivity for simple problems
   B. unit B's level of productivity will be greater than unit A's level of productivity for simple problems
   C. initial levels of profuctivity are higher in unit A than unit B for complex problems
   D. initial levels of productivity are higher in unit B than in unit A for complex problems

7. In the process of communicating an idea, the following five distinct steps are generally involved:
   I. Selection of a media and transmission of the message
   II. Decoding of a message, i.e., meaning is extracted from the message
   III. Message is received
   IV. Idea is organized into a series of symbols designed to give meaning
   V. Action is taken and/or feedback is given

   In what logical, sequential order should these steps be arranged for effective two-way communications to take place?

   A. V, I, II, III, IV   B. II, I, III, IV, V
   C. IV, I, III, II, V   D. I, III, IV, II, V

8. Informal employee groups that share certain norms and strive for member satisfaction through the achievement of group goals are known as work groups.
Which of the following statements can *generally* be considered as being *FALSE* in describing work groups in a moderate size organization?

   A. Formation of work groups is ubiquitous and inevitable.
   B. Work groups strongly influence the overall behavior and performance of their members.
   C. An organization can reap positive and negative consequences as a result of work groups.
   D. Elimination of work groups can be easily achieved by management pressure.

9. Under the management approach known as *management by objectives* which of the following criteria is *generally* used to determine whether the manager has been successful?

   A. Activities performed
   B. Results achieved
   C. Production schedules completed
   D. Financial savings accomplished

10. Of the following, the MOST accurate statement relative to job attitudes is that they

    A. cannot be influenced by only one person
    B. are always the result of work groups
    C. have no relationship to productivity
    D. are strongly influenced by work situation

11. Assume that measures to overcome a budget deficit, including attrition and a hiring freeze, have significantly decreased the work-output of a city agency. The agency administrator desires to develop a plan to restore production to its former level by increasing the work-load and responsibility of the agency's employees.
    In order to obtain *maximum* employee cooperation and *minimize* employee resistance, it would be MOST advisable for the

    A. administrator of the agency to personally describe to the employees the new work changes that they are to follow
    B. employees to decide what the optimal changes in the work load should be
    C. management representatives to consult with employee representatives on these matters
    D. immediate supervisor of the employees to decide on the work changes to be implemented

12. Eliciting the support and cooperation of others often requires a great deal of persuasion. Which one of the following persuasive techniques or practices is generally the LEAST desirable for you, an analyst, to use?

    A. Establish your expertness and authority
    B. Present your arguments without emotion
    C. In presenting your arguments, express yourself in the manner to which you are accustomed
    D. Try to find a face-saving way for your opponent to change his/her mind

13. The following illustration depicts the structure of a municipal agency.

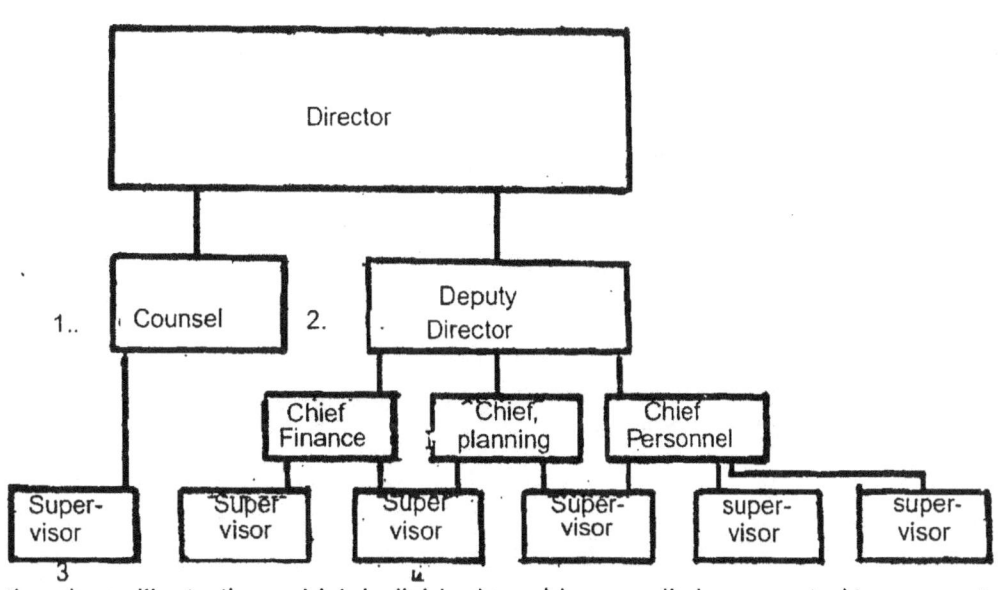

In the above illustration, which individual would generally be expected to encounter the MOST difficulty in carrying out his organizational functions?

    A. 1   B. 2   C. 3   D. 4

14. An agency in which a free flow of communication exists is an agency in which no barriers or structures are erected to control or bar the flow of information and messages between and among management and staff, horizontally or vertically.
Of the following, the GREATEST disadvantage that would be most likely to occur in an agency in which such a free flow of communication exists, is that

    A. it would be difficult to determine which information is important and which is irrelevant
    B. there would be a lesser degree of staff-employee participation and cooperation in communicating
    C. more restrictive controls would be placed on managerial employees
    D. important communications would tend to be eliminated, and and trivial communications over-emphasized

14.___

15. Feedback is generally considered an essential factor in oral communication MAINLY because

    A. it enables the speaker to know whether he is understood
    B. the speed of communication is accelerated
    C. it eliminates the necessity of the speaker to use gestures and facial expressions when speaking
    D. the listener is unable to immediately respond to the speaker until the latter is finished

15.___

16. Assume that two employees are working on a joint project and they have a difference of opinion on the methodology to be used. Each employee not only listens to the other's opinion on methodology but projects him-self into the other's position.
This type of listening is *usually* considered

    A. *ineffective,* mainly because it will be impossible for the employees to reach a satisfactory agreement
    B. *effective,* mainly because each employee will then be more critical of the other's argument
    C. *ineffective,* mainly because each worker will unconsciously and unintentionally accept the other's viewpoint
    D. *effective,* mainly because each speaker can understand the other's viewpoint and can then respond intelligently to his remarks

16.___

17. The arithmetic mean is commonly used in describing data. Which one of the following statements is NOT true about the arithmetic mean?

    A. It is a measure of dispersion.
    B. The sum of the deviations around it is zero.
    C. It is easy to compute, understand and recognize.
    D. It may be treated alegebraically.

17.___

Questions 18 - 20.

DIRECTIONS: Answer Questions 18 through 20 on the basis of the following data. Assume that you are using these data in assessing the impact of Federal and State income taxes on New York City residents, and comparing it to the effect of Federal and State taxes in other areas.

EFFECT OF DEDUCTIBILITY (i.e., deductibility of taxes levied by other jurisdictions in calculating the net base of the tax in the taxing jurisdiction.)

Net income before personal exemption	Effective rate of tax				
	Federal (assuming no state tax)	State		Combined Federal and State	
		New York*	Minnesota (assuming no federal tax)	New York	Minnesota
	(1)	(2)	(3)	(4)	(5)
$20,000	25.0	4.1	6.9	27.6	27.9
50,000	42.2	5.4	9.1	44.0	43.9
100,000	56.0	5.9	9.8	57.5	57.1
200,000	69.2	6.1	10.1	69.9	69.5
1,500,000	88.0	6.3	10.5	89.3	88.9

*New York has no deductibility; the Federal government has deductibility.

18. In which of the following columns is the tax rate shown to be the LEAST progressive?   18._____

   A. 1   B. 2   C. 4   D. 5

19. Which of the following statements is TRUE about the reasons why Columns 1 and 2 do not equal Column 4 for each salary level?   19._____

   A. Personal deductions are taken into account in Column 4 but not in Columns 1 and 2.
   B. Federal deducibility of state taxes only is taken into account in Column 4 but not in Columns 1 and 2.
   C. Reciprocal deductibility is taken into account in Column 4 but not in Columns 1 and 2.
   D. State deductibility of federal taxes only is taken into account in Column 4 but not in Columns 1 and 2.

20. The EFFECT of the State's introducing deductibility, given that the Federal government maintains deductibility, is to   20._____

   A. increase Federal and State income
   B. decrease Federal and State income
   C. decrease Federal income and increase State income
   D. increase Federal income and decrease State income

21. Assume that you have been made project coordinator for a study concerning the implementation of casino gambling in the city. You have assigned each of the professional staff members simple tasks in specialized areas for the duration of the project. For you to make such job assignments would *generally* be

    A. *desirable;* the performance of simple tasks will motivate individuals to work diligently
    B. *desirable;* specialized tasks induce a sense of accomplishment to individuals
    C. *undesirable;* specialized tasks are more difficult to learn
    D. *undesirable;* specialized tasks may lead to a loss of feeling of accomplishment

22. Assume that you have been asked to submit a proposal for the reorganization of a unit that is charged with performing difficult nonroutine work. Frequently decisions must be made quickly and concurrence obtained from high-level agency heads.
    Given the above conditions, of the following it would be *MOST* logical to structure the organization

    A. on the basis of a relatively wide span of control
    B. on the basis of a relatively narrow span of control
    C. with many organizational levels with a wide span of control
    D. with more emphasis on line than staff units

23. Assume that a study has indicated that a recently created city *superagency* has had formal communication difficulties among various component agencies. It appears that jurisdictional overlapping among those agencies has caused frequent rerouting and unnecessary duplication of communications within the organization. Which one of the following proposals would *MOST* effectively deal with the communications problem encountered by this *superagency*?

    A. Create a central communications office to handle all communications for this *superagency.*
    B. Duplicate and distribute all communications to each component within this *superagency.*
    C. Reduce the overlapping areas of jurisdiction among the component agencies
    D. Decentralize the *superagency* on a *borough* basis to expedite mail delivery

24. The utilization of input-output concepts in connection with the application of the systems concept to government raises the problem of the quantification of objectives and performance (the value of the public benefit). The one of the following which is *MOST* easily *quantifiable* is

    A. education
    B. police service
    C. subway car maintenance
    D. the effectiveness of a welfare administrator

25. When an analyst tries to conceive of a city management problem as a *systems* problem, he is, first of all, confronted with establishing the boundaries of the system. Of the following, the city problem which can *most likely* be conceived of within a system whose boundaries are roughly equivalent to those of the city is

    A. taxation
    B. welfare
    C. fire protection
    D. transportation

25.____

KEY (CORRECT ANSWERS)

1. B
2. B
3. D
4. D
5. B
6. C
7. C
8. D
9. B
10. D
11. C
12. B
13. D
14. A
15. A
16. D
17. A
18. B
19. B
20. D
21. D
22. B
23. C
24. C
25. C

TEST 2

DIRECTIONS: Each question or incomplete statement is followed by several suggested answers or completions. Select the one that BEST answers the question or completes the statement. PRINT THE LETTER OF THE CORRECT ANSWER IN THE SPACE AT THE RIGHT.

1. When installing a new *system,* an analyst may choose among several types of installation plans - the *all-at-once type,* the *piecemeal type,* or the *parallel type* each suited to a particular problem or degree of complexity in the system.
The one of the following situations in which the *parallel type* would be MOST appropriate is a situation

   A. in which a minimum installation cost is required
   B. involving a small volume of transactions
   C. in which the change is not radical or does not involve new machines
   D. involving large installation projects and intricate processing

1.___

2. Many decision situations involve a great deal of uncertainty about the future, which is difficult to take into account in the analysis of alternatives. One technique developed for treating such uncertainty is designed to measure the possible effects on alternatives under analysis resulting from variations in uncertain elements. The analyst uses several *expected values* for uncertain parameters in an attempt to ascertain how the results vary (i.e., the relative ranking of the alternatives under consideration) in light of variations in the uncertain parameters. The analyst attempts to determine the alternative (or feasible combination of alternatives) likely to achieve a specified objective, gain or utility at the lowest cost. The one of the following which BEST describes the above technique is:

   A. Contingency analysis employing the fixed-budget approach
   B. Contingency analysis employing the fixed-benefits approach
   C. Sensitivity analysis employing the fixed-budget approach
   D. Sensitivity analysis employing the fixed-benefits approach

2.___

3. In general, the analytical techniques of management science are of the LEAST value when

   A. the effects of a small number of controlled variables must be considered
   B. the number of relevant uncontrolled variables is small
   C. relevant causes and effects are factual in nature and can be stated and measured numerically or symbolically
   D. There are reasons to believe that past relationships will continue to hold in the future

3.___

4. During the installation period of a new system, tight controls must be maintained over every phase of the operation. To do this, an analyst may set up a *warning system* within the system which forecasts potential bottle-necks and affords sufficient clues for correcting any problems, errors or fall-downs.
The one of the following control devices or techniques which would be *most likely* to involve extra effort during the installation, and slow down the processing time is

4.___

A. paper flow controls - log sheets, numerical controls, etc. (a system of logging input and output)
B. timing controls - to inform the analyst about the proper time interval between certain activities with-in the systems
C. program check points - a periodic review of processing to date at each check point
D. accounting control totals, to accumulate invoice numbers as the first and last steps in the system and compare the totals

5. Which of the following types of work measurement techniques would be MOST appropriate for obtaining details of a particular job for cost analysis purposes, such as the operating costs of various types of duplicating machines? 5.____

   A. Work sampling
   B. Predetermined time standards
   C. The time study (stop-watch timing)
   D. Historical

6. It is anticipated that a certain cancer detection program will be capable of detecting many cases at an early stage and that society will be thus enabled to cure twice as many cases as it cures currently. The benefits to society include the reduction in cost of hospitalization, etc., that would have been incurred otherwise. 6.____
   Benefits such as a reduction in the cost of hospitalization are *most usually* called

   A. direct benefits
   B. secondary benefits
   C. intergenerational benefits
   D. external benefits

7. The results of departmental and agency programs can be measured in terms of *EFFECTIVENESS* or *BENEFITS*. Thus, careful budget preparation will permit the calculation of costs which can then be compared, or equated, to these results. Which one of the following statements pertaining to cost-effectiveness measurements is MOST valid? 7.____

   A. In cost-effectiveness measurements, a dollar value is assigned to the output.
   B. The measurement is expressed in terms of quality of output for a given cost.
   C. Cost effectiveness ratios express the relationship between the costs of programs
   D. A cost-effectiveness measurement will show the number of outputs which can be achieved for the expenditure of a given amount of money.

8. Assume that you have been asked to evaluate personnel programs in four city agencies The statistical test that would be MOST appropriate for testing the significance of the differences in the mean number of days absent (normality may be assumed) during the year 2004 in four different agencies is the 8.____

   A. one-way analysis of variance
   B. standard deviation
   C. regression analysis
   D. Chi-square test (x^2-test)

9. Assume that you have been asked to evaluate differences in the children just enrolled in two youth programs. In reviewing the relevant published material you find that in one particular study involving two groups, N = 9 and N = 13, there is a significant difference in the mean scores of the two groups on a characteristic which you believe to be normally distributed.
The statistical test *most likely* used in this study to determine the significance of the difference in the means of the two groups on this characteristic is the

   A. Chi-square test (x^2-test)
   B. Pearson Product-Moment correlation (r)
   C. t-test
   D. two-way analysis of variance

10. In statistics, three common measures of central tendency are the mean, median and mode.
For which of the following conditions would the median generally be the *BEST* choice to use? When the

   A. distribution of scores is skewed
   B. scores are distributed symmetrically around a central point
   C. standard deviation must also be calculated
   D. most frequently occurring value is required

11. Nonparametric statistical tests are *usually* employed when

   A. large samples are used
   B. a very powerful or exact test is needed
   C. data cannot be expressed in ranks
   D. a normally distributed population cannot be assumed

12. Assume that in a report presented to you by an employee under your supervision, a coefficient of correlation of +1.73 is reported between the age at which one first smokes cigarettes and the age at which one first smokes marijuana.
You should *most reasonably* interpret this figure to mean there is a

   A. strong positive correlation
   B. weak positive correlation
   C. weak negative correlation
   D. typographical error

13. One of the major research techniques most often used in studies of organizational behavior problems is the survey. An analyst who utilizes the survey technique should be aware that its *MAJOR* drawback is

   A. the lack of depth obtained from the two major data-collection tolls used in surveys: the mailed question-naire and the personal interview
   B. its impracticality in assessing or estimating the present state of affairs with regard to a variable that changes over time for a large group of subjects
   C. the restriction of this technique to a single, or very few, units of analysis
   D. its absence of dependence upon the collection of empirical data

14. In order for an analyst to understand and interpret statistical data he/she must understand which types of data tend to approximate the normal probability curve, i.e., are normally distributed.
Which of the following types of data falls into this category?
Frequency of

    A. educational test scores for students of a given age, plotted against test score
    B. filing of income tax returns for citizens of a given age, plotted against date of filing
    C. deaths due to childhood disease plotted against age
    D. deaths due to degenerative diseases, plotted against age

15. Which of the following terms describes a line or curve formed by plotting employees salaries that increase yearly by a fixed percentage over the previous year? (In answering the question, assume that time is on the horizontal axis (abscissa) and salary is on the vertical axis (ordinate) - both axes are marked linearly.)

    A. Linear (increasing at a constant rate)
    B. Positively accelerating (increasing at an increasing rate)
    C. Negatively accelerating (increasing at a decreasing rate)
    D. Negatively decelerating (decreasing at a decreasing rate)

Questions 16 - 17

DIRECTIONS: Answer Questions 16 and 17 on the basis of the following groups, both of which depict the same information in different ways.

The x and y axes in graphs A and B are not necessarily drawn in the same scale. The points along the curves on both graphs represent corresponding points, and are the upper limits of class intervals.

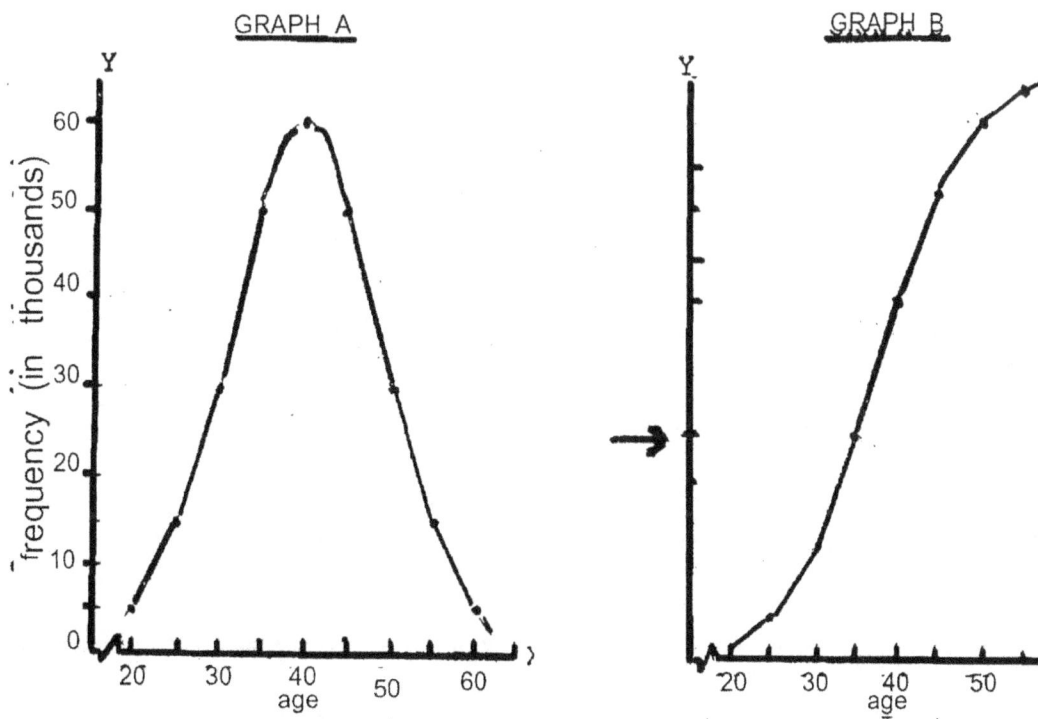

16. The ordinate (y-axis) in graph B is 16.___

   A. frequency
   B. cumulative frequency
   C. average frequency
   D. log frequency

17. The arrow on the y-axis in graph B indicates a particular number. That number is, *most nearly* 17.___

   A. 100 B. 50,000 C. 100,000 D. 150,000

Questions 18 - 19

   DIRECTIONS: Answer Questions 18 and 19 on the basis of the graphs that appear on the following page.

18. In Graph I, the vertical distance between lines E and T within the crosshatched area represents the 18.___

   A. savings to the city if work of less than 50 miles is performed by the city
   B. loss to the city if work of less than 50 miles is performed by the city
   C. savings to the city if work of more than 50 miles is performed by the city
   D. loss to the city if work of more than 50 miles is performed by the city

19. Graph II is identical to Graph I except that contractor costs have been eliminated. Total costs (line E) are the sum of fixed costs (line F) and variable costs. Variable costs are represented by line 19.___

   A. A B. B C. C D. D

ROAD REPAIR COSTS IF PERFORMED BY CITY STAFF OR AN OUTSIDE CONTRACTOR

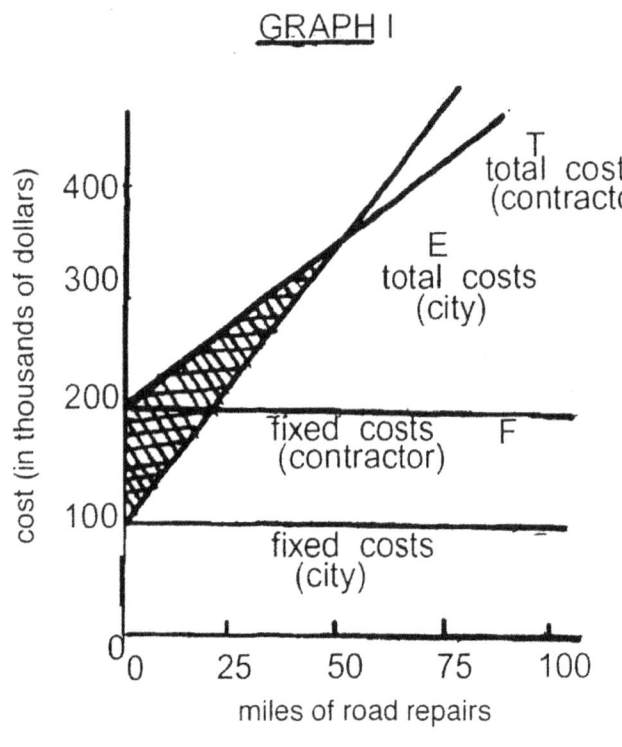
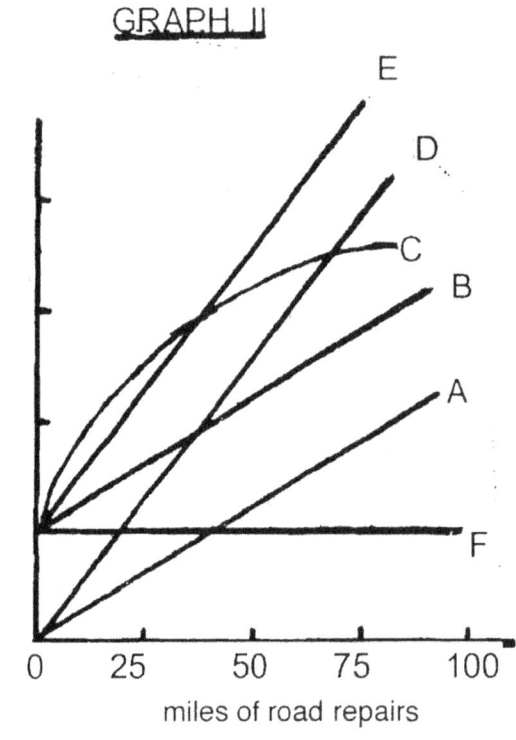

20. Fiscal experts in municipal affairs have contended that the most acute problem facing the city today seems to be the growth of the city's short-term debt.
Of the following, the LEAST likely reason for the city to engage in short-term borrowing is that the city

    A. expects money from long-term borrowing that it plans to undertake
    B. needs to be tided over until funds due from the Federal or State government arrive
    C. needs money to finance big construction outlays
    D. anticipates money from future tax collections

20.____

21. A MAJOR criticism of the *superagency* has been the

    A. additional layers of control and additional lines of command
    B. merger of departmental functions
    C. political manipulation
    D. professional incompetence in administration

21.____

22. The management of a large urban city is different in many ways from the management of other systems, particularly large business organizations.
The one of the following which does NOT exemplify these differences is:

    A. A mayor, in contrast to a manager of a large business, is often held responsible for services, etc., over which he has little authority.
    B. Top management of a large urban city must deal with a greater number of different pressures from diverse interest groups.
    C. The city government, in contrast to a large business organization, often lacks adequate management controls, and goals are often ill-defined.
    D. The multiplicity of alternatives available to city government as opposed to large businesses, are substantially greater, making decision-making haphazard.

22.____

23. The function called internal control applies to those measures taken by a government agency to protect its assets. Internal control has a role to play as an enforcer of administrative edicts as well as for purposes of asset protection.
Of the following statements relating to internal control, as described above, select the *one* usually considered to be LEAST valid.

    A. Internal control makes auditing by an external agency more difficult.
    B. The function of internal control often involves the auditing process.
    C. That people cannot be trusted to act wisely and honestly seems to be implicit in all the principles of internal control.
    D. Internal control is simply a form of self-audit by the agency itself.

23.____

24. In addition to the new effect on workers who are unskilled and undereducated, the severe effect of the high unemployment rate in the city has recently become MOST apparent among

    A. skilled craftsmen in the building trades
    B. clerical employees
    C. middle management personnel
    D. architects and engineers

24.____

25. The fact that the city has the second highest jobless rate of any major U.S. city except Detroit is considered particularly significant because, compared to Detroit, unemployment in the city 25.___

    A. is caused by city government fiscal measures rather than private business conditions
    B. exists in more than one industry
    C. results in an increase in welfare expenditures to a greater extent
    D. more seriously affects the world-wide economy

KEY (CORRECT ANSWERS)

1.	D	11.	D
2.	D	12.	D
3.	A	13.	A
4.	A	14.	A
5.	C	15.	B
6.	A	16.	B
7.	D	17.	C
8.	A	18.	A
9.	C	19.	D
10.	A	20.	C

21. A
22. D
23. A
24. A
25. B

EXAMINATION SECTION
TEST 1

DIRECTIONS: Each question or incomplete statement is followed by several suggested answers or completions. Select the one that BEST answers the question or completes the statement. *PRINT THE LETTER OF THE CORRECT ANSWER IN THE SPACE AT THE RIGHT.*

1. In public agencies, communications should be based PRIMARILY on a
    A. two-way flow from the top down and from the bottom up, most of which should be given in writing to avoid ambiguity
    B. multi-direction flow among all levels and with outside persons
    C. rapid, internal one-way flow from the top down
    D. two-way flow of information, most of which should be given orally for purposes of clarity

    1.____

2. In some organizations, changes in policy or procedures are often communicated by word of mouth from supervisors to employees with no prior discussion or exchange of viewpoints with employees.
    This procedure often produces employee dissatisfaction CHIEFLY because
    A. information is mostly unusable since a considerable amount of time is required to transmit information
    B. lower-level supervisors tend to be excessively concerned with minor details
    C. management has failed to seek employees' advice before making changes
    D. valuable staff time is lost between decision-making and the implementation of decisions

    2.____

3. For good letter writing, you should try to visualize the person to whom you are writing, especially if you know him.
    Of the following rules, it is LEAST helpful in such visualization to think of
    A. the person's likes and dislikes, his concerns, and his needs
    B. what you would be likely to say if speaking in person
    C. what you would expect to be asked if speaking in person
    D. your official position in order to be certain that your words are proper

    3.____

4. One approach to good informal letter writing is to make letters and conversational.
    All of the following practices will usually help to do this EXCEPT:
    A. If possible, use a style which is similar to the style used when speaking
    B. Substitute phrases for single words (e.g., *at the present time* for *now*)
    C. Use contractions of words (e.g., *you're* for *you are*)
    D. Use ordinary vocabulary when possible

    4.____

5. All of the following rules will aid in producing clarity in report-writing EXCEPT:
   A. Give specific details or examples, if possible
   B. Keep related words close together in each sentence
   C. Present information in sequential order
   D. Put several thoughts or ideas in each paragraph

6. The one of the following statements about public relations which is MOST accurate is that
   A. in the long run, appearance gains better results than performance
   B. objectivity is decreased if outside public relations consultants are employed
   C. public relations is the responsibility of every employee
   D. public relations should be based on a formal publicity program

7. The form of communication which is usually considered to be MOST personally directed to the intended recipient is the
   A. brochure   B. film   C. letter   D. radio

8. In general, a document that presents an organization's views or opinions on a particular topic is MOST accurately known as a
   A. tear sheet
   B. position paper
   C. flyer
   D. journal

9. Assume that you have been asked to speak before an organization of persons who oppose a newly announced program in which you are involved. You feel tense about talking to this group.
   Which of the following rules generally would be MOST useful in gaining rapport when speaking before the audience?
   A. Impress them with your experience
   B. Stress all areas of disagreement
   C. Talk to the group as to one person
   D. Use formal grammar and language

10. An organization must have an effective public relations program since, at its best, public relations is a bridge to change.
    All of the following statements about communication and human behavior have validity EXCEPT:
    A. People are more likely to talk about controversial matters with like-minded people than with those holding other views
    B. The earlier an experience, the more powerful its effect since it influences how later experiences will be interpreted
    C. In periods of social tension, official sources gain increased believability
    D. Those who are already interested in a topic are the ones who are most open to receive new communications about it

11. An employee should be encouraged to talk easily and frankly when he is dealing with his supervisor.
    In order to encourage such free communication, it would be MOST appropriate for a supervisor to behave in a(n)
    A. sincere manner; assure the employee that you will deal with him honestly and openly
    B. official manner; you are a supervisor and must always act formally with subordinates
    C. investigative manner; you must probe and question to get to a basis of trust
    D. unemotional manner; the employee's emotions and background should play no part in your dealings with him

11.____

12. Research findings show that an increase in free communication within an agency GENERALLY results in which one of the following?
    A. Improved morale and productivity
    B. Increased promotional opportunities
    C. An increase in authority
    D. A spirit of honesty

12.____

13. Assume that you are a supervisor and your superiors have given you a new-type procedure to be followed.
    Before passing this information on to your subordinates, the one of the following actions that you should take FIRST is to
    A. ask your superiors to send out a memorandum to the entire staff
    B. clarify the procedure in your own mind
    C. set up a training course to provide instruction on the new procedure
    D. write a memorandum to your subordinates

13.____

14. Communication is necessary for an organization to be effective.
    The one of the following which is LEAST important for most communication systems is that
    A. messages are sent quickly and directly to the person who needs them to operate
    B. information should be conveyed understandably and accurately
    C. the method used to transmit information should be kept secret so that security can be maintained
    D. senders of messages must know how their messages are received and acted upon

14.____

15. Which one of the following is the CHIEF advantage of listening willingly to subordinates and encouraging them to talk freely and honestly?
    It
    A. reveals to supervisors the degree to which ideas that are passed down are accepted by subordinates
    B. reduces the participation of subordinates in the operation of the department
    C. encourages subordinates to try for promotion
    D. enables supervisors to learn more readily what the *grapevine* is saying

15.____

16. A supervisor may be informed through either oral or written reports.   16.____
    Which one of the following is an ADVANTAGE of using oral reports?
    A. There is no need for a formal record of the report.
    B. An exact duplicate of the report is not easily transmitted to others.
    C. A good oral report requires little time for preparation.
    D. An oral report involves two-way communication between a subordinate and his supervisor.

17. Of the following, the MOST important reason why supervisors should   17.____
    communicate effectively with the public is to
    A. improve the public's understanding of information that is important for them to know
    B. establish a friendly relationship
    C. obtain information about the kinds of people who come to the agency
    D. convince the public that services are adequate

18. Supervisors should generally NOT use phrases like *too hard*, *too easy*, and   18.____
    a lot PRINCIPALLY because such phrases
    A. may be offensive to some minority groups
    B. are too informal
    C. mean different things to different people
    D. are difficult to remember

19. The ability to communicate clearly and concisely is an important element in   19.____
    effective leadership.
    Which of the following statements about oral and written communication is GENERALLY true?
    A. Oral communication is more time-consuming.
    B. Written communication is more likely to be misinterpreted.
    C. Oral communication is useful only in emergencies.
    D. Written communication is useful mainly when giving information to fewer than twenty people.

20. Rumors can often have harmful and disruptive effects on an organization.   20.____
    Which one of the following is the BEST way to prevent rumors from becoming a problem?
    A. Refuse to act on rumors, thereby making them less believable.
    B. Increase the amount of information passed along by the *grapevine*.
    C. Distribute as much factual information as possible.
    D. Provide training in report writing.

21. Suppose that a subordinate asks you about a rumor he has heard. The rumor   21.____
    deals with a subject which your superiors consider *confidential*.
    Which of the following BEST describes how you should answer the subordinate? Tell

A. the subordinate that you don't make the rules and that he should speak to higher ranking officials
B. the subordinate that you will ask your superior for information
C. him only that you cannot comment on the matter
D. him the rumor is not true

22. Supervisors often find it difficult to *get their message across* when instructing newly appointed employees in their various duties.
The MAIN reason for this is generally that the
    A. duties of the employees have increased
    B. supervisor is often so expert in his area that he fails to see it from the learner's point of view
    C. supervisor adapts his instruction to the slowest learner in the group
    D. new employees are younger, less concerned with job security and more interested in fringe benefits

23. Assume that you are discussing a job problem with an employee under your supervision. During the discussion, you see that the man's eyes are turning away from you and that he is not paying attention.
In order to get the man's attention, you should FIRST
    A. ask him to look you in the eye
    B. talk to him about sports
    C. tell him he is being very rude
    D. change your tone of voice

24. As a supervisor, you may find it necessary to conduct meetings with your subordinates.
Of the following, which would be MOST helpful in assuring that a meeting accomplishes the purpose for which it was called?
    A. Give notice of the conclusions you would like to reach at the start of the meeting.
    B. Delay the start of the meeting until everyone is present.
    C. Write down points to be discussed in proper sequence.
    D. Make sure everyone is clear on whatever conclusions have been reached and on what must be done after the meeting.

25. Every supervisor will occasionally be called upon to deliver a reprimand to a subordinate. If done properly, this can greatly help an employee improve his performance.
Which one of the following is NOT a good practice to follow when giving a reprimand?
    A. Maintain your composure and temper
    B. Reprimand a subordinate in the presence of other employees so they can learn the same lesson
    C. Try to understand why the employee was not able to perform satisfactorily
    D. Let your knowledge of the man involved determine the exact nature of the reprimand

KEY (CORRECT ANSWERS)

1.	C	11.	A
2.	B	12.	A
3.	D	13.	B
4.	B	14.	C
5.	D	15.	A
6.	C	16.	D
7.	C	17.	A
8.	B	18.	C
9.	C	19.	B
10.	C	20.	C

21.	B
22.	B
23.	D
24.	D
25.	B

TEST 2

DIRECTIONS: Each question or incomplete statement is followed by several suggested answers or completions. Select the one that BEST answers the question or completes the statement. *PRINT THE LETTER OF THE CORRECT ANSWER IN THE SPACE AT THE RIGHT.*

1. Usually one thinks of communication as a single step, essentially that of transmitting an idea.
   Actually, however, this is only part of a total process, the FIRST step of which should be
   A. the prompt dissemination of the idea to those who may be affected by it
   B. motivating those affected to take the required action
   C. clarifying the idea in one's own mind
   D. deciding to whom the idea is to be communicated

   1.____

2. Research studies on patterns of informal communication have concluded that most individuals in a group tend to be passive recipients of news, while a few make it their business to spread it around in an organization.
   With this conclusion in mind, it would be MOST correct for the supervisor to attempt to identify these few individuals and
   A. give them the complete facts on important matters in advance of others
   B. inform the other subordinates of the identity of these few individuals so that their influence may be minimized
   C. keep them straight on the facts on important matters
   D. warn them to cease passing along any information to others

   2.____

3. The one of the following which is the PRINCIPAL advantage of making an oral report is that it
   A. affords an immediate opportunity for two-way communication between the subordinate and superior
   B. is an easy method for the superior to use in transmitting information to others of equal rank
   C. saves the time of all concerned
   D. permits more precise pinpointing of praise or blame by means of follow-up questions by the superior

   3.____

4. An agency may sometimes undertake a public relations program of a defensive nature.
   With reference to the use of defensive public relations, it would be MOST correct to state that it
   A. is bound to be ineffective since defensive statements, even though supported by factual data, can never hope to even partly overcome the effects of prior unfavorable attacks
   B. proves that the agency has failed to establish good relationships with newspapers, radio stations, or other means of publicity

   4.____

C. shows that the upper echelons of the agency have failed to develop sound public relations procedures and techniques
D. is sometimes required to aid morale by protecting the agency from unjustified criticism and misunderstanding of policies or procedures

5. Of the following factors which contribute to possible undesirable public attitudes towards an agency, the one which is MOST susceptible to being changed by the efforts of the individual employee in an organization is that
   A. enforcement of unpopular regulations as offended many individuals
   B. the organization itself has an unsatisfactory reputation
   C. the public is not interested in agency matters
   D. there are many errors in judgment committed by individual subordinates

5.____

6. It is not enough for an agency's services to be of a high quality; attention must also be given to the acceptability of these services to the general public.
This statement is GENERALLY
   A. *false*; a superior quality of service automatically wins public support
   B. *true*; the agency cannot generally progress beyond the understanding and support of the public
   C. *false*; the acceptance by the public of agency services determines their quality
   D. *true*; the agency is generally unable to engage in any effective enforcement activity without public support

6.____

7. Sustained agency participation in a program sponsored by a community organization is MOST justified when
   A. the achievement of agency objectives in some area depends partly on the activity of this organization
   B. the community organization is attempting to widen the base of participation in all community affairs
   C. the agency is uncertain as to what the community wants
   D. the agency is uncertain as to what the community wants

7.____

8. Of the following, the LEAST likely way in which a records system may serve a supervisor is in
   A. developing a sympathetic and cooperative public attitude toward the agency
   B. improving the quality of supervision by permitting a check on the accomplishment of subordinates
   C. permit a precise prediction of the exact incidences in specific categories for the following year
   D. helping to take the guesswork out of the distribution of the agency

8.____

9. Assuming that the *grapevine* in any organization is virtually indestructible, the one of the following which it is MOST important for management to understand is:
    A. What is being spread by means of the *grapevine* and the reason for spreading it
    B. What is being spread by means of the *grapevine* and how it is being spread
    C. Who is involved in spreading the information that is on the *grapevine*
    D. Why those who are involved in spreading the information are doing so

10. When the supervisor writes a report concerning an investigation to which he has been assigned, it should be LEAST intended to provide
    A. a permanent official record of relevant information gathered
    B. a summary of case findings limited to facts which tend to indicate the guilt of a suspect
    C. a statement of the facts on which higher authorities may base a corrective or disciplinary action
    D. other investigators with information so that they may continue with other phases of the investigation

11. In survey work, questionnaires rather than interviews are sometimes used. The one of the following which is a DISADVANTAGE of the questionnaire method as compared with the interview is the
    A. difficulty of accurately interpreting the results
    B. problem of maintaining anonymity of the participant
    C. fact that it is relatively uneconomical
    D. requirement of special training for the distribution of questionnaires

12. in his contacts with the public, an employee should attempt to create a good climate of support for his agency.
    This statement is GENERALLY
    A. *false*; such attempts are clearly beyond the scope of his responsibility
    B. *true*; employees of an agency who come in contact with the public have the opportunity to affect public relations
    C. *false*; such activity should be restricted to supervisors trained in public relations techniques
    D. *true*; the future expansion of the agency depends to a great extent on continued public support of the agency

13. The repeated use by a supervisor of a call for volunteers to get a job done is objectionable MAINLY because it
    A. may create a feeling of animosity between the volunteers and the non-volunteers
    B. may indicate that the supervisor is avoiding responsibility for making assignments which will be most productive
    C. is an indication that the supervisor is not familiar with the individual capabilities of his men
    D. is unfair to men who, for valid reasons, do not, or cannot volunteer

14. Of the following statements concerning subordinates' expressions to a supervisor of their opinions and feelings concerning work situations, the one which is MOST correct is that
    A. by listening and responding to such expressions the supervisor encourages the development of complaints
    B. the lack of such expressions should indicate to the supervisor that there is a high level of job satisfaction
    C. the more the supervisor listens to and responds to such expressions, the more he demonstrates lack of supervisory ability
    D. by listening and responding to such expressions, the supervisor will enable many subordinates to understand and solve their own problems on the job

15. In attempting to motivate employees, rewards are considered preferable to punishment PRIMARILY because
    A. punishment seldom has any effect on human behavior
    B. punishment usually results in decreased production
    C. supervisors find it difficult to punish
    D. rewards are more likely to result in willing cooperation

16. In an attempt to combat the low morale in his organization, a high level supervisor publicized an *open-door policy* to allow employees who wished to do so to come to him with their complaints.
    Which of the following is LEAST likely to account for the fact that no employee came in with a complaint?
    A. Employees are generally reluctant to go over the heads of their immediate supervisor.
    B. The employees did not feel that management would help them.
    C. The low morale was not due to complaints associated with the job.
    D. The employees felt that they had more to lose than to gain.

17. It is MOST desirable to use written instructions rather than oral instructions for a particular job when
    A. a mistake on the job will not be serious
    B. the job can be completed in a short time
    C. there is no need to explain the job minutely
    D. the job involves many details

18. If you receive a telephone call regarding a matter which your office does not handle, you should FIRST
    A. give the caller the telephone number of the proper office so that he can dial again
    B. offer to transfer the caller to the proper office
    C. suggest that the caller re-dial since he probably dialed incorrectly
    D. tell the caller he has reached the wrong office and then hang up

19. When you answer the telephone, the MOST important reason for identifying yourself and your organization is to
    A. give the caller time to collect his or her thoughts
    B. impress the caller with your courtesy
    C. inform the caller that he or she has reached the right number
    D. set a business-like tone at the beginning of the conversation

19._____

20. As soon as you pick up the phone, a very angry caller begins immediately to complain about city agencies and *red tape*. He says that he has been shifted to two or three different offices. It turs out that he is seeking information which is not immediately available to you. You believe, you know, however, where it can be found.
    Which of the following actions is the BEST one for you to take?
    A. To eliminate all confusion, suggest that the caller write the agency stating explicitly what he wants.
    B. Apologize by telling the caller how busy city agencies now are, but also tell him directly that you do not have the information he needs.
    C. Ask for the caller's telephone number and assure him you will call back after you have checked further.
    D. Give the caller the name and telephone number of the person who might be able to help, but explain that you are not positive he will get results/

20._____

21. Which of the following approaches usually provides the BEST communication in the objectives and values of a new program which is to be introduced?
    A. A general written description of the program by the program manager for review by those who share responsibility
    B. An effective verbal presentation by the program manager to those affected
    C. Development of the plan and operational approach in carrying out the program by the program manager assisted by his key subordinates
    D. Development of the plan by the program manager's supervisor

21._____

22. What is the BEST approach for introducing change?
    A
    A. combination of written and also verbal communication to all personnel affected by the change
    B. general bulletin to all personnel
    C. meeting pointing out all the values of the new approach
    D. written directive to key personnel

22._____

23. Of the following, committees are BEST used for
    A. advising the head of the organization
    B. improving functional work
    C. making executive decisions
    D. making specific planning decisions

23._____

24. An effective discussion leader is one who 24._____
    A. announces the problem and his preconceived solution at the start of the discussion
    B. guides and directs the discussion according to pre-arranged outline
    C. interrupts or corrects confused participants to save time
    D. permits anyone to say anything at any time

25. The human relations movement in management theory is basically concerned with 25._____
    A. counteracting employee unrest
    B. eliminating the *time and motion* man
    C. interrelationships among individuals in organizations
    D. the psychology of the worker

KEY (CORRECT ANSWERS)

1.	C		11.	A
2.	C		12.	B
3.	A		13.	B
4.	D		14.	D
5.	D		15.	D
6.	B		16.	C
7.	A		17.	D
8.	C		18.	B
9.	A		19.	C
10.	B		20.	C

21.	C
22.	A
23.	A
24.	B
25.	C

EXAMINATION SECTION

TEST 1

DIRECTIONS: Each question or incomplete statement is followed by several suggested answers or completions. Select the one that BEST answers the question or completes the statement. *PRINT THE LETTER OF THE CORRECT ANSWER IN THE SPACE AT THE RIGHT.*

1. Managing conflict effectively by avoiding no-win situations, positively influencing the actions of others and using _____ strategies are what make a great leader.
    A. persuasive   B. ambiguous   C. prosecution   D. performance

    1.____

2. In today's business world, collaboration will bring together people from distinct backgrounds. These collaborative groups may not share common norms, morals or _____, but they can offer unique _____.
    A. vocabulary; perspectives
    B. salaries; vocabulary
    C. modifications; insights
    D. perspectives; salaries

    2.____

3. E-mail is a great tool for communication; however, which of the following should you be careful of when in electronic communication with a colleague?
    A. Font size
    B. E-mail length
    C. Font color
    D. Tone of voice

    3.____

4. A formal relationship can BEST be described as
    A. regulated by procedures or directives
    B. personal and relaxed
    C. emotionally distant and very uncomfortable
    D. confusing and unproductive

    4.____

5. John is in a meeting with his supervisor ad coworkers. He is thinking about what he's going to have for dinner that night when his boss asks him a question. John can repeat back what his supervisor said, but he cannot retain what was said during the meeting.
    This is a classic example of failing to
    A. focus at work
    B. effectively listen
    C. leave personal plans outside the workplace
    D. care about meetings

    5.____

6. A person's choice of _____ can directly affect communication.
    A. clothing   B. food   C. hygiene   D. words

    6.____

7. Why is it important to relax when communicating with team members?
    A. Relaxing always means having better ideas.
    B. People will automatically like you more if you are relaxed.

    7.____

165

    C. If you are nervous, you may talk too quickly and make it hard for others to understand your message or directive.
    D. No one likes someone who is always working, so it is important to relax and not work too hard.

8. In order to show you are genuinely interested in what others have to say, you should
    A. tell them how nice they are
    B. repeat what they say back to them
    C. nod and find something to compliment them about
    D. ask questions and seek clarification from them

8.____

9. Jack and James are always arguing with one another. Their supervisor calls each one in separately to talk to them. He asks Jack to think about things from James' point of view and he asks James to do the same for Jack.
What is the supervisor trying to get each person to do?
    A. Get along   B. Be positive
    C. Communicate effectively   D. Empathize

9.____

10. When working in groups, disagreements
    A. should be avoided at all costs
    B. are often a healthy way of building understanding and camaraderie
    C. lead coworkers to hate one another and the company they work for
    D. don't happen if the supervisor chooses the right people to work together

10.____

11. If things go wrong in a group situation, it is important to AVOID
    A. the boss   B. disagreements or arguments
    C. scapegoating   D. being polite and fair to one another

11.____

12. If you are a listener who likes to hear the rationale behind a message, your listening style would be described as _____ style.
    A. results   B. process   C. reasons   D. eye contact

12.____

13. Which of the following BEST describes a psychological barrier in communication?
    A. Molly is so stressed about her paying for her mortgage that she can't focus at work right now.
    B. John doesn't understand a lot of the terms the IT specialist used in an e-mail sent out to everyone.
    C. Jerry is a little older and has a hard time hearing everything so sometimes he misses parts of a conversation.
    D. Linda doesn't want to be at the company for longer than a few months, so she doesn't really try too hard to fit in.

13.____

14. Body language, also known as _____, is really important when building rapport with coworkers and communicating effectively.
    A. verbal language   B. kinesthetic
    C. non-verbal communication   D. facial expressions

14.____

15. Which of the following might be a good example of someone who has a "closed" posture?
    A. Hands are apart on the arms of the chair.
    B. His/her arms are folded.
    C. They are directly facing you.
    D. They barely speak above a whisper.

16. Which of the following can eye contact be used for?
    A. To give and receive feedback
    B. To let someone know when it is their turn to speak
    C. To communicate how you feel about someone
    D. All of the above

17. Which of the following is NOT a form of non-verbal communication?
    A. Crossing your arms when talking to someone
    B. Using space within the room in a conversation
    C. Clearing your throat before you speak]
    D. Saying "10-4" when asked if you understand

18. Your best friend has just been hired at the company you work for. You notice he has come into work on several occasions after staying out late the night before. His work has not suffered yet, but you fear it will.
    Which of the following actions should you take to help prevent future problems?
    A. Do nothing; he's your friend but it is his life
    B. Try to talk to him and help him see the importance of not creating bad habits.
    C. Talk to your supervisor and tell him your friend isn't suitable for the job
    D. Tell your friend to change his ways or to quit

19. Interacting with coworkers can be positively or negatively affected by _____ when someone's previous biases and assumptions shape their reactions in future situations.
    A. racism
    B. past experience
    C. interpersonal skills
    D. active listening

20. Which of the following scenarios BEST describes a person who is being subjective?
    A. Sally is fair and honest when she listens to coworkers. She does not take sides and wants the best solution to the problem.
    B. Mike doesn't like Steve, because he thinks Steve is only out for himself. Still, Steve offers valuable insights, so Mike tries not to let personal feelings get in the way of working together.
    C. Jamie is dating Veronica's ex and Veronica just found out. Now, Veronica immediately shoots down anything Jamie suggests during a meeting as irrational and superfluous.
    D. None of the above

21. Which important communications tem is MOST closely defined as "the quality of a sound governed by the rate of vibrations producing it; the degree of highness or lowness of a tone"?
    A. Tone
    B. Pitch
    C. Effective communication
    D. Rationalization

22. _____ is when a person tries to make an imprudent and reckless action seem reasonable.
    A. Projection
    B. Self-deception
    C. Past experience
    D. Rationalization

23. When holding conversations with coworkers, you should
    A. do most of the talking
    B. let others do most of the talking
    C. try to split time between talking and listening
    D. zone out and wait for the meeting to finish

24. A new hire just arrived and you are meeting her for the first time. Which of the following actions is MOST appropriate?
    A. Walk up and introduce yourself with a smile and a handshake
    B. Wait for her to come and introduce herself
    C. Approach her and offer a hug to make her feel welcome
    D. Ignore the new hire; she is likely your competition

25. If you are the type of listener who likes to discuss concepts or issues in detail, you would MOST likely fall under which listening style?
    A. Process
    B. Reasons
    C. Results
    D. None of the above

KEY (CORRECT ANSWERS)

1.	A	11.	C
2.	A	12.	C
3.	D	13.	A
4.	A	14.	C
5.	B	15.	B
6.	D	16.	D
7.	C	17.	D
8.	D	18.	B
9.	D	19.	B
10.	B	20.	C

21. B
22. D
23. C
24. A
25. A

TEST 2

DIRECTIONS: Each question or incomplete statement is followed by several suggested answers or completions. Select the one that BEST answers the question or completes the statement. *PRINT THE LETTER OF THE CORRECT ANSWER IN THE SPACE AT THE RIGHT.*

1. Which of the following is an example of the BEST practice when communicating in the workplace?
    A. You are horrible with remembering names so you try to use nicknames to cover up for your poor memory.
    B. You only pay attention to the names of people who you work for or who you deem to be "important."
    C. You try to remember everyone's names and use them whenever possible.
    D. None of the above

2. Words of civility such as "please" and "thank you" should be used _____ when conversing with coworkers and business partners.
    A. always   B. sometimes   C. rarely   D. never

3. When communicating with others, one should _____ stand as close to them as possible and make body contact in order to get an important point across.
    A. always   B. sometimes   C. rarely   D. never

4. The MOST appropriate way to end a conversation is to
    A. seek a mutual resolution, but leave abruptly if it continues
    B. find a way to wrap up the conversation so the other person knows it is time to move on
    C. look impatient so hopefully the person will get the hint
    D. tell the other person the conversation should end

5. Another name for interpersonal communication in an office setting is
    A. peer-to-peer communication   B. mass communication
    C. virtual reality   D. e-mailing

6. Of the following statements, choose the one you feel is the MOST correct.
    A. Devoid of interpersonal communication, people become sick.
    B. Communication is not completely needed for humans.
    C. People are the only animals that need to have relationships in order to survive.
    D. Important communication is not really relevant until after you become an adult.

7. John is giving a presentation on ways to communicate effectively with peers. He is having trouble deciding on what to say in his speech.
   Which of the following statements should he AVOID using?
    A. Always try to understand another person's point of view or perspective
    B. Try to imagine what someone is going to say before they actually say it

C. Be aware of how non-verbal cues like eye contact and body language affect how your message is received
D. Both B and C

8. Which of the following would MOST affect our perception of communication with coworkers?
   A. Past experiences
   B. Marital problems
   C. Rumors spread about coworkers
   D. None of the above

9. Many people think of communication as both _____ and _____ messages.
   A. formal; informal
   B. hearing; listening
   C. sending; receiving
   D. finding; decoding

10. Why is context important in communication?
    A. It's important to know which buttons to push in order to get what you want.
    B. Saying something to one person may not have the same effect as saying it to someone else.
    C. Context is only important if you are worried about what others think.
    D. None of the above

11. If your brother is normally bright and talkative during the summer, but you notice he gets quiet and subdued in the winter, the MOST likely communication context he is dealing with would be
    A. relational   B. cultural   C. inner   D. physical

12. _____ is an example of a negative nonverbal action you can take.
    A. Smiling
    B. Using a tone of voice that matches your message
    C. Maintaining eye contact
    D. Slumping your shoulders

13. Cultural context can BEST be described as
    A. what people think of as it relates to the event they are participating in (i.e., wedding versus a funeral)
    B. the connection between a father and his son
    C. rules and patterns of Americans versus the Japanese
    D. thoughts, feelings, and sensations inside a person's head

14. Which of the following BEST describes feedback?
    A. Staring at the speaker while he talks
    B. Nodding and smiling while listening to a speaker
    C. Standing an appropriate distance away so the speaker does not get uncomfortable
    D. Trying to speak while the other person is speaking because you have something more important to say

15. Being able to communicate more effectively can be improved upon by
    A. continually making an effort to be as flexible as possible when talking to others
    B. committing to one style of speaking until you master it
    C. using the same style of correspondence as the person with whom you are speaking
    D. always using the opposite style of communication from the person you are speaking to

16. John walks up to Sally and compliments her on the dress she wore to work today. In his mind, John was just being friendly, but Sally went to her manager and filed a harassment charge against John.
    This miscommunication could MOST easily be classified as an error in what?
    A. Reality   B. Perception   C. Friendship   D. Loyalty

17. If a speaker's tone is flat and monotone, which of the following is the MOST likely reaction that listeners will have?
    They will
    A. enthused by the message
    B. enjoy the message but not be overly excited about it
    C. be polite and interested but will not seem very engaged
    D. be bored and uninterested in the message

18. When Steve speaks to his group about his ideas, he generally has a higher pitch to his voice and gesticulates frequently.
    This lead his team members to believe that Steve
    A. is enthusiastic and has great ideas for the group
    B. has had too much caffeine and needs to relax
    C. is trying to show off for the boss and make them look bad
    D. is extremely smart and great at his job

19. _____ is used when a person wants to add stress to key words in communication. It lets the audience understand the mood or feelings of particular words or phrases.
    A. Anger   B. Tone   C. Perception   D. Inflection

20. If Barry tells Bill that his haircut looks "great" and Bill can tell Barry is being insincere, which of the following tones is Barry MOST likely using?
    A. Affectionate B. Apologetic   C. Threatening   D. Sarcastic

21. As a supervisor, it is important that everyone clearly comprehends everything you communicate to them.
    In order to ensure this happens, which of the following things should you avoid?
    A. Overusing jargon
    B. Explaining something more than once
    C. Speaking slowly and annunciating everything
    D. Having meetings in the morning

22. If your supervisor is looking down at the ground or has his back to you as he is speaking, it MOST clearly indicates to those who are listening to him that the supervisor
    A. is shy and doesn't like speaking in front of people
    B. is disinterested and doesn't care what he's talking about
    C. is approachable and friendly
    D. dislikes his job and wants to get out as soon as possible

22.____

23. Interpersonal communication helps you
    A. know what others are thinking
    B. turn into an inspiring speaker, especially in public
    C. learn about yourself
    D. communicate with the general public

23.____

24. In general, people who smile more are perceived as
    A. devious   B. friendly
    C. attractive   D. easy to manipulate

24.____

25. If your supervisor constantly takes advantage of you and expresses his or her opinion often at the expense of you or other workers, which communication style are they MOST likely using?
    A. Nonassertive   B. Assertive   C. Aggressive   D. Peacemaking

25.____

KEY (CORRECT ANSWERS)

1.	C		11.	D
2.	A		12.	D
3.	D		13.	C
4.	B		14.	B
5.	A		15.	A
6.	A		16.	B
7.	B		17.	D
8.	A		18.	A
9.	C		19.	D
10.	B		20.	D

21. A
22. B
23. D
24. B
25. C

REPORT WRITING

EXAMINATION SECTION

TEST 1

DIRECTIONS: Each question or incomplete statement is followed by several suggested answers or completions. Select the one that BEST answers the question or completes the statement. *PRINT THE LETTER OF THE CORRECT ANSWER IN THE SPACE AT THE RIGHT.*

Questions 1-4.

DIRECTIONS: Answer Questions 1 through 4 on the basis of the following report which was prepared by a supervisor for inclusion in his agency's annual report.

Line #
1   On Oct. 13, I was assigned to study the salaries paid.
2   to clerical employees in various titles by the city and by
3   private industry in the area.
4   In order to get the data I needed, I called Mr. Johnson at
5   the Bureau of the Budget and the payroll officers at X Corp.—
6   a brokerage house, Y Co. —an insurance company, and Z Inc. —
7   a publishing firm. None of them was available and I had to call
8   all of them again the next day.
9   When I finally got the information I needed, I drew up a
10   chart, which is attached. Note that not all of the companies I
11   contacted employed people at all the different levels used in the
12   city service.
13   The conclusions I draw from analyzing this information is
14   as follows: The city's entry-level salary is about average for
15   the region; middle-level salaries are generally higher in the
16   city government plan than in private industry; but salaries at the
17   highest levels in private industry are better than city em-
18   ployees' pay.

1. Which of the following criticisms about the style in which this report is written is MOST valid?
   A. It is too informal.
   B. It is too concise.
   C. It is too choppy.
   D. The syntax is too complex.

1.____

2. Judging from the statements made in the report, the method followed by this employee in performing his research was
   A. *good*; he contacted a representative sample of businesses in the area
   B. *poor*; he should have drawn more definite conclusions
   C. *good*; he was persistent in collecting information
   D. *poor*; he did not make a thorough study

2.____

3. One sentence in this report contains a grammatical error. This sentence begins on line number
   A. 4
   B. 7
   C. 10
   D. 14

4. The type of information given in this report which should be presented in footnotes or in an appendix is the
   A. purpose of the study
   B. specifics about the businesses contacted
   C. reference to the chart
   D. conclusions drawn by the author

5. The use of a graph to show statistical data in a report is SUPERIOR to a table because it
   A. features approximations
   B. emphasizes facts and relationships more dramatically
   C. presents data more accurately
   D. is easily understood by the average reader

6. Of the following, the degree of formality required of a written report in tone is MOST likely to depend on the
   A. subject matter of the report
   B. frequency of its occurrence
   C. amount of time available for its preparation
   D. audience for whom the report is intended

7. Of the following, a distinguishing characteristic of a written report intended for the head of your agency as compared to a report prepared for a lower-echelon staff member is that the report for the agency head should USUALLY include
   A. considerably more detail, especially statistical data
   B. the essential details in an abbreviated form
   C. all available source material
   D. an annotated bibliography

8. Assume that you are asked to write a lengthy report for use by the administrator of your agency, the subject of which is "The Impact of Proposed New Data Processing Operation on Line Personnel" in your agency. You decide that the *most* appropriate type of report for you to prepare is an analytical report, including recommendations.
   The MAIN reason for your decision is that
   A. the subject of the report is extremely complex
   B. large sums of money are involved
   C. the report is being prepared for the administrator
   D. you intend to include charts and graphs

9. Assume that you are preparing a report based on a survey dealing with the attitudes of employees in Division X regarding proposed new changes in compensating employees for working overtime. Three percent of the respondents to the survey voluntarily offer an unfavorable opinion on the method of assigning overtime work, a question not specifically asked of the employees.
On the basis of this information, the MOST appropriate and significant of the following comments for you to make in the report with regard to employees' attitudes on assigning overtime work is that
    A. an insignificant percentage of employees dislike the method of assigning overtime work
    B. three percent of the employees in Division X dislike the method of assigning overtime work
    C. three percent of the sample selected for the survey voiced an unfavorable opinion on the method of assigning overtime work
    D. some employees voluntarily voiced negative feelings about the method of assigning overtime work, making it impossible to determine the extent of this attitude

10. A supervisor should be able to prepare a report that is well-written and unambiguous.
Of the following sentences that might appear in a report, select the one which communicates MOST clearly the intent of its author.
    A. When your subordinates speak to a group of people, they should be well-informed.
    B. When he asked him to leave, SanMan King told him that he would refuse the request.
    C. Because he is a good worker, Foreman Jefferson assigned Assistant Foreman D'Agostino to replace him.
    D. Each of us is responsible for the actions of our subordinates.

11. In some reports, especially longer ones, a list of the resources (books, papers, magazines, etc.) used to prepare it is included. This list is called the
    A. accreditation	B. bibliography
    C. summary	D. glossary

12. Reports are usually divided into several sections, some of which are more necessary than others.
Of the following, the section which is ABSOLUTELY necessary to include in a report is
    A. a table of contents	B. the body
    C. an index	D. a bibliography

13. Suppose you are writing a report on an interview you have just completed with a particularly hostile applicant.
    Which of the following BEST describes what you should include in this report?
    A. What you think caused the applicant's hostile attitude during the interview
    B. Specific examples of the applicant's hostile remarks and behavior
    C. The relevant information uncovered during the interview
    D. A recommendation that the applicant's request be denied because of his hostility

14. When including recommendations in a report to your supervisor, which of the following is MOST important for you to do?
    A. Provide several alternative courses of action for each recommendation
    B. First present the supporting evidence, then the recommendations
    C. First present the recommendations, then the supporting evidence
    D. Make sure the recommendations arise logically out of the information in the report

15. It is often necessary that the writer of a report present facts and sufficient arguments to gain acceptance of the points, conclusions, or recommendations set forth in the report.
    Of the following, the LEAST advisable step to take in organizing a report, when such argumentation is the important factor, is a(n)
    A. elaborate expression of personal belief
    B. businesslike discussion of the problem as a whole
    C. orderly arrangement of convincing data
    D. reasonable explanation of the primary issues

16. In some types of reports, visual aids add interest, meaning, and support. They also provide an essential means of effectively communicating the message of the report.
    Of the following, the selection of the suitable visual aids to use with a report is LEAST dependent on the
    A. nature and scope of the report
    B. way in which the aid is to be used
    C. aid used in other reports
    D. prospective readers of the report

17. Visual aids used in a report may be placed either in the text material or in the appendix.
    Deciding where to put a chart, table, or any such aid should depend on the
    A. title of the report   B. purpose of the visual aid
    C. title of the visual aid   D. length of the report

18. A report is often revised several times before final preparation and distribution in an effort to make certain the report meets the needs of the situation for which it is designed.
    Which of the following is the BEST way for the author to be sure that a report covers the areas he intended?

A. Obtain a coworker's opinion
B. Compare it with a content checklist
C. Test it on a subordinate
D. Check his bibliography

19. In which of the following situations is an oral report preferable to a written report? When a(n)
    A. recommendation is being made for a future plan of action
    B. department head requests immediate information
    C. long-standing policy change is made
    D. analysis of complicated statistical data is involved

20. When an applicant is approved, the supervisor must fill in standard forms with certain information.
    The GREATEST advantage of using standard forms in this situation rather than having the supervisor write the report as he sees fit is that
    A. the report can be acted on quickly
    B. the report can be written without directions from a supervisor
    C. needed information is less likely to be left out of the report
    D. information that is written up this way is more likely to be verified

21. Assume that it is part of your job to prepare a monthly report for your unit head that eventually goes to the director. The report contains information on the number of applicants you have interviewed that have been approved and the number of applicants you have interviewed that have been turned down.
    Errors on such reports are serious because
    A. you are expected to be able to prove how many applicants you have interviewed each month
    B. accurate statistics are needed for effective management of the department
    C. they may not be discovered before the report is transmitted to the director
    D. they may result in loss to the applicants left out of the report

22. The frequency with which job reports are submitted should depend MAINLY on
    A. how comprehensive the report has to be
    B. the amount of information in the report
    C. the availability of an experienced man to write the report
    D. the importance of changes in the information included in the report

23. The CHIEF purpose in preparing an outline for a report is usually to insure that
    A. the report will be grammatically correct
    B. every point will be given equal emphasis
    C. principal and secondary points will be properly integrated
    D. the language of the report will be of the same level and include the same technical terms

24. The MAIN reason for requiring written job reports is to 24.____
    A. avoid the necessity of oral orders
    B. develop better methods of doing the work
    C. provide a permanent record of what was done
    D. increase the amount of work that can be done

25. Assume you are recommending in a report to your supervisor that a radical 25.____
    change in a standard maintenance procedure should be adopted.
    Of the following, the MOST important information to be included in this report is
    A. a list of the reasons for making this change
    B. the names of others who favor the change
    C. a complete description of the present procedure
    D. amount of training time needed for the new procedure

KEY (CORRECT ANSWERS)

1.	A		11.	B
2.	D		12.	B
3.	D		13.	C
4.	B		14.	D
5.	B		15.	A
6.	D		16.	C
7.	B		17.	B
8.	A		18.	B
9.	D		19.	B
10.	D		20.	C

21. B
22. D
23. C
24. C
25. A

TEST 2

DIRECTIONS: Each question or incomplete statement is followed by several suggested answers or completions. Select the one that BEST answers the question or completes the statement. *PRINT THE LETTER OF THE CORRECT ANSWER IN THE SPACE AT THE RIGHT.*

1. It is often necessary that the writer of a report present facts and sufficient arguments to gain acceptance of the points, conclusions, or recommendations set forth in the report.
Of the following, the LEAST advisable step to take in organizing a report, when such argumentation is the important factor, is a(n)
    A. elaborate expression of personal belief
    B. businesslike discussion of the problem as a whole
    C. orderly arrangement of convincing data
    D. reasonable explanation of the primary issues

    1.____

2. Of the following, the factor which is generally considered to be LEAST characteristic of a good control report is that it
    A. stresses performance that adheres to standard rather than emphasizing the exception
    B. supplies information intended to serve as the basis for corrective action
    C. provides feedback for the planning process
    D. includes data that reflect trends as well as current status

    2.____

3. An administrative assistant has been asked by his superior to write a concise, factual report with objective conclusions and recommendations based on facts assembled by other researchers.
Of the following factors, the administrative assistant should give LEAST consideration to
    A. the educational level of the person or persons for whom the report is being prepared
    B. the use to be made of the report
    C. the complexity of the problem
    D. his own feelings about the importance of the problem

    3.____

4. When making a written report, it is often recommended that the findings or conclusions be presented near the beginning of the report.
Of the following, the MOST important reason for doing this is that it
    A. facilitates organizing the material clearly
    B. assures that all the topics will be covered
    C. avoids unnecessary repetition of ideas
    D. prepares the reader for the facts that will follow

    4.____

5. You have been asked to write a report on methods of hiring and training new employees. Your report is going to be about ten pages long.
For the convenience of your readers, a brief summary of your findings should
   A. appear at the beginning of your report
   B. be appended to the report as a postscript
   C. be circulated in a separate memo
   D. be inserted in tabular form in the middle of your report

6. In preparing a report, the MAIN reason for writing an outline is usually to
   A. help organize thoughts in a logical sequence
   B. provide a guide for the typing of the report
   C. allow the ultimate user to review the report in advance
   D. ensure that the report is being prepared on schedule

7. The one of the following which is MOST appropriate as a reason for including footnotes in a report is to
   A. correct capitalization
   B. delete passages
   C. improve punctuation
   D. cite references

8. A completed formal report may contain all of the following EXCEPT
   A. a synopsis
   B. a preface
   C. marginal notes
   D. bibliographical references

9. Of the following, the MAIN use of proofreaders' marks is to
   A. explain corrections to be made
   B. indicate that a manuscript has been read and approved
   C. let the reader know who proofread the report
   D. indicate the format of the report

10. Informative, readable, and concise reports have been found to observe the following rules:
    Rule I. Keep the report short and easy to understand
    Rule II. Vary the length of sentences.
    Rule III. Vary the style of sentences so that, for example, they are not all just subject-verb, subject-verb.
    Consider this hospital laboratory report: The experiment was started in January. The apparatus was put together in six weeks. At that time, the synthesizing process was begun. The synthetic chemicals were separated. Then they were used in tests on patients.
    Which one of the following choices MOST accurately classifies the above rules into those which are violated by this report ad those which are not?
    A. II is violated, but I and III are not.
    B. III is violated, but I and II are not.
    C. II and III are violated, but I is not.
    D. I, II, and III are violated,

Questions 11-13.

DIRECTIONS: Questions 11 through 13 are based on the following example of a report. The report consists of eight numbered sentences, some of which are not consistent with the principles of good report writing.

(1) I interviewed Mrs. Loretta Crawford in Room 424 of County Hospital. (2) She had collapsed on the street and been brought into emergency. (3) She is an attractive woman with many friends judging by the cards she had received. (4) She did not know what her husband's last job had been, or what their present income was. (5) The first thing that Mrs. Crawford said was that she had never worked and that her husband was presently unemployed. (6) She did not know if they had any medical coverage or if they could pay the bill. (7) She said that her husband could not be reached by telephone but that he would be in to see her that afternoon. (8) I left word at the nursing station to be called when he arrived.

11. A good report should be arranged in logical order.
 Which of the following sentences from the report does NOT appear in its proper sequence in the report?
 A. 1 B. 4 C. 7 D. 8

12. Only material that is relevant to the main thought of a report should be included.
 Which of the following sentences from the report contains material which is LEAST relevant to this report? Sentence
 A. 3 B. 4 C. 6 D. 8

13. Reports should include all essential information.
 Of the following, the MOST important fact that is missing from this report is:
 A. Who was involved in the interview
 B. What was discovered at the interview
 C. When the interview took place
 D. Where the interview took place

Questions 14-15.

DIRECTIONS: Each of Questions 14 and 15 consists of four numbered sentences which constitute a paragraph in a report. They are not in the right order. Choose the numbered arrangement appearing after letter A, B, C, or D which is MOST logical and which BEST expresses the thought of the paragraph.

14. I. Congress made the commitment explicit in the Housing Act of 1949, establishing as a national goal the realization of a decent home and suitable environment for every American family.
 II. The result has been that the goal of decent home and suitable environment is still as far distant as ever for the disadvantaged urban family
 III. In spite of this action by Congress, federal housing programs have continued to be fragmented and grossly under-funded.
 IV. The passage of the National Housing Act signaled a new federal commitment to provide housing for the nation's citizens.

The CORRECT answer is:
A. I, IV, III, II   B. IV, I, III, II   C. IV, I, III, II   D. II, IV, I, III

15. I. The greater expense does not necessarily involve "exploitation," but it is often perceived as exploitative and unfair by those who are aware of the price differences involved, but unaware of operating costs.
    II. Ghetto residents believe they are "exploited" by local merchants, and evidence substantiates some of these beliefs.
    III. However, stores in low-income areas were more likely to be small independents, which could not achieve the economies available to supermarket chains and were, therefore, more likely to charge higher prices, and the customers were more likely to buy smaller-sized packages which are more expensive per unit of measure.
    IV. A study conducted in one city showed that distinctly higher prices were charged for goods sold in ghetto stores than in other areas.

    The CORRECT answer is:
    A. IV, II, I, III   B. IV, I, III, II   C. II, IV, III, I   D. II, III, IV, I

15.____

16. In organizing data to be presented in a formal report, the FIRST of the following steps should be
    A. determining the conclusions to be drawn
    B. establishing the time sequence of the data
    C. sorting and arranging like data into groups
    D. evaluating how consistently the data support the recommendations

16.____

17. All reports should be prepared with at least one copy so that
    A. there is one copy for your file
    B. there is a copy for your supervisor
    C. the report can be sent to more than one person
    D. the person getting the report can forward a copy to someone else

17.____

18. Before turning in a report of an investigation he has made, a supervisor discovers some additional information he did not include in this report. Whether he rewrites this report to include this additional information should PRIMARILY depend on the
    A. importance of the report itself
    B. number of people who will eventually review this report
    C. established policy covering the subject matter of the report
    D. bearing this new information has on the conclusions of the report

18.____

KEY (CORRECT ANSWERS)

1.	A	11.	B
2.	A	12.	A
3.	D	13.	C
4.	D	14.	B
5.	A	15.	C
6.	A	16.	C
7.	D	17.	A
8.	C	18.	D
9.	A		
10.	C		

READING COMPREHENSION
UNDERSTANDING AND INTERPRETING WRITTEN MATERIAL
EXAMINATION SECTION
TEST 1

DIRECTIONS: Each question or incomplete statement is followed by several suggested answers or completions. Select the one that BEST answers the question or completes the statement. *PRINT THE LETTER OF THE CORRECT ANSWER IN THE SPACE AT THE RIGHT.*

Questions 1-5.

DIRECTIONS: Questions 1 through 5 are to be answered SOLELY on the basis of the following passage.

The most effective control mechanism to prevent gross incompetence on the part of public employees is a good personnel program. The personnel officer in the line departments and the central personnel agency should exert positive leadership to raise levels of performance. Although the key factor is the quality of the personnel recruited, staff members other than personnel officers can make important contributions to efficiency. Administrative analysts, now employed in many agencies, make detailed studies of organization and procedures, with the purpose of eliminating delays, waste, and other inefficiencies. Efficiency is, however, more than a question of good organization and procedures; it is also the product of the attitudes and value of the public employees. Personal motivation can provide the will to be efficient. The best management studies will not result in substantial improvement of the performance of those employees who feel no great urge to wok up to their abilities.

1. The above passage indicates that the KEY factor in preventing gross incompetence of public employees is the
   A. hiring of administrative analysts to assist personnel people
   B. utilization of effective management studies
   C. overlapping of responsibility
   D. quality of the employees hired

2. According to the above passage, the central personnel agency staff SHOULD
   A. work more closely with administrative analysts in the line departments than with personnel officers
   B. make a serious effort to avoid jurisdictional conflicts with personnel officers in line departments
   C. contribute to improving the quality of work of public employees
   D. engage in a comprehensive program to change the public's negative image of public employees

3. The above passage indicates that efficiency in an organization can BEST be brought about by
   A. eliminating ineffective control mechanisms
   B. instituting sound organizational procedures
   C. promoting competent personnel
   D. recruiting people with desire to do good work

   3.____

4. According to the above passage, the purpose of administrative analysts in a public agency is to
   A. prevent injustice to the public employee
   B. promote the efficiency of the agency
   C. protect the interests of the public
   D. ensure the observance of procedural due process

   4.____

5. The above passage implies that a considerable rise in the quality of work of public employees can be brought about by
   A. encouraging positive employee attitudes toward work
   B. controlling personnel officers who exceed their powers
   C. creating warm personal associations among public employees in an agency
   D. closing loopholes in personnel organization and procedures

   5.____

Questions 6-8.

DIRECTIONS: Questions 6 through 8 are to be answered SOLELY on the basis of the following passage.

EMPLOYEE NEEDS

The greatest waste in industry and in government may be that of human resources. This waste usually derives not from employees' unwillingness or inability, but from management's ineptness to meet the maintenance and motivational needs of employees. Maintenance needs refer to such needs as providing employees with safe places to work, written work rules, job security, adequate salary, employer-sponsored social activities, and with knowledge of their role in the overall framework of the organization. However, of greatest significance to employees are the motivational needs of job growth, achievement, responsibility, and recognition.

Although employee dissatisfaction may stem from either poor maintenance or poor motivation factors, the outward manifestation of the dissatisfaction may be very much like, i.e., negativism, complaints, deterioration of performance, and so forth. The improvement in the lighting of an employee's work area or raising his level of ay won't do much good if the source of the dissatisfaction is the absence of a meaningful assignment. By the same token, if an employee is dissatisfied with what he considers inequitable pay, the introduction of additional challenge in his work may simply make matters worse.

It is relatively easy for an employee to express frustration by complaining about pay, washroom conditions, fringe benefits, and so forth; but most people cannot easily express resentment in terms of the more abstract concepts concerning job growth, responsibility, and achievement.

It would be wrong to assume that there is no interaction between maintenance and motivational needs of employee. For example, conditions of high motivation often overshadow poor maintenance conditions. If an organization is in a period of strong growth and expansion, opportunities for job growth, responsibility, recognition, and achievement are usually abundant, but the rapid growth may have outrun the upkeep of maintenance factors. In this situation, motivation may be high, but only if employees recognize the poor maintenance conditions as unavoidable and temporary. The subordination of maintenance factors cannot go on indefinitely, even with the highest motivation.

Both maintenance and motivation factors influence the behavior of all employees, but employees are not identical and, furthermore, the needs of any individual do not remain orientation toward maintenance factors and those with greater sensitivity toward motivation factors.

A highly maintenance-oriented individual, preoccupied with the factors peripheral to his job rather than the job itself, is more concerned with comfort than challenge. He does not get deeply involved with his work but does with the condition of his work area, toilet facilities, and his time for going to lunch. By contrast, a strongly motivation-oriented employee is usually relatively indifferent to his surroundings and is caught up in the pursuit of work goals.

Fortunately, there are few people who are either exclusively maintenance-oriented or purely motivation-oriented. The former would be deadwood in an organization, while the latter might trample on those around him in his pursuit to achieve his goals.

6. With respect to employee motivational and maintenance needs, the management policies of an organization which is growing rapidly will probably result
    A. more in meeting motivational needs rather than maintenance needs
    B. more in meeting maintenance needs rather than motivational needs
    C. in meeting both of these needs equally
    D. in increased effort to define the motivational and maintenance needs of its employees

6._____

7. In accordance with the above passage, which of the following CANNOT be considered as an example of an employee maintenance need for railroad clerks?
    A. Providing more relief periods
    B. Providing fair salary increases at periodic intervals
    C. Increasing job responsibilities
    D. Increasing health insurance benefits

7._____

8. Most employees in an organization may be categorized as being interested in
    A. maintenance needs only
    B. motivational needs only
    C. both motivational and maintenance needs
    D. money only, to the exclusion of all other needs

8._____

Questions 9-11.

DIRECTIONS: Questions 9 through 11 are to be answered SOLELY on the basis of the following passage.

GOOD EMPLOYEE PRACTICES

As a city employee, you will be expected to take an interest in you work and perform the duties of your job to the best of your ability and in a spirit of cooperation. Nothing shows an interest in your work more than coming to work on time, not only at the start of the day but also when returning from lunch. If it is necessary for you to keep a personal appointment at lunch hour which might cause a delay in getting back to work on time, you should explain the situation to your supervisor and get his approval to come back a little late before you leave for lunch.

You should do everything that is asked of you willingly and consider important even the small jobs that your supervisor gives you. Although these jobs may seem unimportant, if you forget to do them or if you don't do them right, trouble may develop later.

Getting along well with your fellow workers will add much to the enjoyment of your work. You should respect your fellow workers and try to see their side when a disagreement arises. The better you get along with your fellow workers and your supervisor, the better you will like your job and the better you will be able to do it.

9. According to the above passage, in your job as a city employee, you are expected to
    A. show a willingness to cooperate on the job
    B. get your supervisor's approval before keeping any personal appointments at lunch hour
    C. avoid doing small jobs that seem unimportant
    D. do the easier jobs at the start of the day and the more difficult ones later on

10. According to the above passage, getting to work on time shows that you
    A. need the job
    B. have an interest in your work
    C. get along well with your fellow workers
    D. like your supervisor

11. According to the above passage, the one of the following statements that is NOT true is:
    A. If you do a small job wrong, trouble may develop
    B. You should respect your fellow workers
    C. If you disagree with a fellow worker, you should try to see his side of the story
    D. The less you get along with your supervisor, the better you will be able to do your job

Questions 12-15.

DIRECTIONS: Questions 12 through 15 are to be answered SOLELY on the basis of the following passage.

EMPLOYEE SUGGESTIONS

To increase the effectiveness of the city government, the city asks its employees to offer suggestions when they feel an improvement could be made in some government operation. The Employees' Suggestions Program was started to encourage city employees to do this. Through this Program, which is only for city employees, cash awards may be given to those whose suggestions are submitted and approved. Suggestions are looked for not only from supervisors but from all city employees as any city employee may get an idea which might be approved and contribute greatly to the solution of some problem of city government.

Therefore, all suggestions for improvement are welcome, whether they be suggestions on how to improve working conditions, or on how to increase the speed with which work is done, or on how to reduce or eliminate such things as waste, time losses, accidents or fire hazards. There are, however, a few types of suggestions for which cash awards cannot be given. An example of this type would be a suggestion to increase salaries or a suggestion to change the regulations about annual leave or about sick leave. The number of suggestions sent in has increased sharply during the past few years. It is hoped that it will keep increasing in the future in order to meet the city's needs for more ideas for improved ways of doing things.

12. According to the above passage, the MAIN reason why the city asks its employees for suggestions about government operations is to
    A. increase the effectiveness of the city government
    B. show that the Employees' Suggestion Program is working well
    C. show that everybody helps run the city government
    D. have the employee win a prize

13. According to the above passage, the Employees' Suggestion Program can approve awards ONLY for those suggestions that come from
    A. city employees
    B. city employees who are supervisors
    C. city employees who are not supervisors
    D. experienced employee of the city

14. According to the above passage, a cash award cannot be given through the Employees' Suggestion Program for a suggestion about
    A. getting work done faster
    B. helping prevent accidents on the job
    C. increasing the amount of annual leave for city employees
    D. reducing the chance of fire where city employees work

15. According to the above passage, the suggestions sent in during the past few years have
    A. all been approved
    B. generally been well written
    C. been mostly about reducing or eliminating waste
    D. been greater in number than before

15.____

Questions 16-18.

DIRECTIONS: Questions 16 through 18 are to be answered SOLELY on the basis of the following passage.

The supervisor will gain the respect of the members of his staff and increase his influence over them by controlling his temper and avoiding criticizing anyone publicly. When a mistake is made, the good supervisor will take it over with the employee quietly and privately. The supervisor will listen to the employee's story, suggest the better way of doing the job, and offer help so the mistake won't happen again. Before closing the discussion, the supervisor should try to find something good to say about other parts of the employee's work. Some praise and appreciation, along with instruction, is more likely to encourage an employee to improve in those areas where he is weakest.

16. A good title that would show the meaning of the above passage would be
    A. How to Correct Employee Errors
    B. How to Praise Employees
    C. Mistakes are Preventable
    D. The Weak Employee

16.____

17. According to the above passage, the work of an employee who has made a mistake is more likely to improve if the supervisor
    A. avoids criticizing him
    B. gives him a chance to suggest a better way of doing the work
    C. listens to the employee's excuses to see if he is right
    D. praises good work at the same time he corrects the mistake

17.____

18. According to the above passage, when a supervisor needs to correct an employee's mistake, it is important that he
    A. allow some time to go by after the mistake is made
    B. do so when other employee are not present
    C. show his influence with his tone of voice
    D. tell other employee to avoid the same mistake

18.____

Questions 19-23.

DIRECTIONS: Questions 19 through 23 are to be answered SOLELY on the basis of the following passage.

In studying the relationships of people to the organizational structure, it is absolutely necessary to identify and recognize the informal organizational structure. These relationships are necessary when coordination of a plan is attempted. They may be with *the boss*, line supervisors, staff personnel, or other representatives of the formal organization's hierarchy, and they may include the *liaison men* who serve as the leaders of the informal organization. An acquaintanceship with the people serving in these roles in the organization, and its formal counterpart, permits a supervisor to recognize sensitive areas in which it is simple to get conflict reaction. Avoidance of such areas, plus conscious efforts to inform other people of his own objectives for various plans, will usually enlist their aid and support. Planning *without* people can lead to disaster because the individuals who must act together to make any plan a success are more important than the plans themselves.

19. Of the following titles, the one that MOST clearly describes the above passage is
    A. Coordination of a Function
    B. Avoidance of Conflict
    C. Planning With People
    D. Planning Objectives

20. According to the above passage, attempts at coordinating plans may fail unless
    A. the plan's objectives are clearly set forth
    B. conflict between groups is resolved
    C. the plans themselves are worthwhile
    D. informal relationships are recognized

21. According to the above passage, conflict
    A. may, in some cases, be desirable to secure results
    B. produces more heat than light
    C. should be avoided at all costs
    D. possibilities can be predicted by a sensitive supervisor

22. The above passage implies that
    A. informal relationships are more important than formal structure
    B. the weakness of a formal structure depends upon informal relationships
    C. liaison men are the key people to consult when taking formal and informal structures into account
    D. individuals in a group are at least as important as the plans for the group

23. The above passage suggests that
    A. some planning can be disastrous
    B. certain people in sensitive areas should be avoided
    C. the supervisor should discourage acquaintanceships in the organization
    D. organizational relationships should be consciously limited

Questions 24-25.

DIRECTIONS: Questions 24 and 25 are to be answered SOLELY on the basis of the following passage.

Good personnel relations of an organization depend upon mutual confidence, trust, and good will. The basis of confidence is understanding. Most troubles start with people who do not understand each other. When the organization's intentions or motives are misunderstood, or when reasons for actions, practices, or policies are misconstrued, complete cooperation from individuals is not forthcoming. If management expects full cooperation from employees, it has a responsibility of sharing with them the information which is the foundation of proper understanding, confidence, and trust. Personnel management has long since outgrown the days when it was the vogue to *treat them rough and tell them nothing.* Up-to-date personnel management provides all possible information about the activities, aims, and purposes of the organization. It seems altogether creditable that a desire should exist among employees for such information which the best-intentioned executive might think would not interest them and which the worst-intentioned would think was none of their business.

24. The above passage implies that one of the causes of the difficulty which an organization might have with its personnel relations is that its employees
    A. have not expressed interest in the activities, aims, and purposes of the organization
    B. do not believe in the good faith of the organization
    C. have not been able to give full cooperation to the organization
    D. do not recommend improvements in the practices and policies of the organization

25. According to the above passage, in order for an organization to have good personnel relations, it is NOT essential that
    A. employees have confidence in the organization
    B. the purposes of the organization be understood by the employees
    C. employees have a desire for information about the organization
    D. information about the organization be communicated to employees

KEY (CORRECT ANSWERS)

1.	D	11.	D
2.	C	12.	A
3.	D	13.	A
4.	B	14.	C
5.	A	15.	D
6.	A	16.	A
7.	C	17.	D
8.	C	18.	B
9.	A	19.	C
10.	B	20.	D

21. D
22. D
23. A
24. B
25. C

TEST 2

DIRECTIONS: Each question or incomplete statement is followed by several suggested answers or completions. Select the one that BEST answers the question or completes the statement. *PRINT THE LETTER OF THE CORRECT ANSWER IN THE SPACE AT THE RIGHT.*

Questions 1-8.

DIRECTIONS: Questions 1 through 8 are to be answered SOLELY on the basis of the following passage.

    Important figures in education and in public affairs have recommended development of a private organization sponsored in part by various private foundations which would offer installment payment plans to full-time matriculated students in accredited colleges and universities in the United States and Canada. Contracts would be drawn to cover either tuition and fees, or tuition, fees, room and board in college facilities, from one year up to and including six years. A special charge, which would vary with the length of the contract, would be added to the gross repayable amount. This would be in addition to interest at a rate which would vary with the income of the parents. There would be a 3% annual interest charge for families with total income, before income taxes, of $50,000 or less. The rate would increase by 1/10 of 1% for every $1,000 of additional net income in excess of $50,000 up to a maximum of 10% interest. Contracts would carry an insurance provision on the life of the parent or guardian who signs the contract; all contracts must have the signature of a parent or guardian. Payment would be scheduled in equal monthly installments.

1. Which of the following students would be eligible for the payment plan described in the above passage? A
    A. matriculated student taking six semester hours toward a graduate degree
    B. matriculated student taking seventeen semester hours toward an undergraduate degree
    C. graduate matriculated at the University of Mexico taking eighteen semester hours toward a graduate degree
    D. student taking eighteen semester hours in a special pre-matriculation program

1.____

2. According to the above passage, the organization described would be sponsored in part by
    A. private foundations
    B. colleges and universities
    C. persons in the field of education
    D. persons in public life

2.____

3. Which of the following expenses could NOT be covered by a contract with the organization described in the above passage?
    A. Tuition amounting to $20,000 per year
    B. Registration and laboratory fees
    C. Meals at restaurants near the college
    D. Rent for an apartment in a college dormitory

3.____

4. The total amount to be paid would include ONLY the
   A. principal
   B. principal and interest
   C. principal, interest, and special charge
   D. principal, interest, special charge, and fee

5. The contract would carry insurance on the
   A. life of the student
   B. life of the student's parents
   C. income of the parents of the student
   D. life of the parent who signed the contract

6. The interest rate for an annual loan of $25,000 from the organization described in the above passage for a student whose family's net income was $55,000 should be
   A. 3%   B. 3.5%   C. 4%   D. 4.5%

7. The interest rate for an annual loan of $35,000 from the organization described in the above passage for a student whose family's net income was $100,000 should be
   A. 5%   B. 8%   C. 9%   D. 10%

8. John Lee has submitted an application for the installment payment plan described in the above passage. John's mother and father have a store which grossed $500,000 last year, but the income which the family received from the store was $90,000 before taxes. They also had $5,000 income from stock dividends. They paid $10,000 in income taxes.
   The amount of income upon which the interest should be based is
   A. $85,000   B. $90,000   C. $95,000   D. $105,000

Questions 9-13.

DIRECTIONS: Questions 9 through 13 are to be answered SOLELY on the basis of the following passage.

Since the organization chart is pictorial in nature, there is a tendency for it to be drawn in an artistically balanced and appealing fashion, regardless of the realities of actual organizational structure. In addition to being subject to this distortion, there is the difficulty of communicating in any organization chart the relative importance or the relative size of various component parts of an organizational structure. Furthermore, because of the need for simplicity of design, an organization chart can never indicate the full extent of the interrelationships among the component parts of an organization.

These interrelationships are often just as vital as the specifications which an organization chart endeavors to indicate. Yet, if an organization chart were to be drawn with all the wide variety of criss-crossing communication and cooperation networks existent within a typical organization, the chart would probably be much more confusing than informative. It is also obvious that no organization chart as such can prove or disprove that the organizational structure it represents is effective in realizing the objectives of the organization. At best, an organization chart can only illustrate some of the various factors to be taken into consideration in understanding, devising, or altering organizational arrangements.

9. According to the above passage, an organization chart can be expected to portray the
    A. structure of the organization along somewhat ideal lines
    B. relative size of the organizational units quite accurately
    C. channels of information distribution within the organization graphically
    D. extent of the obligation of each unit to meet the organizational objectives

9.____

10. According to the above passage, those aspects of internal functioning which are NOT shown on an organization chart
    A. can be considered to have little practical application in the operations of the organization
    B. might well be considered to be as important as the structural relationships which a chart does present
    C. could be the cause of considerable confusion in the operations of an organization which is quite large
    D. would be most likely to provide the information needed to determine the overall effectiveness of an organization

10.____

11. In the above passage, the one of the following conditions which is NOT implied as being a defect of an organization chart is that an organization chart may
    A. present a picture of the organizational structure which is different from the structure that actually exists
    B. fail to indicate the comparative size of various organizational units
    C. be limited in its ability to convey some of the meaningful aspects of organizational relationships
    D. become less useful over a period of time during which the organizational facts which it illustrated have changed

11.____

12. The one of the following which is the MOST suitable title for the above passage is
    A. The Design and Construction of an Organization Chart
    B. The Informal Aspects of an Organization Chart
    C. The Inherent Deficiencies of an Organization Chart
    D. The Utilization of a Typical Organization Chart

12.____

13. It can be inferred from the above passage that the function of an organization chart is to
    A. contribute to the comprehension of the organization form and arrangements
    B. establish the capabilities of the organization to operate effectively
    C. provide a balanced picture of the operations of the organization
    D. eliminate the need for complexity in the organization's structure

13.____

Questions 14-16.

DIRECTIONS: Questions 14 through 16 are to be answered SOLELY on the basis of the following passage.

In dealing with visitors to the school office, the school secretary must use initiative, tact, and good judgment. All visitors should be greeted promptly and courteously. The nature of their business should be determined quickly and handled expeditiously. Frequently, the secretary should be able to handle requests, deliveries, or passes herself. Her judgment should determine when a visitor should see members of the staff or the principal. Serious problems or doubtful cases should be referred to a supervisor.

14. In general, visitors should be handled by the 14.____
 A. school secretary
 B. principal
 C. appropriate supervisor
 D. person who is free

15. It is wise to obtain the following information from visitors: 15.____
 A. Name
 B. Nature of business
 C. Address
 D. Problems they have

16. All visitors who wish to see members of the staff should 16.____
 A. be permitted to do so
 B. produce identification
 C. do so for valid reasons only
 D. be processed by a supervisor

Questions 17-19.

DIRECTIONS: Questions 17 through 19 are to be answered SOLELY on the basis of the following passage.

Information regarding payroll status, salary differentials, promotional salary increments, deductions, and pension payments should be given to all members of the staff who have questions regarding these items. On occasion, if the secretary is uncertain regarding the information, the staff member should be referred to the principal or the appropriate agency. No question by a staff member regarding payroll status should be brushed aside as immaterial or irrelevant. The school secretary must always try to handle the question or pass it on to the person who can handle it.

17. If a teacher is dissatisfied with information regarding her salary status, as given 17.____
 by the school secretary, the matter should be
 A. dropped
 B. passed on to the principal
 C. passed on by the secretary to proper agency or the principal
 D. made a basis for grievance procedures

18. The following is an adequate summary of the above passage: 18.____
 A. The secretary must handle all payroll matters
 B. The secretary must handle all payroll matter or know who can handle them
 C. The secretary or the principal must handle all payroll matters
 D. Payroll matter too difficult to handle must be followed up until they are solved

19. The above passage implies that
    A. many teachers ask immaterial questions regarding payroll status
    B. few teachers ask irrelevant pension questions
    C. no teachers ask immaterial salary questions
    D. no question regarding salary should be considered irrelevant

Questions 20-22.

DIRECTIONS: Questions 20 through 22 are to be answered SOLELY on the basis of the following passage.

The necessity for good speech on the part of the school secretary cannot be overstated. The school secretary must deal with the general public, the pupils, the members of the staff, and the school supervisors. In every situation which involves the general public, the secretary serves as a representative of the school. In dealing with pupils, the secretary's speech must serve as a model from which students may guide themselves. Slang, colloquialisms, malapropisms, and local dialects must be avoided.

20. The above passage implies that the speech pattern of the secretary must be
    A. perfect
    B. very good
    C. average
    D. on a level with that of the pupils

21. The last sentence indicates that slang
    A. is acceptable
    B. occurs in all speech
    C. might be used occasionally
    D. should be shunned

22. The above passage implies that the speech of pupils
    A. may be influenced
    B. does not change readily
    C. is generally good
    D. is generally poor

Questions 23-25.

DIRECTIONS: Questions 23 through 25 are to be answered SOLELY on the basis of the following passage.

The school secretary who is engaged in the task of filing records and correspondence should follow a general set of rules. Items which are filed should be available to other secretaries or to supervisors quickly and easily by means of the application of a modicum of common sense and good judgment. Items which, by their nature, may be difficult to find should be cross-indexed. Folders and drawers should be neatly and accurately labeled. There should never be a large accumulation of papers which have not been filed.

23. A good general rule to follow in filing is that materials should be
    A. placed in folders quickly
    B. neatly stored
    C. readily available
    D. cross-indexed

24. Items that are filed should be available to
    A. the secretary charged with the task of filing
    B. secretaries and supervisors
    C. school personnel
    D. the principal

25. A modicum of common sense means _____ common sense.
    A. an average amount of
    B. a great deal of
    C. a little
    D. no

KEY (CORRECT ANSWERS)

1.	B		11.	D
2.	A		12.	C
3.	C		13.	A
4.	C		14.	A
5.	D		15.	B
6.	B		16.	C
7.	B		17.	C
8.	C		18.	B
9.	A		19.	D
10.	B		20.	B

21. D
22. A
23. C
24. B
25. C

TEST 3

DIRECTIONS: Each question or incomplete statement is followed by several suggested answers or completions. Select the one that BEST answers the question or completes the statement. *PRINT THE LETTER OF THE CORRECT ANSWER IN THE SPACE AT THE RIGHT.*

Questions 1-4.

DIRECTIONS: Questions 1 through 4 are to be answered SOLELY on the basis of the following passage.

The proposition that administrative activity is essentially the same in all organizations appears to underlie some of the practices in the administration of private higher education. Although the practice is unusual in public education, there are numerous instances of industrial, governmental, or military administrators being assigned to private institutions of higher education and, to a lesser extent, of college and university presidents assuming administrative positions in other types of organizations. To test this theory that administrators are interchangeable, there is a need for systematic observation and classification. The myth that an educational administrator must first have experience in the teaching profession is firmly rooted in a long tradition that has historical prestige. The myth is bound up in the expectations of the public and personnel surrounding the administrator. Since administrative success depends significantly on how well an administrator meets the expectations others have of him, the myth may be more powerful than the special experience in helping the administrator attain organizational and educational objectives. Educational administrators who have risen through the teaching profession have often expressed nostalgia for the life of a teacher or scholar, but there is no evidence that this nostalgia contributes to administrative success.

1. Which of the following statements as completed is MOST consistent with the above passage?
   The greatest number of administrators has moved from
   A. industry and the military to government and universities
   B. government and universities to industry and the military
   C. government, the armed forces, and industry to colleges and universities
   D. colleges and universities to government, the armed forces, and industry

1.____

2. Of the following, the MOST reasonable inference from the above passage is that a specific area requiring further research is the
   A. place of myth in the tradition and history of the educational profession
   B. relative effectiveness of educational administrators from inside and outside the teaching profession
   C. performance of administrators in the administration of public colleges
   D. degree of reality behind the nostalgia for scholarly pursuits often expressed by educational administrators

2.____

3. According to the above passage, the value to an educational administrator of experience in the teaching profession
   A. lies in the first-hand knowledge he has acquired of immediate educational problems
   B. may lie in the belief of his colleagues, subordinates, and the public that such experience is necessary
   C. has been supported by evidence that the experience contributes to administrative success in educational fields
   D. would be greater if the administrator were able to free himself from nostalgia for his former duties

4. Of the following, the MOST suitable title for the above passage is
   A. Educational Administration, Its Problems
   B. The Experience Needed For Educational Administration
   C. Administration in Higher Education
   D. Evaluating Administrative Experience

Questions 5-6.

DIRECTIONS: Questions 5 and 6 are to be answered SOLELY on the basis of the following passage.

Management by objectives (MBO) may be defined as the process by which the superior and the subordinate managers of an organization jointly define its common goals, define each individual's major areas of responsibility in terms of the results expected of him and use these measure as guides for operating the unit and assessing the contribution of each of its members.

The MBO approach requires that after organizational goals are established and communicated, targets must be set for each individual position which are congruent with organizational goals. Periodic performance reviews and a final review using the objectives set as criteria are also basic to this approach.

Recent studies have shown that MBO programs are influenced by attitudes and perceptions of the boss, the company, the reward-punishment system, and the program itself. In addition, the manner in which the MBO program is carried out can influence the success of the program. A study done in the late sixties indicates that the best results are obtained when the manager sets goals which deal with significant problem areas in the organizational unit, or with the subordinate's personal deficiencies. These goals must be clear with regard to what is expected of the subordinate. The frequency of feedback is also important in the success of a management-by-objectives program. Generally, the greater the amount of feedback, the more successful the MBO program.

5. According to the above passage, the expected output for individual employees should be determined
   A. after a number of reviews of work performance
   B. after common organizational goals are defined
   C. before common organizational goals are defined
   D. on the basis of an employee's personal qualities

6. According to the above passage, the management-by-objectives approach requires
   A. less feedback than other types of management programs
   B. little review of on-the-job performance after the initial setting of goals
   C. general conformance between individual goals and organizational goals
   D. the setting of goals which deal with minor problem areas in the organization

Questions 7-10.

DIRECTIONS: Questions 7 through 10 are to be answered SOLELY on the basis of the following passage.

Management, which is the function of executive leadership, has as its principal phases the planning, organizing, and controlling of the activities of subordinate groups in the accomplishment of organizational objectives. Planning specifies the kind and extent of the factors, forces, and effects, and the relationships among them, that will be required for satisfactory accomplishment. The nature of the objectives and their requirements must be known before determinations can be made as to what must be done, how it must be done and why, where actions should take place, who should be responsible, and similar programs pertaining to the formulation of a plan. Organizing, which creates the conditions that must be present before the execution of the plan can be undertaken successfully, cannot be done intelligently without knowledge of the organizational objectives. Control, which has to do with the constraint and regulation of activities entering into the execution of the plan, must be exercised in accordance with the characteristics and requirements of the activities demanded by the plan.

7. The one of the following which is the MOST suitable title for the above passage is
   A. The Nature of Successful Organization
   B. The Planning of Management Functions
   C. The Importance of Organizational Functions
   D. The Principle Aspects of Management

8. It can be inferred from the above passage that the one of the following functions whose existence is essential to the existence of the other three is the
   A. regulation of the work needed to carry out a plan
   B. understanding of what the organization intends to accomplish
   C. securing of information of the factors necessary for accomplishment of objectives
   D. establishment of the conditions required for successful action

9. The one of the following which would NOT be included within any of the principal phases of the function of executive leadership as defined in the above passage is
   A. determination of manpower requirements
   B. procurement of required material
   C. establishment of organizational objectives
   D. scheduling of production

10. The conclusion which can MOST reasonably be drawn from the above passage is that the control phase of managing is most directly concerned with the
    A. influencing of policy determinations
    B. administering of suggestion systems
    C. acquisition of staff for the organization
    D. implementation of performance standards

10.____

Questions 11-12.

DIRECTIONS: Questions 11 and 12 are to be answered SOLELY on the basis of the following passage.

Under an open-and-above-board policy, it is to be expected that some supervisors will gloss over known shortcomings of subordinates rather than face the task of discussing team face-to-face. It is also to be expected that at least some employees whose job performance is below par will reject the supervisor's appraisal as biased and unfair. Be that as it may, these are inescapable aspects of any performance appraisal system in which human beings are involved. The supervisor who shies away from calling a spade a spade, as well as the employee with a chip on his shoulder, will each in his own way eventually be revealed in his true light—to the benefit of the organization as a whole.

11. The BEST of the following interpretations of the above passage is that
    A. the method of rating employee performance requires immediate revision to improve employee acceptance
    B. substandard performance ratings should be discussed with employees even if satisfactory ratings are not
    C. supervisors run the risk of being called unfair by the subordinates even though their appraisals are accurate
    D. any system of employee performance rating is satisfactory if used properly

11.____

12. The BEST of the following interpretations of the above passage is that
    A. supervisors generally are not open-and-above-board with their subordinates
    B. it is necessary for supervisors to tell employees objectively how they are performing
    C. employees complain when their supervisor does not keep them informed
    D. supervisors are afraid to tell subordinates their weaknesses

12.____

Questions 13-15.

DIRECTIONS: Questions 13 through 15 are to be answered SOLELY on the basis of the following passage.

During the last decade, a great deal of interest has been generated around the phenomenon of *organizational development,* or the process of developing human resources through conscious organization effort. Organizational development (OD) stresses improving interpersonal relationships and organizational skills, such as communication, to a much greater degree than individual training ever did. The kind of training that an organization should emphasize depends upon the present and future structure of the organization. If future organizations are to be unstable, shifting coalitions, then individual skills and abilities, particularly those emphasizing innovativeness, creativity, flexibility, and the latest technological knowledge, are crucial and individual training is most appropriate.

But if there is to be little change in organizational structure, then the main thrust of training should be group-oriented or organizational development. This approach seems better designed for overcoming hierarchical barriers, for developing a degree of interpersonal relationships which make communication along the chain of command possible, and for retaining a modicum of innovation and/or flexibility.

13. According to the above passage, group-oriented training is MOST useful in in
    A. developing a communications system that will facilitate understanding through the chain of command
    B. highly flexible and mobile organizations
    C. preventing the crossing of hierarchical barriers within an organization
    D. saving energy otherwise wasted on developing methods of dealing with rigid hierarchies

14. The one of the following conclusions which can be drawn MOST appropriately from the above passage is that
    A. behavioral research supports the use of organizational development training methods rather than individualized training
    B. it is easier to provide individualized training in specific skills than to set up sensitivity training programs
    C. organizational development eliminates innovative or flexible activity
    D. the nature of an organization greatly influences which training methods will be most effective

15. According to the above passage, the one of the following which is LEAST important for large-scale organizations geared to rapid and abrupt change is
    A. current technological information
    B. development of a high degree of interpersonal relationships
    C. development of individual skills and abilities
    D. emphasis on creativity

Questions 16-18.

DIRECTIONS: Questions 16 through 18 are to be answered SOLELY on the basis of the following passage.

The increase in the extent to which each individual is personally responsible to others is most noticeable in a large bureaucracy. No one person *decides* anything; each decision of any importance, is the product of an intricate process of brokerage involving individuals inside and outside the organization who feel some reason to be affected by the decision, or two have special knowledge to contribute to it. The more varied the organization's constituency, the more inside *veto-groups* will need to be taken into account. But even if no outside consultations were involved, sheer size would produce a complex process of decision. For a large organization is a deliberately created system of tensions into which each individual is expected to bring workways, viewpoints, and outside relationships markedly different from those of his colleagues. It is the administrator's task to draw from these disparate forces the elements of wise action from day to day, consistent with the purposes of the organization as a whole.

16. The above passage is essentially a description of decision-making as 16.____
    A. an organization process
    B. the key responsibility of the administrator
    C. the one best position among many
    D. a complex of individual decisions

17. Which one of the following statements BEST describes the responsibilities of 17.____
    an administrator?
    A. He modifies decisions and goals in accordance with pressures from within and outside the organization.
    B. He creates problem-solving mechanisms that rely on the varied interests of his staff and *veto-groups*.
    C. He makes determinations that will lead to attainment of his agency's objectives.
    D. He obtains agreement among varying viewpoints and interests

18. In the context of the operations of a central public personnel agency, a 18.____
    veto-group would LEAST likely consist of
    A. employee organizations
    B. professional personnel societies
    C. using agencies
    D. civil service newspapers

Questions 19-25.

DIRECTIONS: Questions 19 through 25 are to be answered SOLELY on the basis of the following passage, which is an extract from a report prepared for Department X, which outlines the procedure to be followed in the case of transfers of employees.

Every transfer, regardless of the reason therefore, requires completion of the record of transfer, Form DT411. To denote consent to the transfer, DT411 should contain the signatures of the transferee and the personnel officer(s) concerned, except that, in the case of an involuntary transfer, the signatures of the transferee's present and prospective supervisors shall be entered in Boxes 8A and 8B, respectively, since the transferee does not consent. Only a permanent employee may request a transfer; in such cases, the employee's attendance record shall be duly considered with regard to absences, latenesses, and accrued overtime balances. In the case of an inter-district transfer, the employee's attendance record must be included in Section 8A of the transfer request, Form DT410, by the personnel officer of the district from which the transfer is requested. The personnel officer of the district to which the employee requested transfer may refuse to accept accrued overtime balances in excess of ten days.

An employee on probation shall be eligible for transfer. If such employee is involuntarily transferred, he shall be credited for the period of time already served on probation. However, if such transfer is voluntary, the employee shall be required to serve the entire period of his probation in the new position. An employee who has occurred a disability which prevents him from performing his normal duties may be transferred during the period of such disability to other appropriate duties. A disability transfer requires the completion of either DT414 if the disability is job-connected, or Form DT415 if it is not a job-connected disability. In either case, the personnel officer of the district from which the transfer is made signs in Box 6A of the first two copies and the personnel officer of the district to which the transfer is made signs in Box 6B of the last two copies, or, in the case of an intra-district disability transfer, the personnel officer must sign in Box 6A of the first two copies and Box 6B of the last two copies.

19. When a personnel officer consents to an employee's request for transfer from his district, this procedure requires that the personnel officer sign Forms
    A. DT411
    B. DT410 and DT411
    C. DT411 and either Form DT414 or DT415
    D. DT410 and DT411, and either Form DT414 or DT415

20. With respect to the time record of an employee transferred against his wishes during his probationary period, this procedure requires that
    A. he serve the entire period of his probation in his present office
    B. he lose his accrued overtime balance
    C. his attendance record be considered with regard to absences and latenesses
    D. he be given credit for the period of time he has already served on probation

21. Assume you are a supervisor and an employee must be transferred into your office against his wishes.
    According to this procedure, the box you must sign on the record of transfer is
    A. 6A   B. 8A   C. 6B   D. 8B

22. Under this procedure, in the case of a disability transfer, when must Box 6A on Forms DT414 and DT415 be signed by the personnel officer of the district to which the transfer is being made?
    A. In all cases when either Form DT414 or Form DT415 is used
    B. In all cases when Form DT414 is used and only under certain circumstances when Form DT415 is used
    C. In all cases when Form DT415 is used and only under certain circumstances when Form DT414 is used
    D. Only under certain circumstances when either Form DT414 or Form DT415 is used

23. From the above passage, it may be inferred MOST correctly that the number of copies of Form DT414 is
    A. no more than 2
    B. at least 3
    C. at least 5
    D. more than the number of copies of Form DT415

23._____

24. A change in punctuation and capitalization only which would change one sentence into two and possibly contribute to somewhat greater ease of reading this report extract would be MOST appropriate in the
    A. 2nd sentence, 1st paragraph
    B. 3rd sentence, 1st paragraph
    C. next to the last sentence, 2nd paragraph
    D. 2nd sentence, 2nd paragraph

24._____

25. In the second paragraph, a word that is INCORRECTLY used is
    A. *shall* in the 1st sentence
    B. *voluntary* in the 3rd sentence
    C. *occurred* in the 4th sentence
    D. *intra-district* in the last sentence

25._____

KEY (CORRECT ANSWERS)

1.	C	11.	C
2.	B	12.	B
3.	B	13.	A
4.	B	14.	D
5.	B	15.	B
6.	C	16.	A
7.	D	17.	C
8.	B	18.	B
9.	C	19.	A
10.	D	20.	D

21. D
22. D
23. B
24. B
25. C

INTERPRETING STATISTICAL DATA GRAPHS, CHARTS, AND TABLES

EXAMINATION SECTION

TEST 1

DIRECTIONS: Each question or incomplete statement is followed by several suggested answers or completions. Select the one that BEST answers the question or completes the statement. *PRINT THE LETTER OF THE CORRECT ANSWER IN THE SPACE AT THE RIGHT.*

Questions 1-5.

DIRECTIONS: Questions 1 through 5 are to be answered SOLELY on the basis of the following table.

ANNUAL SALARIES PAID TO SELECTED CLERICAL TITLES IN FIVE MAJOR CITIES IN 2017 AND 2019					
2019					
	Clerk	Typist	Steno	Legal Steno	Computer Operator
Newton	$33,900	$34,800	$36,300	$43,800	$35,400
Barton	$32,400	$34,200	$35,400	$43,500	$24,200
Phelton	$32,400	$32,400	$34,200	$42,000	$33,000
Washburn	$33,600	$34,800	$35,400	$43,800	$34,800
Biltmore	$33,000	$34,200	$35,100	$43,500	$34,500
2017					
Newton	$31,800	$33,600	$35,400	$41,400	$34,500
Barton	$30,000	$31,500	$33,000	$39,600	$31,500
Phelton	$29,400	$30,600	$31,800	$37,800	$31,200
Washburn	$30,600	$32,400	$33,600	$40,200	$32,400
Biltmore	$30,000	$31,800	$33,00	$39,600	$32,100

1. Assume that the value of the fringe benefits offered to clerical employees in 2019 amounted to 14% of their annual salaries in Newton, 17% in Barton, 18% in Phelton, 15% in Washburn, and 16% in Biltmore.
   The total cost of employing a computer operator for 2019 was GREATEST in
   A. Newton   B. Barton   C. Phelton   D. Washburn

   1._____

2. During negotiations for their 2020 contract, the stenographers of Biltmore are demanding that their rate of pay be fixed at 85% of the legal stenographer salary.
   If this demand is granted and if the legal stenographer salary increases by 7% in 2020, the 2020 stenographer salary will be MOST NEARLY
   A. $36,972   B. $37,560   C. $39,564   D. $40,020

   2._____

3. Of the following, the GREATEST percentage increase in salary from 2017 to 2019 was gained by
   A. clerks in Newton
   B. stenographers in Barton
   C. legal stenographers in Washburn
   D. computer operators in Biltmore

   3.____

4. The title which achieved the SMALLEST average percentage increase in salary from 2017 to 2019 was
   A. clerk
   B. typist
   C. stenographer
   D. legal stenographer

   4.____

5. Assume that, in 2019, clerks accounted for 60% of the clerical work force in Barton. The clerical work force consists of 140 employees. In 2017, the clerks accounted for 65% of the clerical work force in Barton. The clerical work force then consisted of 120 employees.
   The difference between the 2017 and 2019 payroll for clerks in Barton is MOST NEARLY
   A. $120,000   B. $240,000   C. $360,000   D. $480,000

   5.____

KEY (CORRECT ANSWERS)

1. A
2. C
3. C
4. C
5. C

TEST 2

DIRECTIONS: Each question or incomplete statement is followed by several suggested answers or completions. Select the one that BEST answers the question or completes the statement. *PRINT THE LETTER OF THE CORRECT ANSWER IN THE SPACE AT THE RIGHT.*

Questions 1-9.

DIRECTIONS: Questions 1 through 9 are to be answered SOLELY on the basis of the facts given in the following table, which contains certain information about employees in a city bureau.

| RECORD OF EMPLOYEES IN A CITY BUREAU ||||||
NAME	TITLE	AGE	ANNUAL SALARY	YEARS OF SERVICE	EXAMINATION RATING
Jones	Clerk	34	$40,800	10	82
Smith	Stenographer	25	$38,400	2	72
Black	Typist	19	$28,800	1	71
Brown	Stenographer	36	$50,400	12	88
Thomas	Accountant	49	$82,400	21	91
Gordon	Clerk	31	$60,000	8	81
Johnson	Stenographer	26	$52,800	5	75
White	Accountant	53	$72,000	30	90
Spencer	Clerk	42	$55,200	19	85
Taylor	Typist	24	$43,200	5	74
Simpson	Accountant	37	$100,000	1	87
Reid	Typist	20	$24,000	2	72
Fulton	Accountant	55	$110,000	31	100
Chambers	Clerk	22	$31,200	4	75
Calhoun	Stenographer	48	$57,600	16	80

1. The name of the employee whose salary would be the middle one if all the salaries were ranked in order of magnitude is
   A. White B. Johnson C. Brown D. Spencer

2. The combined monthly salary of all the stenographers EXCEEDS the combined monthly salary of all the clerks by
   A. $12,000 B. $1,000 C. $45,600 D. $1,200

3. The age of the employee who received the HIGHEST rating in the examination among those who have less than 10 years of service is _____ years.
   A. 22 B. 31 C. 55 D. 34

4. The average examination rating of those employees who had 15 years of service or more as compared with the average examination rating of those employees who had 5 years of service or less is MOST NEARLY _____ points _____.
   A. 16; greater   B. 7; greater   C. 10; less   D. 25; greater

5. The name of the youngest employee whose monthly salary is more than $2,000 per month and who has more than one year of service is
   A. Reid   B. Black   C. Chambers   D. Taylor

6. The name of the employee who received an examination rating of over 85%, who has more than 15 years of service, and who earns a yearly salary of more than $50,000 but less than $80,000 is
   A. Thomas   B. Spencer   C. Calhoun   D. White

7. The annual salary of the HIGHEST paid stenographer is
   A. more than twice as great as the salary of the youngest employee
   B. greater than the salary of the oldest typist but not as great as the salary of the oldest clerk
   C. greater than the salary of the highest paid typist but not as great as the salary of the lowest paid accountant
   D. less than the combined salaries of the two youngest typists

8. The number of employees whose annual salary is more than $31,200 but less than $57,600 and who have at least 5 years of service is
   A. 11   B. 8   C. 6   D. 5

9. Of the following, it would be MOST accurate to state that the
   A. youngest employee is lowest with respect to number of years of service, examination rating, and salary
   B. oldest employee is highest with respect to number of years of service, examination rating, but not with respect to salary
   C. annual salary of the youngest clerk is $2,400 more than the annual salary of the youngest typist and $4,800 less than the annual salary of the youngest stenographer
   D. difference in age between the youngest and oldest typist is less than one-fourth the difference in age between the youngest and oldest stenographer

KEY (CORRECT ANSWERS)

1. B
2. B
3. B
4. A
5. C
6. D
7. C
8. D
9. D

TEST 3

DIRECTIONS: Each question or incomplete statement is followed by several suggested answers or completions. Select the one that BEST answers the question or completes the statement. *PRINT THE LETTER OF THE CORRECT ANSWER IN THE SPACE AT THE RIGHT.*

Questions 1-10.

DIRECTIONS: Questions 1 through 10 are to be answered SOLELY on the basis of the Personnel Record of Division X shown below.

DIVISION X PERSONNEL RECORD – CURRENT YEAR					
				No. of Days Absent	
Employee	Bureau in Which Employed	Title	Annual Salary	On Vacation	On Sick Leave	No. of Times Late
Abbot	Mail	Clerk	$31,200	18	0	1
Barnes	Mail	Clerk	$25,200	25	3	7
Davis	Mail	Typist	$24,000	21	9	2
Adams	Payroll	Accountant	$42,500	10	0	2
Bell	Payroll	Bookkeeper	$31,200	23	2	5
Duke	Payroll	Clerk	$27,600	24	4	3
Gross	Payroll	Clerk	$21,600	12	5	7
Lane	Payroll	Stenographer	$26,400	19	16	20
Reed	Payroll	Typist	$22,800	15	11	11
Arnold	Record	Clerk	$32,400	6	15	9
Cane	Record	Clerk	$24,500	14	3	4
Fay	Record	Clerk	$21,100	20	0	4
Hale	Record	Typist	$25,200	18	2	7
Baker	Supply	Clerk	$30,000	20	3	2
Clark	Supply	Clerk	$27,600	25	6	5
Ford	Supply	Typist	$22,800	25	4	22

1. The percentage of the total number of employees who are clerks is MOST NEARLY
   A. 25%   B. 33%   C. 38%   D. 56%

2. Of the following employees, the one who receives a monthly salary of $2,100 is
   A. Barnes   B. Gross   C. Reed   D. Clark

3. The difference between the annual salary of the highest paid clerk and that of the lowest paid clerk is
   A. $6,000   B. $8,400   C. $11,300   D. $20,900

4. The number of employees receiving more than $25,000 a year but less than $40,000 a year is
   A. 6   B. 9   C. 12   D. 15

4._____

5. The TOTAL annual salary of the employees of the Mail Bureau is _____ the total annual salary of the employees of the _____.
   A. one-half of; Payroll Bureau
   B. less than; Record Bureau by $21,600
   C. equal to; Supply Bureau
   D. less than; Payroll Bureau by $71,600

5._____

6. The average annual salary of the employees who are not clerks is MOST NEARLY
   A. $23,700   B. $25,450   C. $26,800   D. $27,850

6._____

7. If all the employees were given a 10% increase in pay, the annual salary of Lane would then be
   A. *greater* than that of Barnes by $1,320
   B. *less* than that of Bell by $4,280
   C. *equal to* that of Clark
   D. *greater* than that of Ford by $3,600

7._____

8. Of the clerks who earned less than $30,000 a year, the one who was late the FEWEST number of times was late _____ time(s).
   A. 1   B. 2   C. 3   D. 4

8._____

9. The bureau in which the employees were late the FEWEST number of times on an average is the _____ Bureau.
   A. Mail   B. Payroll   C. Record   D. Supply

9._____

10. The MOST accurate of the following statements is that
    A. Reed was late more often than any other typist
    B. Bell took more time off for vacation than any other employee earning $30,000 or more annually
    C. of the typists, Ford was the one who was absent the fewest number of times because of sickness
    D. three clerks took no time off because of sickness

10._____

KEY (CORRECT ANSWERS)

1. D
2. A
3. C
4. B
5. C

6. D
7. A
8. C
9. A
10. B

TEST 4

DIRECTIONS: Each question or incomplete statement is followed by several suggested answers or completions. Select the one that BEST answers the question or completes the statement. *PRINT THE LETTER OF THE CORRECT ANSWER IN THE SPACE AT THE RIGHT.*

Questions 1-10.

DIRECTIONS: Questions 1 through 10 are to be answered SOLELY on the basis of the Weekly Payroll Record shown below of Bureau X in a public agency. In answering these questions, note that gross weekly salary is the salary before deductions have been made; take-home pay is the amount remaining after all indicated weekly deductions have been made from the gross weekly salary. In answering questions involving annual amounts, compute on the basis of 52 weeks per year.

			BUREAU X WEEKLY PAYROLL PERIOD			
				Weekly Deductions From Gross Salary		
Unit in Which Employed	Employee	Title	Gross Weekly Salary (Before Deductions)	Medical Insurance	Income Tax	Pension System
Accounting	Allen	Accountant	$950	$14.50	$125.00	$53.20
Accounting	Barth	Bookkeeper	$720	$19.00	$62.00	$40.70
Accounting	Keller	Clerk	$580	$6.50	$82.00	$33.10
Accounting	Peters	Typist	$560	$6.50	$79.00	$35.30
Accounting	Simons	Stenographer	$610	$14.50	$64.00	$37.80
Information	Brown	Clerk	$560	$13.00	$56.00	$42.20
Information	Smith	Clerk	$590	$14.50	$61.00	$58.40
Information	Turner	Typist	$580	$13.00	$59.00	$62.60
Information	Williams	Stenographer	$620	$19.00	$44.00	$69.40
Mail	Conner	Clerk	$660	$13.00	$74.00	$55.40
Mail	Farrell	Typist	$540	$6.50	$75.00	$34.00
Mail	Johnson	Stenographer	$580	$19.00	$36.00	$37.10
Records	Dillon	Clerk	$640	$6.50	$94.00	$58.20
Records	Martin	Clerk	$540	$19.00	$29.00	$50.20
Records	Standish	Typist	$620	$14.50	$67.00	$60.10
Records	Wilson	Stenographer	$690	$6.50	$101.00	$75.60

1. Dillon's annual take-home pay is MOST NEARLY
   A. $25,000   B. $27,000   C. $31,000   D. $33,000

2. The difference between Turner's gross annual salary and his annual take-home pay is MOST NEARLY
   A. $3,000   B. $5,000   C. $7,000   D. $9,000

3. Of the following, the employee whose weekly take-home pay is CLOSEST to that of Keller's is
   A. Peters   B. Brown   C. Smith   D. Turner

4. The average gross annual salary of the typists is
   A. less than $27,500
   B. more than $27,500 but less than $30,000
   C. more than $30,000 but less than $32,500
   D. more than $32,500

5. The average gross weekly salary of the stenographers EXCEEDS the gross weekly salary of the clerk by
   A. $20   B. $30   C. $40   D. $50

6. Of the following employees in Accounting Unit, the one who pays the HIGHEST percentage of his gross weekly salary for the Pension System is
   A. Barth   B. Keller   C. Peters   D. Simons

7. For all of the Accounting Unit employees, the total annual deductions for Medical Insurance are less than the total annual deductions for the Pension System by MOST NEARLY
   A. $6,000   B. $7,000   C. $8,000   D. $9,000

8. Of the following, the employee whose total weekly deductions are MOST NEARLY 27% of his gross weekly salary is
   A. Barth   B. Brown   C. Martin   D. Wilson

9. The total amount of the gross weekly salaries of all the employees in the Records Unit is MOST NEARLY
   A. 95% of the total amount of the gross weekly salaries of all the employees in the Information Unit
   B. 10% greater than the total amount of the gross weekly salaries of all the employees in the Mail Unit
   C. 75% of the total amount of the gross weekly salaries of all the employees in the Accounting Unit
   D. four times as great as the total amount deducted weekly for tax for all the employees in the Records Unit

10. For the employees in the Information Unit, the AVERAGE weekly deductions for Income Tax _____ the average weekly deduction for _____.
    A. exceeds; Income Tax for the employees in the Records Unit
    B. is less than; the Pension System for the employees in the Mail Unit
    C. exceeds; Income Tax for the employees in the Accounting Unit
    D. is less than; the Pension System for the employees in the Records Unit

KEY (CORRECT ANSWERS)

1.	A	6.	C
2.	C	7.	B
3.	C	8.	D
4.	B	9.	C
5.	B	10.	D

TEST 5

DIRECTIONS: Each question or incomplete statement is followed by several suggested answers or completions. Select the one that BEST answers the question or completes the statement. *PRINT THE LETTER OF THE CORRECT ANSWER IN THE SPACE AT THE RIGHT.*

Questions 1-9.

DIRECTIONS: Questions 1 through 9 are to be answered SOLELY on the basis of the following information.

Assume that the following rules for computing service ratings are to be used experimentally in determining service ratings of seven permanent city employees. (Note that these rules are hypothetical and are NOT to be confused with the existing method of computing service ratings for city employees). The personnel record of each of these seven employees is given in Table II. You are to determine the answer to each of the questions on the basis of the rules given below for computing service ratings and the data contained in the personnel records of these seven employees.

All computations should be made as of the close of the rating period ending March 31, 2017.

Service Rating
The service rating of each permanent competitive class employee shall be computed by adding the following three scores: (1) a basic score, (2) the employee's seniority score, and (3) the employee's efficiency score.

Seniority Score
An employee's seniority score shall be computed by crediting him with ½% per year for each year of service starting with the date of the employee's entrance as a permanent employee into the competitive class, up to a maximum of 15 years (7½%).
A residual fractional period of eight months or more shall be considered as a full year and credited with ½%. A residual fraction of from four to, but not including, eight months shall be considered as half-year and credited with ¼%. A residual fraction of less than four months shall receive no credit in the seniority score.
For example, a person who entered the competitive class as a permanent employee on August 1, 2014 would, as of March 31, 2017, be credited with a seniority score of 1¼% for his 2 years and 8 months of service.

Efficiency Score
An employee's efficiency score shall be computed by adding the annual efficiency ratings received by him during his service in his present position. (Where there are negative efficiency ratings, such ratings shall be subtracted from the sum of the positive efficiency ratings.) An employee's annual efficiency rating shall be based on the grade he receives from his supervisor for his work performance during the annual efficiency rating period.

Basic Score
A basic score of 70% shall be given to each employee upon permanent appointment to a competitive class position.

An employee shall receive a grade of A for performing work of the highest quality and shall be credited with an efficiency rating of plus (+)3%. An employee shall receive a grade of F for performing work of the lowest quality and shall receive an efficiency rating of minus (-)2%. Table I, entitled BASS FOR DETERMINING ANNUAL EFFICIENCY RATINGS, lists the six grades of work performance with their equivalent annual efficiency ratings. Table I also lists the efficiency ratings to be assigned for service in a position for less than a year during the annual efficiency rating period.

The annual efficiency rating period shall run from April 1 to March 31, inclusive.

TABLE I – BASIS FOR DETERMINING ANNUAL EFFICIENCY RATINGS				
			Annual Efficiency Rating for Service in a Position For	
Quality of Work Performed	Grade Assigned	8 Months to a Full Year	At Least 4 Months But Less Than 8 Months	Less Than 4 Months
Highest	A	+3%	+1½%	0%
Good	B	+2%	+1%	0%
Standard	C	+1%	+ ½%	0%
Substandard	D	0%	0%	0%
Poor	E	-1%	-4%	0%
Lowest	F	-2%	-1%	0%

Appointment or Promotion During an Efficiency Rating Period

An employee who has been appointed or promoted during an efficiency rating period shall receive for that period an efficiency rating only for work performed by him during the portion of the period that he served in the position to which he was appointed or promoted. His efficiency rating for the period shall be determined in accordance with Table I.

Sample Computation of Service Rating

John Smith entered the competitive class as a permanent employee on December 1, 2012 and was promoted to his present position as a Clerk, Grade 3, on November 1, 2015. As a Clerk, Grade 3, he received a grade of B for work performed during the five-month period extending from November 1, 2015 to March 31, 2016 and a grade of C for work performed during the full annual period extending from April 1, 2016 to March 31, 2017.

On the basis of the RULES FOR COMPUTING SERVICE RATINGS, John Smith should be credited with:

70%   Basic Score
2¼%   Seniority Score – for 4 years and 4 months of service (from 12/1/12 to 3/31/17)
2%   Efficiency Score – for 5 months of B service and a full _____ year of C service
74¼%

TABLE II
PERSONNEL RECORD OF SEVEN PERMANENT COMPETITIVE CLASS EMPLOYEES

Employee	Present Position	Date of Appointment or Promotion to Present Position	Date of Entry as Permanent Employment in Competitive Class
Allen	Clerk, Gr. 5	6-1-13	7-1-00
Brown	Clerk, Gr. 4	1-1-15	7-1-17
Cole	Clerk, Gr. 3	9-1-13	11-1-10
Fox	Clerk, Gr. 3	10-1-13	9-1-08
Green	Clerk, Gr. 2	12-1-11	12-1-11
Hunt	Clerk, Gr. 2	7-1-12	7-1-12
Kane	Steno, Gr. 3	11-16-14	3-1-11

GRADES RECEIVED ANNUALLY FOR WORK PERFORMED IN PRESENT POSITION

Employee	4-1-11 to 3-31-12	4-1-12 to 3-31-13	4-1-13 to 3-31-14	4-1-14 to 3-31-15	4-1-15 to 3-31-16	4-1-16 to 3-31-17
Allen			C*	C	B	C
Brown				C*	C	B
Cole			A*	B	C	C
Fox			C*	C	D	C
Green	C*	D	C	D	C	C
Hunt		C*	C	E	C	C
Kane				B*	B	C

EXPLANATORY NOTES
* Served in present position for less than a full year during this rating period. (Note date of appointment, or promotion, to present position.)
All seven employees have served continuously as permanent employees since their entry into the competitive class.

Questions 1 through 9 refer to the employees listed in Table II. You are to answer these questions SOLELY on the basis of the preceding RULES FOR COMPUTING SERVICE RATINGS and on the information concerning these seven employees given in Table II. You are reminded that all computations are to be made as of the close of the rating period ending March 31, 2017. Candidates may find it helpful to arrange their computations on their scratch paper in an orderly manner since the computations for one question may also be utilized in answering another question.

1. The seniority score of Allen is
   A. 7½%   B. 8½%   C. 8%   D. 8¼%

2. The seniority score of Fox EXCEEDS that of Cole by
   A. 1½%   B. 2%   C. 1%   D. ¾%

3. The seniority score of Brown is
    A. *equal* to Hunt's
    B. *twice* Hunt's
    C. *more* than Hunt's by 1½%
    D. *less* than by Hunt's by ½%

4. Green's efficiency score is
    A. *twice* that of Kane
    B. *equal* to that of Kane
    C. *less* than Kane's by ½%
    D. *less* than Kane's by 1%

5. Of the following employees, the one who has the LOWEST efficiency score is
    A. Brown
    B. Fox
    C. Hunt
    D. Kane

6. A comparison of Hunt's efficiency score with his seniority score reveals that his efficiency score is
    A. *less* than his seniority score by ½%
    B. *less* than his seniority score by ¾%
    C. *equal* to his seniority score
    D. *greater* than his seniority score by ½%

7. Fox's service rating is
    A. 72½%
    B. 74%
    C. 76½%
    D. 76¾%

8. Brown's service rating is
    A. less than 78%
    B. 78%
    C. 78¼%
    D. more than 78¼%

9. Cole's service rating EXCEEDS Kane's by
    A. less than 2%
    B. 2%
    C. 2¼%
    D. more than 2¼%

KEY (CORRECT ANSWERS)

1.	A	6.	D
2.	C	7.	D
3.	B	8.	B
4.	C	9.	A
5.	B		

www.ingramcontent.com/pod-product-compliance
Lightning Source LLC
Chambersburg PA
CBHW081806300426
44116CB00014B/2261